CHOICE WORDS

CHOICE WORDS

A collection of writing about abortion

Edited by Louise Swinn

ALLEN&UNWIN
SYDNEY • MELBOURNE • AUCKLAND • LONDON

'The slutty whore from whoresville making us all look bad' is an excerpt from *Every Lie I've Ever Told*, Rosie Waterland, HarperCollins, Sydney, 2017.

'A slice of life, 1965' is an excerpt from *Ducks on the Pond: an autobiography 1945–1976*, Anne Summers, Viking, Ringwood, 1999.

First published in 2019

Copyright © in the collection Louise Swinn 2019.
Copyright © in individual pieces with their authors

All rights reserved. No part of this book may be reproduced or transmitted in any form or by any means, electronic or mechanical, including photocopying, recording or by any information storage and retrieval system, without prior permission in writing from the publisher. The Australian *Copyright Act 1968* (the Act) allows a maximum of one chapter or 10 per cent of this book, whichever is the greater, to be photocopied by any educational institution for its educational purposes provided that the educational institution (or body that administers it) has given a remuneration notice to the Copyright Agency (Australia) under the Act.

Allen & Unwin
83 Alexander Street
Crows Nest NSW 2065
Australia
Phone: (61 2) 8425 0100
Email: info@allenandunwin.com
Web: www.allenandunwin.com

 A catalogue record for this book is available from the National Library of Australia

ISBN 978 1 76087 522 0

Set in 11.25/15.75 pt Sabon by Midland Typesetters, Australia
Printed and bound in Australia by Griffin Press

10 9 8 7 6 5 4 3 2 1

 The paper in this book is FSC® certified. FSC® promotes environmentally responsible, socially beneficial and economically viable management of the world's forests.

Proceeds from the sale of this book will be donated to the Marie Stopes Australia Choice Fund.

In Australia abortion is unfortunately still deeply stigmatised. There is limited provision or funding of the service through the public health system. Addressing this stigma and ensuring people can access the service without fear of judgement is at the heart of Marie Stopes Australia's advocacy work.

In 2017, in recognition of the limited public funding for abortion services, Marie Stopes Australia launched the Choice Fund. This philanthropic fund helps women experiencing financial and other hardships to access abortion care if and when they need it. Since its launch the fund has assisted 170 women to access abortion and contraception. Of the women the fund has assisted:

- 34 per cent reported domestic violence
- 33 per cent reported pre-existing mental health issues
- 13 per cent reported experiencing reproductive coercion
- 20 women were from rural and remote Australia
- 51 women were from New South Wales
- 88 women were from Queensland
- 28 women were from Victoria

Marie Stopes Australia is a national award-winning not-for-profit provider of sexual and reproductive health services. These services include abortion, contraception, vasectomy, tubal ligation and sexual health screening and treatment. The organisation advocates for Australians to have access to safe and high quality care. Any surplus funds generated by Marie Stopes Australia are invested into its Australian operations, Choice Fund and its regional sexual and reproductive health programs.

For more information visit https://www.mariestopes.org.au/

Contents

Tanya Plibersek	Foreword: unfinished business	ix
Louise Swinn	Introduction	xxi
Abortion laws across Australia		xxiv
Claudia Karvan	Free and relieved	1
Shirley Barrett	Doctor Marshall	3
Angela Williamson	The Apple Isle	31
Caroline de Costa	Who are the abortion providers, and what does the future hold?	42
Caroline de Costa	Out of the shadows: abortion in Queensland	48
Melissa Lucashenko	Together we are powerful	66
Laura Jean	Day of	70
Clem Bastow	I dreamed I lost my reproductive rights in my Maidenform bra	77
Meredith Burgmann	For the long haul	86
Ellena Savage	Unwed teen mum Mary	95
Gideon Haigh	The racket	101

Anne Summers	A slice of life, 1965	110
Sarah Firth	Given the options	120
Gabrielle Stanley Blair	A Twitter thread: abortion, unwanted pregnancies and irresponsible ejaculation	139
Brooke Davis	Snorkel	149
Michelle Law	Choosing	160
Monica Dux	My silent scream	162
Catherine Deveny	How abortion set me free	174
Jess Scully	Still dancing	183
Louise Swinn	In conversation: Jenny Kee and Grace Heifetz	186
Samantha Maiden	RU486 in Australia	191
Rosie Waterland	The slutty whore from whoresville making us all look bad	205
Van Badham	Waiting room: a villanelle	221
Bri Lee	An absurd threshold	223
Jane Caro	An old story	234
Tony Birch	The manger	247
Gina Rushton	From the frontline	260
Tara June Winch	Letter to my teenage daughter	270
Eleanor Limprecht	Her history, my silence	276
Jane Gleeson-White	My womb is not *terra nullius*	284
Emily Maguire	The abortions I have known	297
Zoya Patel	Provision: an interview with Dr Kamala Emanuel	310
Maxine Beneba Clarke	Weight	320
Amy Gray	Against choice	325
Melanie Cheng	A test unlike any other	335
Contributors		340
Notes		348

Tanya Plibersek

Foreword: unfinished business

Back in 2005 a doctor told me a story about a young woman from a small rural community in Queensland. She was a mother of two children under the age of three. Both her children had been born premature because she suffered from severe pre-eclampsia.

She was not in a happy relationship. Her partner was unsupportive.

She was eight weeks pregnant with her third child when she travelled to a small country hospital some distance from her home, wanting to terminate her pregnancy. The doctor she saw wanted to help but was unable to arrange a surgical termination at the hospital. Her only option was to take the bus to the nearest large town, hundreds of kilometres away, to have an abortion at a private clinic.

Can you imagine? Catching a bus for hundreds of kilometres with two children under three so you could have a medical procedure. What would you even do with the toddlers while you were anaesthetised for surgery?

It did not come to that anyway, because the procedure would have cost more than $700. The young woman simply could not afford it, so she returned home from the hospital still pregnant.

At 26 weeks, she was back at the hospital severely ill for the third time with pre-eclampsia. She was airlifted to the same town where she might have had the pregnancy terminated. She had an emergency caesarean, the infant died and she spent a week in the high dependency unit.

So much unnecessary trauma. Unnecessary risk to a woman's life. The loss of a baby. Unnecessary expense to the health system. This should not happen in a country like Australia.

It was this story, told to me by a Queensland doctor, and others like it, that made me understand how necessary it was to add RU486, the drugs used for a medical abortion, to the Pharmaceutical Benefits Scheme back in 2013.

I wanted to make sure a woman facing the difficult decision to terminate her pregnancy had more options available to her.

Adding RU486 to the PBS undoubtedly made it easier for some women to end an unwanted pregnancy. But the reality is that for many Australian women who have decided they want an abortion, it is still unaffordable and unattainable.

Abortion is one of the most common medical procedures that Australian women require in their lives.[1] Over 80 per cent of Australians support a woman's right to choose.

When I first delivered this speech at the annual Emily's List Oration in 2017, having an abortion was still a criminal act in both Queensland and New South Wales. That meant that it was a crime for half the women in Australia. The Queensland legislation originated in 1899, but it was not a law that was defunct in practice. A Brisbane couple were prosecuted for purchasing abortion drugs in 2010, and just last year a woman was prosecuted in New South Wales. But half of Queenslanders did not even know that abortion was illegal in their state.

A lot changed in a year. Generations of activists have fought for decriminalisation of abortion in Queensland, and Premier Annastacia Palaszczuk and Deputy Premier Jackie Trad took a momentous step forward for Australian women by passing decriminalisation legislation in October 2018. It is time for New South Wales to follow suit.

But decriminalisation is not the end of the battle. Since the last Labor government added RU486 to the PBS, the drug itself costs only $6.40 with a healthcare card. But the average price women actually pay for a medical termination is close to $600.[2]

Access to safe, legal and affordable abortions is crucial but it is not the beginning and end of the fight for reproductive rights in Australia. Real reproductive freedom means the freedom to say yes or no to sex, being able to access appropriate contraception and maternal healthcare, and being able to have children without experiencing discrimination.

What is reproductive freedom?

I want to say up front that when I am talking about reproductive freedom I get that it is a lot messier than demanding rights, changing laws and providing health services.

We would like to hope that as women we can control our bodies, but too many of us have had unexpected pregnancies, or struggled to become pregnant when we desperately wanted a child, to imagine that we *really* control our bodies. We do the best we can to influence our fertility, but life and relationships and accidents, both tragic and happy, all play a role.

But when it comes to something as important as carrying and raising a child we deserve as much say as possible, as much choice as possible. Every child born should be loved and wanted.

Legislating reproductive rights

Around two-thirds of women in Australia can legally access an abortion. For the other four million, it is still a crime you could be jailed for.

This does not mean that it is impossible to get an abortion in New South Wales, but the legal risk can make it far more difficult and costly. Most medical practitioners put providing abortion services in the too-hard basket. Outdated laws are a serious barrier to the provision of healthcare.

Gaps in services in different parts of Australia lead to the ridiculous situation of 'abortion tourism'. One in 25 women who have an abortion had to travel interstate to have it.[3] When Tasmania's last private abortion clinic had to close in 2018, reproductive health providers in Melbourne reported a big increase in women travelling to the mainland to access services.

It is also not as simple as abortion being a crime in New South Wales and legal and easily available everywhere else in the country. In many cases the legal conditions attached to how and when you can get an abortion are almost as restrictive as prohibition.

In South Australia, a woman can only terminate her pregnancy if her mental or physical health or life is at risk. It then becomes the doctor's prerogative to decide whether a woman can have an abortion. Abortion is the only medical procedure in the country where the patient's wishes are inconsequential.

In early 2016, a twelve-year-old girl presented to the Central Queensland Hospital and Health Service because she wanted to end her early-term pregnancy. The girl had the support of her mother, the social worker, two obstetricians and a psychiatrist.

The hospital would not perform the abortion and the decision ended up having to be made by the Queensland Supreme Court, even though the girl and her parents were consenting. Of course, no court approval would have been required if she had decided to continue the pregnancy, even though that would have placed her health at far higher risk.

There has been notable success recently in changing outdated laws. The Northern Territory Labor government passed reforms to abortion laws in March 2017 that made medical terminations available for the first time. The ACT Labor government followed suit in September 2018. New South Wales has introduced safe access zones around abortion clinics after the success of Penny Sharpe's Private Member's Bill. In October this year, Queensland successfully decriminalised abortion.

More is needed than changed laws

Even in states where abortion is legal, there is a huge gap between the law and the reality on the ground. For many women, abortions are unaffordable and unattainable. The legal right to access a termination is not much use to a homeless teenager when the upfront cost of an abortion is more than $500.

Adding RU486 to the Pharmaceutical Benefits Scheme in 2013 is one of the more important things I did as Health minister because the pills went from costing around $300 to just $6 with a healthcare card. But uptake of medical terminations by women who want an abortion is still very low by international standards. Women seeking abortions are often charged more for medical terminations than they are for traditional surgical terminations. The cost for medical terminations can rise to around $800 in some parts of the country. This can be completely unaffordable when one in three Australians does not have $500 available in case of an emergency.[4]

Not being able to afford an abortion is a ridiculous situation to be put in when you consider the longer term cost of raising a child. It still seems tragic to me that a woman would have a child for no reason other than that she could not afford an abortion when she needed one. A 2017 survey found one in three women found it difficult to pay for their abortion. Two-thirds needed financial assistance and had to miss paying bills or cut back on food to afford it.[5]

Things are made worse by how difficult it can be to find a doctor or clinic to help. Abortion services in the public health system are rare and poorly coordinated. Services are restricted to a few facilities in major cities. Most services are provided in private clinics and very few general practice doctors will perform medical terminations. Less than 1.5 per cent of GPs are registered to prescribe RU486 and far fewer are actively doing so.[6] This must change.

Another 2017 survey in Western Australia found one in five women seeking an abortion had difficulty finding a provider or were refused a referral by their GP.[7] It gets even harder to find an affordable service if you live in a rural or remote area. These are the women we are truly letting down.

I have been told about clients living in remote areas of Queensland who have travelled over 1300 kilometres to get a termination.[8] One in ten women have to stay overnight in the town they have travelled to – drastically increasing the cost.[9]

The reality of the situation is that if you are a middle-class woman living in a capital city, maybe you will agonise over the decision, there may be barriers and stigma around you getting an abortion, but you will probably be able to get one if you need to.

If you live in a rural or remote area, if you are experiencing poverty, if you do not speak much English, or if you are young – it is going to be a whole lot harder, if it is possible at all.

It is a serious restriction on women's reproductive freedom and it is a terrible start for children brought into the world in these circumstances.

Unplanned pregnancy

There is clearly a lot of work that needs to be done to improve legal and practical access to abortion, but as we know, true reproductive freedom is about much more than that.

Most women spend a lot of their lives trying not to get pregnant when the time does not seem right. We are not always successful. Studies show around one in four pregnancies in Australia is unintended,[10] and that can be a lovely happy surprise. But often it is not. One in three unplanned pregnancies is terminated.[11]

Contraceptive failure is the cause of 70 per cent of unwanted pregnancies.[12] Lots of Australian women are not using the best form of contraception for them because they are not fully informed about their options. Around 8 per cent of Australian women use long-acting removable contraceptives (LARCs) compared to 32 per cent in Europe.[13] Far more people rely on condoms and The Pill, but condoms are only 82 per cent effective and The Pill 91 per cent effective. Long-acting removable contraceptives such as implants and intrauterine devices are over 99 per cent effective.[14] The difference between 91 and 99 per cent is thousands of unplanned pregnancies.

As well as being more effective, LARCs cost less than The Pill. Of course, this does not mean they will be the best choice for everyone or that they should be foisted on women who do not want them. Part of the reason there are misconceptions about LARCs is because in the past they have been given to vulnerable people, including Indigenous women and young mothers, without their proper consent. But, at the moment, lots of young women do not learn about all options in school and are not always told about them when they visit their GP.

Reproductive coercion
There is another aspect of reproductive freedom that I believe needs to be urgently included in our efforts to eliminate violence against women.

Reproductive coercion can take on a number of forms. It happens when your partner controls or sabotages your birth control, when they make threats or are violent if you insist on using a condom, and when they take the condom off without telling you. It is disturbing that this is so common it has a name: 'stealthing'. It should be known as rape.

Reproductive coercion happens when a man emotionally blackmails or coerces you into falling pregnant or keeping a pregnancy you do not want – or, the flipside, forces you to have an abortion.

None of this behaviour is okay, but it is shockingly common. Children by Choice, a Queensland-based pregnancy counselling provider, has found one in seven of their clients has experienced reproductive coercion.

Reproductive coercion is a way for perpetrators of violence to exercise power over their partner's life. A third of women reporting domestic violence to Children by Choice also reported reproductive coercion. It is a sickening truth, but the risk of women experiencing domestic violence increases while they are pregnant.[15]

Reproductive coercion is also a form of violence that has lasting impacts. Having a child creates a legal tie with your abuser that can last a lifetime and makes it far harder to leave a violent relationship. Combatting reproductive coercion needs to become part of our national effort to prevent violence against women.

Anti-choice demonstrators often use the fact that some women may be coerced into having a termination as a reason that no women should ever be able to choose one. Certainly, we should ensure no one is ever forced to have an abortion. We should also recognise that harassing, attacking or shaming vulnerable women who are trying to end a pregnancy is also a form of reproductive coercion.

Social and economic constraints

Women's reproductive choice can also be limited by our society.

Half of Australian mothers report having been discriminated against in the workplace while they were pregnant, on maternity leave or when they returned to work.

It is no wonder then that women are waiting later and later to have their first child, in part because of fears about what it will mean for their careers. This creates its own barriers. If you wait too long and have to rely on IVF, the cost runs into the thousands and is prohibitive for many. Only 18 per cent of IVF cycles in Australia result in a live birth. This drops off even further for women over forty.

Making our society and workplaces family friendly gives women more genuine choice about when they start their family if they want one.

Consent and respectful relationships

Above all, reproductive freedom begins with knowing how to say yes or no to having sex. 76 per cent of girls say their sex education classes at school were useless in preparing them to deal with sex and relationships.[16]

For the most part, it is a combination of scientific diagrams of genitals and descriptions of how fertilisation occurs, with some warnings about STIs thrown in for extra measure. Yet many young people do not know that asymptomatic sexually transmitted diseases can compromise your fertility later in life.

We are kidding ourselves if we think kids are not finding out about sex elsewhere. In Australia, the average age young boys first see porn is thirteen.[17] Smart phones and social media are creating a whole range of new expectations and peer pressure for young people. Two-thirds of teenagers surveyed reported having received a 'sext'.[18] It is not possible anymore to just avoid mentioning sex to teenagers and hope ignorance will lead to abstinence. That approach has never worked.

Young Australians are developing unhealthy ideas about what sex and sexual relationships look like because we are not talking to them clearly enough about healthy relationships. Misinformation is only a click away. We need comprehensive and honest sex and relationships education. We need to teach young people about consent: what it is, what it is not, how to ask for it, how to express it, how to know if you are not ready and to have the freedom to say no – not with you; not that way; not today.

Australia needs sex and relationship education that is age-appropriate and covers respect, online safety, diversity and sexual violence. Honest education is essential to equipping young people with the tools to form safe, healthy relationships when they are ready.

This would benefit all young people, but the benefits are not gender-neutral. It is girls who are more likely to be pressured to have sex when they do not want to, to be publically shamed for sending selfies, to be ostracised for being too frigid or too promiscuous. It is girls who will end up pregnant, who are less likely to experience pleasure, and who are more likely to be victims of violence. When our sex education system fails, girls pay a higher price.

Reproductive freedom in Australia

It is so clear that our current approach is not good enough. Abortion is a crime for four million Australian women. Reproductive healthcare can be prohibitively expensive – if you can even find a service that will help you.

Yet one in four pregnancies is unplanned and a third of those pregnancies end in abortion. If the intention behind all these barriers and restrictions is to stop women having abortions, it is not working.

We need to improve reproductive freedom in Australia through decent sex education to ensure young people have safe, fun, healthy, respectful relationships when they are ready. We need a comprehensive approach to improve use of effective contraception. We need to ensure all women can access healthcare – to get pregnant, deliver safely, avoid pregnancy or end a pregnancy as a woman chooses. We need strong public health systems to take responsibility for supporting each of these reproductive options. We need to eliminate reproductive coercion and violence against women. We need to make sure that women have autonomy over their bodies.

Reproductive freedom is intimately tied to gender equality. For the Australian Labor Party to be pro-women, we must be pro-choice. For Australia to be pro-women, we must be pro-choice.

Australia still has unfinished business on reproductive health.

Louise Swinn

Introduction

In Year 9 my class watched an anti-abortion video – perhaps it was the film Monica refers to here – and I went home utterly bereft. The image that stayed with me was of dead babies being tossed into a bin, left piled on top of each other.

I now know how inaccurate it was, but it took a lot of unlearning. Misinformation persists. When we began this project, I didn't know the extent of the legal differences across Australia's states and territories. Even in places where abortion is legal it is sometimes nearly impossible to access, and costs can be prohibitive.

I spoke to an abortion provider who wouldn't go on record because in her small town people would cross the street if they knew what she does for a living. She mentioned that it can be hard to access training. It's legal where she is, and she isn't ashamed, but she doesn't want to make waves. She spoke in a hushed voice. 'How did you get my name?' she asked.

The uniform summer dress that I had to wear to school was thin, see-through cotton. I would never choose to wear a dress like that, now or then. For a week a month we wrapped our jumpers around us for fear of bloody leakages. Many girls still have to wear them today, but now there is period-proof underwear; it should be government subsidised. I would have – we all would have – continued with sport, self-defence and dancing. Girls' bodies are policed and they aren't protected and they're over-protected, and it's just the start of it.

While we were putting this book together, the law in QLD changed and abortion became legal – Caroline encapsulates the excitement of witnessing the vote. Around the same time, Michelle Obama released a memoir that revealed she had experienced a miscarriage and that her daughters were conceived through IVF. Why can't all of this be dinner table conversation? It's an arcane fallacy that these are just women's issues. Abortion is a human rights issue.

These debates force us to think about when life begins, and many grapple with this through a religious lens. After my 1990s Catholic education that was so anti-abortion and scared of unwanted pregnancies, I grew up in a generation of women who have left babies till later and rely heavily on IVF. Women petrified of getting pregnant became women desperate to do so.

Who has a right to talk about abortion was much debated while putting this book together, and some people who hadn't had abortions felt as though they couldn't write about it. One writer wanted to tell his abortion story but when he contacted his former partner she didn't want the story told. Some women were unable to write about their own abortions because they were still a secret or because the memory of it – going back decades – was too painful.

The stories in these pages are from people who have experienced abortion first-hand, people who are working in the field, and people who have thought long and hard about it. This is not a facile subject and many of the people included here did a lot of soul-searching, for which I am utterly grateful. At least one in four women have abortions – we all know people. We are all affected. These are our stories.

Abortion laws across Australia

Western Australia

- *Acts Amendment (Abortion) Act 1998, Health Act 1911.*
- Abortion lawful up to 20 weeks after counselling by medical practitioner (not the practitioner providing abortion), with referral for additional counselling before and after abortion.
- After 20 weeks at least two members of a government-appointed panel must agree that woman or foetus has severe medical condition.
- Conscientious objection clause.
- All abortions reported to WA Director of Public Health.
- Criminal Code 1913 if non-medical practitioner performs abortions – five years prison.

South Australia

- *Criminal Law Consolidation Act 1935 (Amended 1969).*
- Legal decision by two doctors if pregnancy risks woman's physical or mental health or there is severe foetal anomaly.
- Abortions must be carried out in prescribed hospital.
- Woman must be SA resident for at least two months.
- Conscientious objection clause.
- Women who attempts abortion – life imprisonment.
- Person who provides abortion – life imprisonment.
- Provision of instrument of 'noxious thing' knowing it will be used for abortion – three years prison.

Victoria

- *Abortion Law Reform Act 2008, Public Health and Wellbeing Amendment (Safe Access Zones) Act 2015.*
- Up to 24 weeks abortions can be carried out by registered medical practitioner with woman's consent.
- After 24 weeks, two doctors must consider abortion appropriate in all circumstances.
- Registered pharmacists or nurses can supply prescription abortion drugs.
- Conscientious objection clause requires referral to another medical practitioner.
- 150m safe access zones around clinics.

Tasmania

- *Reproductive Health (Access to Terminations) Act 2013.*
- Up to 16 weeks, abortion provided by medical practitioner with woman's consent.
- After 16 weeks, two medical practitioners (one must be obstetrician or gynaecologist) must agree pregnancy would injure woman's physical or mental health.
- Conscientious objection clause and medical practitioner to provide list of who can assist.
- 150m safe access zones around clinics.

Northern Territory

- *Termination of Pregnancy Law Reform Act 2017, Regulation and Chief Health Officer Credentials.*
- Up to 14 weeks, legal decision with one 'suitably qualified medical practitioner'.
- 14–23 weeks, two 'suitably qualified medical practitioners'.
- 'Suitably qualified medical practitioner' must decide that abortion appropriate in all circumstances having regard to woman's medical, current and future physical, psychological and social circumstances, and professional standards and guidelines.
- In an emergency, abortion is lawful if medical practitioner deems it necessary to preserve life of woman.
- 'Suitably qualified medical practitioner' is an obstetrician or gynaecologist or is 'credentialed' in abortion provision.
- Conscientious objection clause requires referral to another medical practitioner.
- 150m safe access zones around clinics.
- All abortions reported to Chief Health Officer.
- If not 'qualified person' who procures, supplies drugs or instruments for abortion – 7 years imprisonment (includes not 'suitably qualified' healthcare professionals).

Queensland

- Termination of Pregnancy Bill 2018.
- Up to 22 weeks abortion can be carried out by a medical practitioner.
- After 22 weeks practitioner must consult with another practitioner who must agree that in all circumstances the abortion should be performed.
- Conscientious objection clause requires referral to another medical practitioner or service.
- 150m safe access zones around clinics.

Australian Capital Territory

- *Medical Practitioners (Maternal Health) Amendment Act 2002, Health Act 1993* (Amended 2005).
- Legal decision is a woman's to make.
- No gestational limits in the law.
- Registered practitioner can perform abortion.
- Abortion must be carried out in a medical facility or part of facility approved by minister for Health.*
- Conscientious objection clause.
- 50m safe access zones around clinics.

Legislation will come into effect shortly to broaden this.

New South Wales

- *Crimes Act 1900.*
- Woman who attempts abortion – 10 years prison.
- Person who provides abortion – 10 years prison.
- Supplying instruments or drugs for abortion – 5 years prison.
- Levine ruling (1971): abortion considered lawful if two doctors agree that continuing pregnancy will cause 'serious danger' to woman's physical or mental health.
- 150m safe access zones around clinics.

Claudia Karvan

Free and relieved

16 years old – got my first period.
17 years old – got pregnant.

How fucking stupid am I? I couldn't fault the extraordinarily thorough sex-ed I'd had at high school. But my mother never talked about contraception. Nor did either of my boyfriends. Not even the one who was 25. The one I got pregnant with.

I flipped through the Yellow Pages, an ancient tome that millennials would laugh at, looking for abortion clinics. Or family-planning something. I called the clinics and couldn't get through the calls without crying. I felt so stupid, like I was in some crass soap opera. A teen pregnancy. It seemed so melodramatic and not me. How could this happen? It was inconceivable. Ha, ha . . . Get it? A woman could make a baby. Not a girl. I was still a girl. A really fucking dumb girl.

Thank God I lived in Sydney, Australia, and it was 1989.

I walked from my home in Paddington to Woollahra. The operation was performed by a lovely, handsome doctor. When he administered the sedative, he asked me to count down from ten. At number ten I was blubbering. By number three I was groggy, free and relieved.

Thank you, thank you, thank you, to all the men and women who made that procedure possible. Thank you.

Shirley Barrett
Doctor Marshall

Rummaging around in the bowels of the internet one day, idly researching family history, I stumbled across an extraordinary, if somewhat ghoulish, document: *The Register of Dead Bodies Taken to North Sydney Morgue Between 1881 And 1908.* Inscribed entirely by hand, in two volumes running to over 1100 pages, it offers a fascinating insight into life (or more accurately, death) in Sydney at the time. The North Sydney Morgue, located at the bottom of Argyle Place in Circular Quay, was described as little more than 'an old tin shed' ('a less suitable building could scarcely be imagined,' harrumphed the *Evening News,* 11 June 1901). It was one of two morgues operating in Sydney for much of that period – the South Sydney Morgue closed in 1901 to make way for the construction of Central Railway Station.

Trawling through the pages of this register, I began to notice certain types of deaths recurring with regularity:

drownings in Sydney Harbour (no one could swim, of course); wharf labourers falling to their deaths into the holds of ships; deaths as a result of violence, domestic or otherwise; deaths attributable to alcoholism. But most startling and horrifying is the number of newborn babies and foetuses listed within these pages. Between 1901 and 1903 alone, I counted 58 newborns and thirty foetuses brought to the morgue. The few details supplied are pitiful: 'the body of a newly born female infant wrapped up in some brown paper, a piece of old bath towel and a sock,' 'found in a low-level sewer,' 'found on the doorstep of Mr James Chemist, supposed left there by some female,' 'on the beach at Manly, wrapped up in a piece of towel with a stone tied in it,' 'in the Ladies Lavatory of no. 5 platform, Redfern railway station, wrapped up in a copy of the *Daily Telegraph*.' And this: 'foetus lying on the footpath in Victoria St, Darlinghurst, the body evidently trodden on by some passer-by during the night.'

Page after page, these newborns and foetuses appear. It takes a moment to process what you're reading. Babies given birth to and then abandoned, tossed into the harbour or smothered or strangled or stabbed or left to die in a paddock. A hundred years ago, in my own city, this was commonplace. What desperate circumstances prompted these horrifying acts? And foetuses – the pathetic product of an agonising, mortifying and highly dangerous procedure that likely took place in a darkened room somewhere – trodden on or stumbled across by a passer-by.

Just as shocking to the modern reader is the steady succession of young women who appear in the pages of the Morgue Register, dead of septicaemia or peritonitis brought on by backyard abortions. Consider this selection, ten women dead in a period of just over nine months:

12 November 1903: Florence White, 19, domestic servant, 'at the lying-in home of Nurse Charlotte Binder as the result of a miscarriage.' ('Death due to septicaemia following a certain event, brought about by someone unknown.' *Maitland Daily Mercury*, 18 March 1903)

8 December 1903: Alice Leighton, 28, domestic servant, 'from peritonitis ... resulting from a recent miscarriage, but the cause of the miscarriage is unknown.'

5 December 1903: Elizabeth Booth, 28, married. 'Death was due to septicaemia, following a certain event.' (*Sydney Morning Herald*, 12 December 1903)

16 December 1903: Fanny Foster, 19, 'septic peritonitis.' ('Died from septicaemia following upon a certain event.' (*Sydney Morning Herald*, 18 December 1903)

27 April 1904: Clara Throlfo, 26, found dead in bed at the house of Nurse Jeffries. ('Acute septicaemia following an event which had been partially caused.' *Maitland Weekly Mercury*, 7 May 1904)

19 June 1904: Ellen Prendergast, 27, domestic servant, 'the foetus of a child found amongst her blood-stained clothing.'

28 June 1904: Clara Farmer, 26, domestic duties, 'at residence of Nurse Brown.' ('Died from septic peritonitis.' *Daily Telegraph*, 30 June 1904)

23 July 1904: Dolly Whiffen, 24, domestic servant, 'blood poisoning caused through an illegal operation.'

24 July 1904: Margaret Dawson, 23, single, domestic servant, 'the result of an illegal operation.'

28 August 1904: Amelia Lynch, 26, single, dressmaker, 'at the house of Nurse Ruby Mayne . . . from septic peritonitis and haemorrhage following a miscarriage.'

They're all so young. I think of my own daughters in their early twenties, out in the world and sexually active, and my heart thuds in gratitude for the miracle of contraception. And so many of these young women were domestic servants! It's not difficult to imagine the predicament they had found themselves in: pregnant and unmarried in a time when this combination bore a shameful stigma, the danger of losing their livelihoods a certainty if they didn't do something quickly. What did they do, one wonders – how did they go about seeking help? And perusing the back pages of the newspapers of the day, in the columns headed 'Medical', you begin to get an idea, because there are rows of brief, cryptically worded advertisements:

Ladies – My New Female Pills Restore Regularity instantly, no matter what has failed. Post 5s. 6d. Prof. W. W. Garfield, Collins St, Melbourne.

Dr Rock's Reliable Female Pills Never Fail: They act like Magic. 5s 6d per box. Extra strong 10s. 6d. Post Free, under cover from 436 Oxford St, Paddington.

NURSE RAY receives Patients for Medical Surgery and Midwifery. Doctors attend daily. Beauchamp, Edgecliffe Road, Woollahra. Tel. 18 Wav.

LADIES – For safe and successful treatment in all cases, call at Nurse Pender's Reg. Lying-in Hospital, 142 Glenmore Rd, Glenmore. Bus passes door.

LADIES – Your Troubles at an End by Applying to MADAME ORME, MD, SYDNEY'S ONLY LADY SPECIALIST, for a list of her REMEDIES and genuine testimonials, FAILURE IMPOSSIBLE . . . 279 Elizabeth St, Hyde Park. (*Evening News*, 10 March 1900)

As hopeful and reassuring as these advertisements must have sounded to a nineteen-year-old in trouble, the reality was, of course, very different. 'Many a girl, more sinned against than sinning, has cause to regret that she ever read of the "magic female pills" or the "regularity restored without pain" business,' railed *Truth* (12 August 1900). 'The pills contain either ergot, tansy, iron, cottonweed, permanganate of potash, or pennyroyal, and science teaches that none of these things . . . will wreck the course of nature of themselves. It's all a fallacy and women should be taught to know it.'

If the magic pills failed, as they did invariably, what next? What of the kindly sounding nurses, offering safety and 'success', even convenience ('bus passes door'), in the privacy and comfort of their homes? Many of these nurses appeared again and again at the inquests of those who had died from the effects of abortion. Nurse Ray ('receives patients for medical surgery and midwifery') was called at the inquest for Alice Hutchinson (aged nineteen, domestic servant), who died of 'acute pleurisy and heart failure'. When the Coroner got wind of the fact that an illegal abortion had taken place, he had the funeral stopped, the body returned to the morgue and a postmortem conducted – it was found, unsurprisingly, that the young woman had died of septic peritonitis following an abortion. And the illustriously titled Madame Orme MD, Sydney's Only Lady Specialist (real name: Rosaline Brown), had, only a couple of weeks prior to the publication of the advertisement above, appeared at the inquest of Elizabeth Billington, a widow with five children, found dead after apparently administering to herself an injection of fluids. A box of powders, an instrument and printed material bearing the name of Madame Orme MD had been found in Billington's bedroom. At the inquest, Rosaline Brown underwent the following interrogation:

> The Coroner: What is the meaning of 'MD'?
> Witness: There is no special significance in the letters 'MD'. They are used more for attraction than anything else.
> The Coroner: Have you ever studied medicine or drugs of any kind? For instance, can you tell me anything about permanganate of potash?
> Witness: No, sir. I have studied medical books.
> The Coroner: Have you had any special training?
> Witness: No, sir. (*Truth*, 11 March 1900)

Madame Orme MD was just twenty years old and had started her business at the age of seventeen.

Given the grave physical danger associated with undergoing an abortion at that time, it's not surprising that some women with sufficient means sought out that rare creature, a qualified doctor who was willing to perform what was, of course, an illegal procedure. The New South Wales *Crimes Act 1900*, still in effect today, states that supplying 'any drug or noxious thing, or any instrument or thing whatsoever' for the purpose of procuring an abortion is punishable by imprisonment for up to five years. (The woman herself could face a prison term of ten years.) Consequently, these doctors did not, of course, advertise themselves. How did these women find them? It must have been almost entirely word of mouth. For going back to that list of ten women who died in a period of just over nine months between 1903 and 1904, four of them – Elizabeth Booth, Fanny Foster, Ellen Prendergast and Amelia Lynch – had been treated by Dr Frederick Marshall, a respected Sydney doctor with rooms on Macquarie Street.

My interest piqued by the recurrence of Dr Marshall's name. I dug a little deeper and found, to my mounting horror, that in the space of just over four years, between 1901 and 1905, Dr Marshall was implicated in the deaths of eight women and faced serious charges in the cases of another two women who had almost died – all from the effects of abortion. On every occasion but one, juries failed to convict him of wrongdoing.

Pause here to stare at a photo of Dr Marshall, which the internet obligingly offers up. He cuts a dashing figure, sporting a dark moustache – his expression (am I imagining this?) a little arrogant, even disdainful. With a track record of so many deaths, each well-publicised in the newspapers, why did women continue to go to him? More to the point: given, at the very least, the legal peril he faced so regularly, why did he continue to offer abortions? Was it financially lucrative? (It was. 'The cash gains are enormous, and the risk is ridiculously small,' declared the *Australian Star*, 8 June 1888. 'It is no secret that practitioners are known to make yearly thousands by this species of industry.') Or, to take a more charitable view, was he simply unable to say no to a woman who came to him in trouble?

The first case in which Dr Marshall found himself in significant difficulty was in April 1901, when a young woman named Florence Treffeny made a dying deposition as she hovered between life and death in Prince Alfred Hospital. She claimed that Dr Marshall had unlawfully used an instrument with intent to bring about that overworked euphemism, 'a certain event'. He was promptly arrested and taken to the hospital (incredibly, when a witness had given a dying deposition, the accused was afforded the opportunity to cross-examine her). En route, Dr Marshall became suddenly unwell, necessitating a stop at a hotel for a couple of fortifying glasses of brandy. (One can't help but marvel at how obliging the accompanying detectives were to accommodate this request.)

> He was taken to the girl's bedside, and said to her, 'Did you ever see me before?' Miss Treffeny replied, 'Yes, at the surgery, 229 Macquarie St.' After leaving the hospital, accused said, 'No, I never saw her; she is telling lies. She has a bad chin.' (*Truth*, 6 October 1901)

Presumably, in this golden age of phrenology, 'a bad chin' was a sign of poor character. Eventually Dr Marshall conceded that he may have treated her for catarrh.

Florence Treffeny did not die, however, and when she was finally well enough, some months later, for the case to go to trial, she showed a sudden reluctance to co-operate. Her answers to questioning were almost inaudible; sometimes she would barely shake her head in response.

> His Honour: What is it that is frightening you?
> Witness replied that nothing was frightening her . . .
> His Honour: You have sworn to tell the truth and the whole truth. It is time I warned you. You must not hold anything back.
> Witness remarked that her memory had not been good since her illness.

Mr Wade: What illness?
Witness: The illness after Dr Marshall attended me.
(*Telegraph,* 4 October 1901)

Dr Marshall's barrister, Mr J. C. Gannon, 'in the course of two hours vigorous speech, ridiculed the idea of a medical man of Dr Marshall's standing jeopardising his position and liberty . . . He asked the jury to weigh the clean, highly skilled experience of the doctor with the hysterical statement of an unfortunate girl who now could not remember what she had said. There was no evidence of miscarriage, and if there had been it might have been occasioned by the girl toying with herself.' (*Truth,* 6 October 1901)

In his summing up, the judge warned the jury that it would be a very dangerous thing to convict Dr Marshall without corroboration of events. After a brief deliberation, the jury found Dr Marshall not guilty.

'I know I refused to examine her unless in some friend's presence,' Dr Marshall said in an unsworn statement at the Florence Treffeny trial. 'It is dangerous for a medical man to do so sometimes, although I know eminent medical men in Sydney who would rather be alone when examining a woman in order to avoid a blackmailing conspiracy that might be trumped up if there were a witness present.' (*Truth,* 6 October 1901)

Well, Dr Marshall would know: he had himself very recently scraped through a blackmailing attempt by an angry husband whose wife had just died.

Emily Ritchie, aged forty, mother of five, died in June 1901 from a haemorrhage after an extended period of being treated by Dr Marshall. Her husband, unable to pay for the funeral, had demanded £500 from Dr Marshall, knowing full well that the Florence Treffeny case was at the time hanging over his head. 'Go to the devil; I will not be blackmailed by any d------- scoundrel,' retorted Marshall, adding that he'd have him arrested if he called upon him again. (*Evening News,* 16 July 1901) The newspaper articles covering the inquest make fascinating reading for the oblique detail they provide on Marshall's modus operandi, in testimony from Emily Ritchie's married daughter, Winnifred Helton, who had accompanied her mother on her visits to Dr Marshall:

> At the end of April, Dr Marshall examined her mother, who paid him £2 2s. Witness was present during the examination. They remained only about five or ten minutes altogether. They went to see the doctor three days later, when, in answer to an inquiry, her mother told Dr Marshall that she was not getting on very well and felt very bad. Witness then described what she saw the doctor do. She accompanied her mother to the surgery about a week after that, when Dr Marshall gave her certain instructions, and told her to call and see him again if a certain thing did not happen. Four days later, witness went once more with her mother to the surgery, but Dr Marshall was not there. They waited for four hours, then went away without seeing him. That was on a Saturday. On the following Monday she went with her mother to see the doctor again. He said he was in a hurry then and asked her mother to come and see him by-and-bye. They returned the same night but did not see the doctor. On the following morning they went to the surgery again, when Dr Marshall used the same instrument on her mother as before. (*Evening News,* 16 July 1901)

Shortly thereafter, Emily Ritchie became gravely ill. She asked her daughter to get Nurse Mayne, who Dr Marshall had recommended if he was unavailable. 'Dr Marshall came a little later and whilst he was examining her mother she groaned very much with pain. Once the doctor said to her mother, "Hold your d------ tongue: do you want the neighbours to hear you?" and the nurse slipped some of the bedclothes over her mother's mouth in order that she would not make a noise.' (*Evening News,* 16 July 1901) Within a day or so, Emily Ritchie was dead.

Unable to sleep at night thinking about her mother's terrible death, Winnifred finally told her father what had transpired. He immediately seized the opportunity to try to extort £500 from Dr Marshall, and this prompted a panicked visit to Winnifred in the middle of the night:

> Her husband and she heard a knocking from about 2 a.m. to 3.30 a.m. At last her husband went to the door, and as it was opened Dr Marshall came in. He said he wanted to see witness, and he was shown into the room where she was in bed. He complained about her father having made a noise about the case, and said to her, 'If you stick with me, I'll stick to you.' He asked her not to give any information about the instrument to the police if they came to her . . . Before finally leaving the place, Dr Marshall asked her not to mention to anybody – not even her father – that he had been there.

(Reading this, one can't help wonder if Florence Treffeny had received a similar pre-dawn visit from the doctor, hence her sudden unwillingness to testify.)

The Coroner: You say the doctor treated your mother twelve months ago?

Witness [Winnifred Helton]: Yes.
The Coroner: What was that for?
Witness: The same thing.
The Coroner: Did the doctor ever treat you?
Witness: Yes.
The Coroner: Mind, you have been cautioned: you need not answer any question you think might incriminate you.
Witness: I must speak the truth . . .
The Coroner: Well, what did he treat you for?
Witness: The same thing.
The Coroner: How long ago was that?
Witness: About eight months ago.
The Coroner: Did you pay him anything for it?
Witness: Yes; five guineas. (*Evening News*, 16 July 1901)

Ultimately, despite what seems like plenty of corroborative evidence from Winnifred Helton, the jury was unable to agree upon a verdict and Dr Marshall was subsequently discharged. The Attorney-General declined to pursue the matter further and Dr Marshall continued to practise.

In fact, his business appeared to be booming.

There were 13 or 14 persons waiting – all of them being either young girls or middle-aged women. On no occasion when they visited the place did witness see any men waiting about. (*Evening News*, 16 July 1901)

So Winnifred Helton described the crowd in Dr Marshall's waiting room. Perhaps one of these women was Clara Chivers (27 years), who died weeks later of blood poisoning, having been treated by Dr Marshall. At her inquest, the jury delivered an open verdict.

Another of his patients, May Palmer (thirty years) died in December 1902, at the home of the previously mentioned Nurse Mayne. (Although married, Dr Marshall admitted to occasionally residing at Nurse Mayne's place.) 'The jury found that death was due to septicaemia following upon a certain event, but whether that event was brought about naturally or artificially the evidence did not enable them to state.' (*Australian Star*, 22 December 1902)

A year later, in December 1903, Elizabeth Booth (27 years, married with three children) died, having been attended by Dr Marshall, apparently in the very house where he lived in Rushcutters Bay. Once again, the jury brought an open verdict, and Dr Marshall was free to continue practising.

Within days of the Elizabeth Booth verdict, nineteen-year-old Fanny Foster died. On discovering that she was pregnant, a friend had recommended that she see Dr Marshall, but her mother (who must have read the newspapers) strongly advised her against it. Fanny managed to get hold of ten shillings and went to see Dr Marshall anyway, but she was turned away after being told it was not enough money. Somehow, she must have got hold of the required amount, because ultimately Dr Marshall did treat her and three weeks later, she was dead. 'The jury returned a verdict that death was due to septic peritonitis, following on a certain event, but how that certain event occurred they were unable to say.' (*Australian Star*, 18 December 1903)

Less than three months later, Dr Marshall was back in the newspapers. 'MEDICO MARSHALL: IS HE AN ABORTIONIST?' demanded *Truth*, 6 March 1904, finally asking what everyone surely had already concluded. Dr Marshall was charged with having unlawfully used an instrument with intent to procure a miscarriage on Elsie Burgess, 22 years old, recently arrived in Sydney from a convent in Bathurst. Elsie had tried pills first, but when they failed, she had gone to see Dr Marshall:

> He said, 'You won't tell anyone if I do something for you?' She said, 'No, certainly not.' Witness got on a couch, and he told her to turn well on her left side. He then used an instrument which felt like a pair of pincers ... She saw him the following Saturday in the evening. She said she had been vomiting, and he said, 'Take a good dose of salts and use a syringe.' She paid the accused 16s 6d. (*Truth*, 6 March 1904)

Elsie's condition worsened and finally she was admitted to Prince Alfred Hospital, suffering the effects of an incomplete abortion and blood poisoning. She was operated upon and eventually recovered. It appears that a police detective may have talked her into giving evidence against Dr Marshall, but without warning her that she might herself be prosecuted. She was also required to give her sexual history in court:

> She had known the man three weeks when intercourse took place. He met her in the street, said he had just come from Melbourne, and thought he knew her. Intercourse with him took place in the Waverley Park on the second occasion on which she went out with him. It was the very first time any man had had intercourse with her. (*Truth*, 6 March 1904)

Dr Marshall declared himself to be 'absolutely innocent'. In yet another unsworn statement, he divulged that Elsie Burgess had 'asked him to do something for her. Witness was annoyed, and "cleared her out, quick and lively" because he had a crowd of patients waiting, and he did not like to be asked to do such a thing. His Honour said that if the jury had a reasonable doubt they must give the benefit of it to the prisoner. The girl was unquestionably, according to her own evidence, an accomplice, and it was quite open to them to refuse to believe her because she was a criminal herself.' (*Truth*, 10 April 1904)

The jury acquitted Dr Marshall. As to what happened to Elsie Burgess, I have not been able to discover if she was ever charged or convicted.

'There were about thirty people in the hall – nearly all women.' (*Truth*, 6 March 1904) So Elsie Burgess described the waiting area at Dr Marshall's surgery, and one's heart sinks at the thought that, if waiting room attendances were a reliable measure, Dr Marshall's business seemed to have doubled. Far from scaring women off, perhaps this regular succession of inquests worked as a means of advertising his services. Within three months, Dr Marshall was again implicated in the death of a young woman in 'mysterious circumstances'.

Ellen Prendergast was 27 years old and worked as a servant for the McPherson family of Glebe. When the young man of the household heard her groaning in pain at three in the morning, he gave her brandy and sent for her mother. Ellen told her mother that she had seen Dr Marshall 'for her leg,' but that she did not know what was the matter with her. Too ill to make her way back to his surgery, telegrams were sent to Dr Marshall, but he failed to come. The next day, Ellen somehow found her way back to him. At the inquest, Dr Marshall gave the following testimony:

'Of course, I could see from her appearance that she was ill,' he continued, 'and I took her pulse, which was very feeble, put the stethoscope on her heart and found it was weak, and from the symptoms I came to the conclusion that she had haemorrhaged ... I could see she had lost blood, so I said, "If there is anything wrong with you, you must give me the whole of the symptoms before I can proceed to treat you."'

She then told him certain things, and he had reason to believe she might have had a miscarriage ... He asked her if she had been under any medical man or nurse. 'She answered me evasively,' he continued, 'and told me she had taken drugs.' He told her he would not treat her unless she went to a hospital or lying-in home, and he gave her the address of Nurse Starkey, 'a good little nurse', in Macquarie St. 'As the woman was dying on her feet ... he thought it was only an act of humanity to see what he could do for her.' (*Australian Star,* 22 June 1904)

Somehow, with her feeble pulse, 'dying on her feet', Ellen Prendergast managed to get to Nurse Starkey's house. She told Nurse Starkey that Dr Marshall had sent her, and that he would be around shortly. 'When the doctor arrived, he said something about what the deceased wanted done to her, and a nurse said she had a certain thing for the purpose ... the doctor did something and left.' (*Australian Star,* 21 June 1904) Ellen Prendergast was dead within hours.

When the police called upon Dr Marshall to inform him of Ellen Prendergast's death, he remarked that 'women did certain things and came to him when they were nearly dead, to be cured.' (*Australian Star,* 21 June 1904) Reading that, I wondered if it was true, and if this explained his high mortality rate. Had Ellen Prendergast gone elsewhere for the abortion, or even 'toyed with herself', thus inducing a haemorrhage and leaving Dr Marshall having to attempt to curette her in 'an act of humanity'? I suppose it's possible. But then I remembered that Ellen had told her mother she had been to see Dr Marshall 'about her leg'. And in fact, Dr Marshall would often use this as his defence: that he was simply mopping up as best he could after somebody else had wrought all the damage.

After a very brief deliberation, the jury delivered an open verdict at the Prendergast inquest. And with sickening predictability, three months later Dr Marshall was back in court. This time, it was over the death of Amelia Lynch, the seventh of the eight women in whose deaths he was implicated. But this time, evident especially in the testimony of other doctors, there seems to have been a will to finally convict the man.

Amelia Lynch ('Millie'), 26 years of age, a dressmaker from Young, had travelled to Sydney on the 8.30 a.m. train, ostensibly to do some dressmaking work in the city. Within a week or so, her brother Arthur, who lived at Enfield, received a telegram that his sister was ill, and to go to Nurse Mayne's house. There Millie told her brother that she had fallen and hurt herself, and not to send word home as she was feeling much better. Arthur asked Nurse Mayne if he could get another doctor in to see her, but Nurse Mayne assured Arthur that Dr Marshall was treating her and that she was getting every care and attention.

> Next morning, he received a wire, 'Sister dying. Nurse Mayne.' The time on the telegram was 9.15. When he arrived, his sister was dead, and when he asked at what time she had died, he was told 9.15. Witness said, 'At exactly the time you sent the telegram.' She replied, 'Yes.' He had instructed Nurse Mayne to send for him should any change take place, and to call in another doctor. He asked her why she had not done as he desired. She said she had knocked up three doctors, but none would come. Dr Fred Marshall was with her for two or three hours. Nurse Mayne gave him

Dr Marshall's certificate of death ... she said Dr Fred Marshall was a legally qualified medical man, and they could not question the certificate. (*Australian Star*, 30 August 1904)

On the death certificate, Dr Marshall had stated that Amelia Lynch had died from septic peritonitis following a miscarriage. The Coroner regarded this certificate very dubiously:

They had been told by Dr Marshall himself that septic peritonitis was more often the result of criminal efforts to secure an abortion. What were his reasons in giving a certificate? Was he afraid that a public inquiry into the circumstances of her death would get him into trouble? (*Sydney Morning Herald*, 9 September 1904)

Well, yes, he was afraid, and he had good reason to be this time. The postmortem had revealed that Amelia Lunch suffered a serious perforation to the uterus.

Dr Marshall's panic is evident in his attempt to have the inquest postponed as 'his wife was in such a critical state of health that he might be called to her bedside at any moment.' (*Australian Star,* 2 September 1904) The City Coroner showed a marked reluctance to accommodate this request and demanded more evidence of Mrs Marshall's condition. In the meantime, he heard testimony from Nurse Mayne, who stated firmly that she did not receive cases that were the result of abortion. And here the ghosts of May Palmer and Emily Ritchie rose up to disprove her, for she was reminded of her involvement in the deaths of these two women by the Coroner.

The next witness called was a young woman named Elizabeth Pound, a paying lodger at Nurse Mayne's house at the time. Elizabeth Pound is an interesting witness, as she was sharing a house in Rushcutters Bay with Dr Marshall at the time of the death of Elizabeth Booth, only eight months previously – in fact, she gave evidence in defence of Dr Marshall at that inquest. 'She had known Dr Marshall for seven years . . . Dr Marshall had helped her in her studies as a nurse. She was studying from books, and the doctor took her out to three accouchement cases.' (*Australian Star*, 2 September 1904) Dr Marshall went on to marry her in March 1906.

Elisabeth Pound gave evidence that she had shown Amelia Lynch to her room when she first turned up at Nurse Mayne's house:

> 'She was very white and said she was cold. She asked for a glass of milk or a cup of tea. She looked ill, and weak and pale, but it did not appear to the witness that she had recently given birth to a child.' She described how Dr Marshall had visited over ensuing days, and that Amelia had taken a bad turn in the early hours of Saturday morning. 'Witness ran out for doctors at half past one on Saturday morning. She ran to College St, and rang the bell of the first house, but got no answer. She then rang the bell of another house but got no answer there. She did not know the names of the doctors whose bells she rang. Then she went to Dr Marshall. She did not see him but saw Miss Marshall and she said that she would send the doctor down. Dr Marshall came at 2.' (*Australian Star*, 2 September 1904)

And at this point, the inquest was adjourned, as the Coroner had received confirmation that Mrs Marshall was very seriously ill. However, when the inquest was resumed a week later, the Coroner was clearly furious that the adjournment had been granted on false pretexts. 'All I know is that the statement made then has since been discovered to be without foundation, and if I had known as much then as I know now I should not have called the adjournment.' (*Australian Star*, 8 September 1904) It seems that Mrs Marshall was not as critically ill as she had been made out to be. (In fact, she died six months later.)

Nurse Mayne was promptly recalled:

The Coroner: You first discovered the existence of peritonitis on the Wednesday. Did you communicate the fact to Dr Marshall?
Witness: Yes . . .
The Coroner: Did he examine her?
Witness: Yes.
The Coroner: And did he say anything as to the existence of peritonitis?
Witness: He said he did not think it was anything serious . . .
In answer to further questions, the witness said that Dr Marshall did not use forceps.
The Coroner: On this point you have made three different statements. First, you said that he did; then you said you did not know whether he did or not; and now you say definitely that he did not. These are three different statements. Now which is true?
Witness: He did not use the forceps. (*Australian Star*, 8 September 1904)

The evidence is a little hard to make sense of at times, as the newspapers are coy about naming the instruments referred to. 'Frederick William Marshall, re-called, denied having used a certain instrument on the deceased. He produced the instrument that he had used on the Saturday and said that he did not use any other instrument.' (*Australian Star*, 8 September 1904)

Possibly, the instrument he produced was a flushing curette, a surgical hand tool with a small scoop at the end, used for uterine scraping of 'retained products'; that is, placental or foetal tissue remaining in the uterus after a miscarriage or abortion.

Whichever instrument was used, Amelia suffered a devastating injury. Dr G. H. Taylor, Government Medical Officer, described the perforation to her uterus as 'about an inch in diameter. It was fairly circular with ragged edges. The wound could have been caused by the instrument produced. The interior appeared to have been scraped ... The perforation showed that an unusual amount of violence had been used.' (*Sydney Morning Herald,* 9 September 1904.

Dr Sydney Jamieson, a physician of over sixteen years' experience and a specialist in pathology, stated that if the organ was septic, 'it was bad treatment because it was recognised that there was a danger of perforation in using an instrument. If it was not septic, great force must have been used to cause the wound.' (*Sydney Morning Herald,* 9 September 1904) He went on to say that any medical man would know if he had made a perforation, and if he didn't, it showed a great lack of skill. He should then have got the patient to hospital, his failure to do so constituting 'gross inattention'.

This was the first time that other doctors had openly criticised Dr Marshall's ability, and they did so vehemently. The idea of violence and force used against this poor, weakened young woman (her request for a glass of milk or a cup of tea particularly poignant) must have resonated. The jury returned a verdict that Amelia Lynch had died from septic peritonitis following a certain event, and that her death was accelerated by the gross carelessness and unskilful treatment of Dr Marshall.

The Coroner (to the foreman): Did you understand my definition of malpractice?
The Foreman: Yes.
The Coroner: Then you find Dr Marshall guilty of manslaughter?
The Foreman: Yes.
Dr Marshall was then committed for trial. (*Sydney Morning Herald*, 9 September 1904)

Dr Marshall's manslaughter trial commenced later that same month, but not before he was hauled over the coals at the District Court for having attempted to do a runner. Arrested by the bailiff for having 'ignored certain court procedures' (what these procedures were is unclear, but one wonders if he was unable to cough up his £300 bail), Dr Marshall had told the bailiff he was ill, and needed to go to the lavatory. He then 'slipped away', evading arrest for some time. 'The court cannot be played with in that way,' thundered the judge. 'The bailiff should not have been deceived in that fashion.' (*Evening News*, 26 September 1904) Clearly things were beginning to seriously unravel for the doctor. On the first morning of the trial, his barrister, the beleaguered Mr Gannon, failed to show because he had not yet received his money.

The trial lasted several days, with various leading specialists brought in to give their professional opinions. Dr Joseph Foreman, a Macquarie St specialist in women's diseases, stated that the wound to the uterus 'indicated gross carelessness or ignorance on the part of the medical practitioner responsible'. (*Daily Telegraph*, 28 September 1904)

(His Honour): If an ordinary medical man made that puncture, that rupture, would he have known it? – Certainly.

If he did not know it, what would it show? – Ignorance. What kind of ignorance? – Culpable ignorance. (*Australian Star*, 27 September 1904)

Even more damning was the following statement by Dr Sydney Jamieson:

Witness said that he thought the organ must have been septic for the instrument to have perforated it, unless the curetting instrument had been used by a grossly ignorant or intoxicated person. (*Daily Telegraph*, 28 September 1904)

Dr Marshall made a lengthy statement from the dock:

He had studied in Edinburgh, Vienna, Berlin, Leipzig, Dresden, Budapest and London. He had been for three years district surgeon of the Sydney Hospital, having treated 16,700 cases there. On Saturday, August 20, Nurse Mayne had sent for him to see a patient . . . he found a girl suffering from severe bleeding. There was no time to send for another medical man and the only thing he could do – and it was an act of humanity – was to stop the haemorrhage . . . On the following Tuesday he saw her, and he noticed indications that there might be septic trouble. He used a douche but did not curette . . . On Wednesday she seemed to have improved. She did not exhibit any septic trouble until Friday August 26 . . . On the Saturday morning, continued the accused, he was called to see the deceased at 2 o'clock. She was very hysterical but seemed better when he left her. Her pulse was then normal. The next information he got was at 9 or 10 o'clock on the telephone, it being stated that she had collapsed and died at 9 o'clock ... It would be impossible for him, with his experience, to have made that puncture. 'I am inclined to think,' said the accused, 'that the puncture may have been caused during the postmortem.' (*Daily Telegraph*, 29 September 1904)

The idea that the puncture could have been caused during the postmortem was promptly shot down by Dr Taylor and Dr Palmer, both recalled separately by the Solicitor-General. In response to another question, they answered that it would have been impossible for Amelia Lynch to have had a normal pulse at 2 a.m. on the morning of her death, but that it would have been rapid, a characteristic symptom of septic peritonitis. Dr Marshall had either not known this fact or ignored its significance, because at that point, if not earlier, the young woman should have been taken to hospital.

Locked up overnight, the gentlemen of the jury could not agree on a verdict, and the next morning assured the judge that there was no possible chance they would ever agree. They were subsequently discharged. The case was set for a re-trial in November, but in fact did not go ahead until June of the following year.

In the second trial, the medical experts – clearly desperate for a conviction – pulled no punches:

Mr Pollock: After such an injury had been caused, what should a medical man do?
Dr Foreman: Assistance should be called in to see what could be done, and an operation should follow ...
Supposing that he knew what had been done and did not take this course, what would that show? – A great want of humanity, and disregard for the life of the patient.

And this from Dr Jamieson, who had previously hinted that perhaps Dr Marshall had been intoxicated:

> Mr Pollock: What did such an injury on the part of the operator indicate?
> Dr Jamieson: Either gross ignorance of the anatomy of the part, carelessness, or, to be more charitable, one might say that a man producing it was under the influence of a drug, and not in possession of his senses. (*Evening News*, 7 June 1905)

Dr Marshall – desperate to stay out of gaol – let out all stops in his statement from the dock:

> 'I was called in after midnight,' said the accused, 'by Nurse Mayne to go and see a patient in her house at Palmer Street. Being her family doctor, and having attended cases with her on many occasions, I went there without asking any questions. When I got there I found a young woman lying in bed . . .
>
> I thought that I should enjoy the privilege and honour of saving her life, thinking I was serving the best interests of humanity. I pulled off my coat, rolled up my sleeves, and tried to save that woman from death – from imminent death . . .'
>
> 'And,' went on accused, 'because I risked my liberty to save a life, I am persecuted by these trials at a time after I had met with a serious accident and had suffered from spinal meningitis. When I came back, it was only to see my wife die, and in three or four weeks – nay, not so much as four weeks – I am called upon after her death to present myself to this court to be tried on a charge of which I am entirely innocent.' (*Evening News*, 8 June 1905)

It took the jury two hours to find Dr Marshall not guilty of manslaughter, and he was accordingly discharged. And almost unbelievably, just five months later he was back in court, this time charged with murder. Martha Walker, head nurse at Gladesville Asylum, engaged to be married, had died of septicaemia. Before she died, she made a dying deposition in which she described her difficulty in seeing Dr Marshall, owing to the police presence now maintained outside his premises. Instead, she had rented a room at the home of a nurse, Mrs Steppe, and sent a telegram to her fiancé, Andrew Moorhead, asking him to fetch Dr Marshall. They paid Dr Marshall £10 in two £5 notes. She was six months pregnant. At the trial, the judge deemed the dying deposition inadmissible on a technicality – a copy of it had not been presented to Dr Marshall upon his arrest. Once again, he was acquitted.

And here the brutal tally comes to an end, or at least as far as I can tell. Just after his acquittal in March 1906, a small, sinister advertisement appears in the *Sydney Morning Herald* (19 April 1906), under *Professions, Trades Etc*: 'Dr Fred Marshall has resumed practice at Bengal House, 23 Jamieson St, nr Hunter St.'

But – perhaps mercifully – shortly thereafter he was declared bankrupt:

> His bankruptcy was caused by falling off of his business, caused by being prosecuted on several occasions for manslaughter, and other offences, and police having been stationed in front of his place taking notes of everyone who came to him. He had a big practice amongst the Chinese, and the Chinese refused to come to him when they saw the police in front of his place. (*Evening News*, 6 June 1906)

He died in December 1906, of epileptic seizures. He was 48 years old.

Of course, I feel no sympathy for Dr Marshall. Reading through all those inquest details, I have formed the impression that he was in the game for money; separated from his first wife, he seemed to have several households to support, and the abortion trade was known to be highly profitable. I have a sneaking suspicion that he may have been an opium addict, and I wonder if that is what Dr Jamieson was alluding to in his remarks at the Amelia Lynch trial. But in any case, it's plain to see from the way he spoke to Emily Ritchie ('shut your d------- mouth') and the terrible injury that he wreaked upon Amelia Lynch that he was rough and careless at best and treated these young women with contempt. And how chillingly cavalier it seems to lurch from inquest to inquest, one dead girl after another, only apparently ever lamenting the eventual drop-off in his business. These women died in agony, awash with blood. Why did he not stop?

And why was he not stopped? Why was he never convicted, despite overwhelming evidence against him? Why all those open verdicts and acquittals? Why did the police have to resort to maintaining a presence outside his premises, armed with notebooks, in the hope of deterring would-be patients? 'It is almost impossible to get a conviction, even in the most flagrant cases,' lamented *Australian Star* (8 June 1888), 'because the bars to the proof of the technical case are almost insuperable'. And certainly, the fact that the women often told stories to conceal the true cause of their sufferings did not help matters. But even beyond the onerous burden of proof required to convict, perhaps something else was at play. This small quote from the inquest into the death of Emily Ritchie, in the testimony of her daughter, Winnifred Helton, sheds some light on the matter:

Her mother told her she thought she would be all right, but if she did not recover she wished witness never to say a word against the doctor. (*Evening News,* 16 July 1901)

After all, Dr Marshall had given her an abortion before, successfully; he'd given Winnifred Helton an abortion. He had told Emily Ritchie to shut her d------- mouth when she groaned with pain, but she still wanted to protect him – even though she must have suspected by then that she wasn't going to recover. The fact is, he was providing – albeit ineptly and dangerously – a necessary service. His waiting rooms were filled with anxious women guarding their shameful secrets. All they had to do, apart from hand over the necessary cash, and pray that it turned out all right, was promise him that they wouldn't tell anyone. The risk was worthwhile, it seemed, when the alternative was disposing of a newborn in a sewer or a drain.

> It is all very well for grim lawyers and stern moralists to shriek at the deeds of the abortionist, but the public, from whom the juries are drafted, look at the terrible amount of shame and ruin and heartbreak and suicide and hellish-cruel bastardy that is spared by abortion, and it is a very hard thing to find twelve citizens of this advanced age who will convict the abortionist. (*Truth, 5* March 1899)

Angela Williamson
The Apple Isle

This is the first time I've thought about who I am without starting with my work CV. I'm a confident, educated and able woman. Yet, I'm sitting here feeling beyond vulnerable; I'm feeling less of a person. I'm feeling invisible. I'm feeling alone. I'm feeling ashamed.

I just turned 39, I have three beautiful kids, I've been a mum since I was 21. My kids are seventeen, ten and seven. I'm divorced. I'm into the second year of a loving relationship with someone I love unconditionally. We have a beautiful life.

My story represents one part of the unspoken face of terminations – I'm the mother in my late thirties who has a family, works hard in my career, doesn't always pay attention to my car . . . and my body (I need to see a dentist, I need to get a pap smear, I need to not eat and drink as much over Xmas, I need to work out what my regular cycle is . . .), who thinks about everyone else, and forgets about what I need.

I'm not reckless, a term often assigned to those who end up in this situation.

I'm also a Tasmanian female who had to fly to Melbourne because I couldn't access affordable and available abortion services in Tasmania. Even though the media releases tell me I'm not disadvantaged because I live in Tasmania, that the services have been restored, that I just have to see my GP, I've flown to Melbourne.

I'm an advocate, but I've never been an activist. I'm now both.

Tasmania has gone from leading Australia in reproductive health legislation, to shining a light on how easily access can be eroded. Reproductive health has not yet secured tripartisan policy, in particular abortion-related legislation, policy and operational environment. It's clearly viewed from a political lens in many cases, and not from a public health or personal lens. I know what a political lens is and what it leads to, especially in Tasmania. I worked in Premier Will Hodgman's Office after working for both Labor and Liberal federal Environment ministers, including our now federal Health minister, Greg Hunt. This is in addition to working in the Australian Public Service for thirteen years.

The Health portfolio has hardly impacted on me in my life. I have private health insurance and I'm fortunate to have a healthy family, so this is my first true intersection with a health policy that fails Tasmanians, that failed me. As I look back now, it's so clear to me that these times were dark and raw, and changed my life. This is how it went for me:

Decision is made.

Now what?

Where do I go?

The public debate and the official line and what the government is saying don't match the results of my internet searching.

Where do I go? I'm intelligent, but why aren't I moving? Just call a doctor. Call a doctor.

It's not clear what I need to do. I don't want to be judged. I don't want to have to see three different people. I just want this to be straightforward. To be easy to understand. I stop looking.

One week later

I don't fit into my pants. Everything feels tighter.

I need to do something.

I search the biographies of all the doctors at a semi-local clinic I go to more to than any other. I make an appointment with a female GP. I can't find my handbag. I miss the appointment. Maybe it's meant to be. Maybe this is the universe telling me not to do this.

Um, wtf? I need to stop making excuses. There's no time for excuses.

I ring the doctor's surgery to find a new time for an appointment and then spend an hour looking for my bag. It's in the back of the other car. Yep. I'm not making this easy on myself. Alex can't come. He's working. He's campaigning. He wants to win the election.

I'm talking to the GP. She's so great. But like me, she's not clear about what's available. She needs to find out. We agree that I'll get a blood test and an ultrasound, as I'm not sure what stage I'm at. I'm talking about the differences in my last period and I can see she's not confident, and now I'm not confident. We need facts. She's going to talk to her colleagues and get details. She gives me a medical certificate to focus on the tests and sorting out where I go ASAP. We will get back together next week once we have the test results. $82.50

It's Friday afternoon. I leave the GP and walk up the road for a blood test. One thing down. FREE

It's a long weekend.

I can't focus. It all seems too hard. It weighs me down. It's all consuming. Three days of trying to distract myself.

4 p.m. on Tuesday, long weekend behind us.

I'm getting an ultrasound. Alex is in the waiting room. I don't want him to see it. This is just process.

Oh fuck. It's bigger than I'd expected. Shit. It's got form. I'm crying but trying to be all humorous. I think I'm funny. But I'm really not. We are talking a month more than I had suspected. They're measuring the parts. The calculations are done and they've settled on fifteen weeks and five days. I'm fucked.

We're talking about the options available in Tasmania for aborting after fifteen weeks. Public hospitals don't do this. There's one provider offering a few a month. It's clear to me that nobody really knows what to do or what to say. Everyone wants to help, but the pathway isn't there. During my session it becomes clear that it might be easier to do this in Melbourne.

Next part down. $265.00

I'm back at the GP's office. She's got me all the details. We're excited that we both have info. It's like a show and tell. We talk about medical terminations and look awkward because I'm past that. So it's surgical. I explain that we should refer to the public, just to see if I can be one of those looked after there. Hopeful. And I also get referred to the local provider. I can confirm there are options. I'm excited. Progress. $82.50

I need information. I call the local provider. Explain that my referral was faxed earlier that day. She reads the referral and I hear it in her voice. Fuck. This isn't going to be easy.

I'm in a waiting room at an obstetrician. There are pregnant women, new babies. I can't make eye contact. I'm filling out the personal form. I just want him to do this. I don't want to go to Melbourne. I want this done now. I want my life to be normal. I'm busy. We have lots going on. The kids are back at school. The election is fast approaching. I need normality.

He's really nice. We talk and laugh. I tear up, but then make more bad jokes. Worst reflex/defence I've ever had. Really bad humour to hide utter devastation. If I didn't put this persona on, I think I'd die. I say that lightly, but there's part of me trying to work out how to escape this situation. I refuse to admit it, but these are the darkest days for me. I've never felt as low as I do at this point. Trapped. Not sure what to do or what to believe. I don't want to burden people. I feel like I've stuffed up. I feel stupid. I feel invisible. He can't do it. I'm sixteen weeks on the day. He only does a certain number of procedures and on only one day of the week. That day. Under legislation, it's illegal if we proceed after that day unless two doctors sign off. I explain all my reasons why two doctors should sign off. But it's not strong enough. He commits to talk to another doctor. He will call me once that's done. But he fills out the referral to Melbourne telling me it's going to be best, quickest and cheapest to do it in Melbourne. I resist a little. I don't want to go to Melbourne. He tells me how he'd do a sixteen-plus week termination. It's the medical pill taken in hospital and me miscarrying while under observation. I walk out and I call Melbourne. $190

Melbourne. They explain what services they offer, who they are, what needs to happen. I get in my car and I feel empty.

I go home and I google Victorian services. I look at everything. I trawl through it. There's only one place that can really do this for me. It's thirty minutes from my parents. I can't tell them. Fuck. Look at my life. Full circle. I google and look at feedback. Where are the stars and feedback like you'd have for a restaurant? It's still so taboo. But the website says it's a very common minor surgery. Why won't anyone treat it like that?

Weekend comes and goes. I'm on auto-pilot by now.

Monday
I'm back at work. I feel fat. I look fat. I have crazy eyes. I'm unsettled.

I call Melbourne. They explain the days they undertake the procedure. It's a three-day process for second trimester surgery. Starts on a Thursday. I can fly home on a Sunday. But I can't be booked in until I speak to a nurse for an assessment. I want to be booked in this Thursday. So I can move forward. So I can be normal again. If I can't get in this week, it goes from $2750 to $3300 the following week. I hate that money is playing a role in this, but I can't afford that increase. This is already going to push me outside my limits.

I have a phone consult with the nurse booked for Tuesday, the next day.

I sleep better. I can see a way forward.

I don't sleep better. I'm so uncomfortable.

Tuesday
10.30 a.m. Alex stands alongside Bec White and Tanya Plibersek as they make the state and federal Labor election pledges for terminations in Tasmania. Tanya announces that a federal Labor government would contribute $1 million to construction of a stand-alone reproductive clinic in Tasmania. Bec re-confirms that they will also cover medical and surgical terminations in the public system.

They have no idea that we are living this. They have no idea how much I want this now. They have no idea how close to tears Alex is throughout the whole announcement – what this commitment would mean for us at home.

When you wear a brave face, but there's pure anxiety and fear and pain underneath. Women aren't the only ones who carry these feelings. This moment is etched in my memories; it's a turning point in our relationship.

Lunch time, I'm outside on the phone to the nurse. She goes through the procedures. It's over three days. I can't fly until Sunday. I need a carer. We go through my details. Sixteen-plus weeks. Termination will be at seventeen or eighteen weeks. I beg for a slot this week. I have to wait to see what they can do.

Can't focus. Feel sick.

I get a phone call. I'm booked in for Thursday. I can focus again.

When I get home, I pay my deposit. $500
Flights booked. $411.50
Accommodation. $507.45

What am I doing? I've stopped talking about it with Alex. I'm internalising everything. I'm lying to him that I'll be fine. I'm telling him not to worry. I'm scared I'm going to die over there. Irrational. I buy pads. I buy Easter eggs for the kids and hide them in the cupboard. In case I die, I want him to still have Easter with the kids.

It's not a rational fear. I know that. But it's what's inside me. Dying alone. Being alone. Just alone.

I pack. A million knickers, fat pants, T-shirts, jumpers.

Thursday
We drive to the airport.

I'm really heavy. I'm bigger. We sort of talk. The rhythm isn't there. We're both afraid. I see it in his eyes. I hate that he's different. I am angry that I'm doing this alone. I lie again that I'll be fine and that I'll get a carer. I don't want a carer. I don't want anyone to know.

Distracting myself with an election. At the airport doing work. Maybe it looks like I'm off on work? Not off for termination. Not minor surgery.

I'm on the plane. I see a colleague further down the plane. I smile and wave awkwardly.

We take off. I'm alone. I'm doing this. I'm so angry and disappointed at my government. I'm disappointed with my former employer. I don't believe anyone has briefed them on what is really going on.

I see my colleague again as I'm leaving the airport. I feel a hot blush of shame creeping over me. I tell her that I'm off for minor surgery. She looks at me with a quizzical expression.

I catch the SkyBus then a train and then a taxi to the centre. I call my brother and ask if he or his nurse wife (she's pregnant, six weeks more than I am) will be my carer. I don't tell them everything. It gets confusing. I tell them everything.

The centre is great; the staff are amazing. My humour is ridiculously bad. Argh, stop it! I've decided we need this in Hobart. It's discreet. It makes sense. It feels right. I'm no longer being judged. I'm safe.

Back at the hotel, it's all very real. I'm alone. I'm scared. I'm hungry. I miss Alex. I miss the kids. I wonder: if I died would he know there were Easter eggs in the cupboard? I don't think I even told him about them.

Friday
I'm like a scientist, getting as much information as I can. I go through the processes, I'm so impressed with the people. I feel so safe.

I pay the remainder: $2250

I get into the gown and hat and booties. There are six of us in the waiting room. We keep to ourselves, looking at the TV for a while, smiling nervously if we catch each other's eyes. Finally, we start talking in the waiting room. We all have such different and similar stories. Some are local, some are from regional areas, some are from overseas. We are all here because this is the only place we could go to have this procedure.

I'm walking into the theatre and I notice on the TV that Barnaby Joyce has resigned.

I lie down. I feel safe. But I'm so frightened. I'm really far away from my home.

I wake up and tell the nurse that Barnaby Joyce resigned. I am a nerd!

I've told all the staff that I want to advocate for solving the surgical termination situation in Tasmania. It's clear to me that the public system, doing this in a hospital, is different to doing this in a standalone centre. Tanya Plibersek's addition makes so much more sense to me now. These two actions are essential. It's the counselling, the care, the discretion, the privacy, the security. These aren't on offer in Tasmania under the current system. The combination is a really good option. It's very clear what I need to do when I get home. I'm going to talk to the decision makers, tell them my experience confidentially. I'm going to use social media to highlight this injustice. I'm not ashamed or afraid of speaking out on this issue. Reproductive health directly affects 51 per cent of the population, and has indirect impact on the remainder of our population. My connections from my former roles mean that my story may have weight. They'll be able to put a face to the policy.

My brother and his wife take me to my hotel. I talk and eat and do everything I can to be distracted. They leave. I'm alone.

I go to sleep knowing that the foetus is already asleep. It's the first night I've been in bed these past weeks without feeling anything. I feel numb. I miss Alex. I'm alone.

I don't sleep. I cry all night. I wake up dehydrated.

Saturday
This is the big day.

I get there a little later than the others. I go through the process. It's hard and fast for me. I'm angry at Alex, but I don't know why. Because he couldn't come? Because I wanted them to win the election so that this doesn't happen to anyone else?

I'm telling the staff my intention to advocate when I get home. They are all supportive, but want me to focus on myself first.

Fuck, it's all so fast. I have a high pain threshold, so by the time I'm asking for pain relief, I'm pretty much ready for surgery.

I wake up and I'm shaking.

The staff are all so good to me. At least I wasn't talking about Barnaby Joyce this time.

I'm sitting down in recovery. I have a million cups of Milo. Well, four. Maybe five. I haven't had Milo for years and years. I get picked up and I leave everything behind.

I have lunch like everyone else. I watch a movie. I catch up with a colleague. I grab some take-away dinner.

I think about the Easter eggs. I'm not dead.

I talk to Alex, but I have nothing to say.

I still feel invisible. I go to sleep.

Sunday
We head to the airport and I can't stop telling my sister-in-law how amazing the staff were. I'm a living review. I can't stop gushing.

I'm not that person who flew to Melbourne four days earlier. I'm even more complex. I'm armed with information, statistics, and a purpose. But I'm also tired. And I'm not sure how to start a conversation with the government.

Thanks Jetstar for making me pay $60 in excess baggage because of all the pads I'm now carrying with me. I fucking weigh less than I did on my way over! I'm so mad.

I cry quietly on the plane. I'm strong and vulnerable all at once.

I'm invisible. No one knows why I'm crying.

This is grief. I'm alone. I'm empty. I can't make any more jokes. I'm done.

No one should have to pay over $4000 for this procedure, and no one should have to leave their home and fly interstate. This is a disgrace.

Caroline de Costa

Who are the abortion providers, and what does the future hold?

In Australia, we do not have a country-wide public health system which provides safe, timely, local, legal and financially accessible abortion services from experienced and sympathetic health professionals, as part of holistic women's reproductive healthcare, and available to all women resident in Australia.

Like abortion laws, abortion services in Australia are different – sometimes very different – from one state to another. Abortion law was initially state law that from the time of colonisation was included in criminal legislation; as law reform gradually took place, service provision followed, in a piecemeal state-by-state process. All jurisdictions do now have some safe and legal abortion services, but where these are located, and who actually performs abortions, is very variable.

We must strive to achieve uniformity, accessibility and high standards across the country. This is what has been provided, for example, in the United Kingdom (apart from Northern Ireland) since the passing of their *Abortion Act* of 1967. An essential first step is much better education and training of medical students and doctors in the need for accessible abortion services, and in the techniques of abortion.

Most early abortions, up to fourteen weeks' gestation, both surgical and medical, take place in the private sector; the main exception is South Australia, where a public abortion service is provided. Early procedures make up nearly 95 per cent of all abortions. With some exceptions, the doctors performing or supervising these procedures are registered medical practitioners, sometimes with diplomas in obstetrics and gynaecology or other qualifications, but they are not specialist gynaecologists. They have undertaken training and education in the practice of abortion in various ways and are highly skilled and experienced in the area; the doctors working for Marie Stopes Australia, which is the largest organisation providing abortion care in the country, are an example.

The majority of later abortions (5 to 6 per cent of all abortions) are performed because some abnormality has been detected in the pregnancy, mostly a severe foetal abnormality revealed by the very sensitive screening and diagnostic tests now available to pregnant women, but sometimes because a condition in the woman makes continuing the pregnancy risky for her. All later abortions must, under the health regulations of all states and territories, be performed in a relatively small number of accredited hospitals or clinics. Like early abortions, they may be performed surgically or medically. While some are performed, and very competently, by non-specialist doctors with appropriate training in dedicated private clinics, most are done by specialist obstetricians and gynaecologists, many of whom have further qualifications in Maternal Foetal Medicine (MFM).

Until recently, abortion was a topic not publicly discussed in Australia; women felt stigmatised if they revealed an abortion, and in most jurisdictions abortion was unlawful. Doctors also avoided the topic; general practitioners wanted to be able to refer women requesting abortion to safe legal services but were reluctant to perform abortions themselves, and most specialist gynaecologists did not perform early procedures either. Early abortions took place in free-standing clinics divorced from other medical institutions, and this continues to be the case. In both society generally, and among the medical profession in particular, abortion remained in a grey area, the last taboo.

Fortunately, over the past eighteen years of the 21st century this has started to change; there have been major law reforms in five states and territories, and lesser changes in others. The topic is now widely discussed in the media, and many research papers on abortion practice are being published in medical journals.

However, only around half of the nineteen Australian medical schools include abortion in their curriculum, and even in these it is often limited to a one-hour lecture, which may not be compulsory in order not to offend a small number of students. Because most medical students undertake their clinical training in public hospitals, where virtually no early abortions are performed, medical students do not meet women requesting and undergoing abortion, and do not witness their procedures.

While the Royal Australian and New Zealand College of Obstetricians and Gynaecologists (RANZCOG) is now actively promoting the education of trainee doctors in the care of women requesting abortion, at the time of writing the online education around abortion that the College provides has only just become mandatory, and there are no requirements for trainees to undergo clinical experience in the practice of abortion. This means that most doctors undertaking the six years of training required to become a Fellow of RANZCOG have emerged as specialists but with little or no direct knowledge of a vitally important part of women's reproductive healthcare. Some of these young Fellows go on to become MFM specialists and therefore become expert in late abortion care, but recruitment of doctors trained in early abortion services remains problematic.

All forms of abortion require doctors to be involved, both by law and because it is in the best interests, physically and emotionally, of the women seeking and undergoing abortion, to have trained medical practitioners available. Mostly the involvement of doctors is minimal, because most abortions take place before fourteen weeks and most women are healthy and have made their decision for abortion themselves, or with the help of partners, family or friends. Early medical abortion allows the woman herself to control the time she self-administers the drugs; the consultation around why she is requesting abortion, her general health, and the information about the process necessary to her giving informed consent can all be conducted by a trained nurse or midwife, with access to a supervising doctor if questions arise. In many countries, early medical abortion care is provided almost entirely by nurses and midwives, something we could emulate here. Later abortions need the skills of appropriately trained doctors, often Fellows of RANZCOG with MFM qualifications, working together with nursing staff, midwives, social workers, psychologists and others as needed.

Education about abortion needs to start in medical school. At James Cook University medical school in Cairns we provide lectures on the topic in the fifth year of training, attendance at early medical abortion (EMA) clinics in our Sexual Health service for one day in that year, and two weeks further experience in the sexual health clinic in their sixth and final year. Students with conscientious objections to abortion may opt out; in fourteen years, none has done so. The students learn about the reasons women request abortion, which often involve complex medical, social, employment and family issues – they discover that financial hardship, difficulty accessing reliable contraception, domestic violence and long-term social disadvantage play a huge role in these requests. They take part in consultations where women are counselled and informed about the process of EMA performed in the woman's home, and they observe follow-up visits and the provision of long-acting contraception. I know that similar education is provided in other medical schools, particularly in South Australia and Victoria, but I believe it should be available to all medical students. Most will never actively practice abortion but they need to come to regard it as part of mainstream medical practice, like neurosurgery and appendectomies. My views are strongly supported by the Australian Medical Students' Association.

Equally, there should be mandatory education about abortion for all RANZCOG trainees, as well as trainees of the Royal Australian College of General Practitioners; GPs are a group ideally placed to provide accurate information to women about abortion, and to provide EMA in their practices. I am not suggesting that the trainees of either College should be obliged to perform abortions, simply that they need to know that around one in four Australian women undergoes an abortion at some time in her reproductive years, women's reasons for doing so, and how procedures are performed. Apart from anything else, these trainees, once qualified and working, are likely to care for some women presenting post-abortion; as well, many trainees will find that this is an area that is not as frightening or off-putting as they perhaps thought, and incorporate it into their practices.

I am strongly supportive of all the doctors currently working in abortion care across Australia; they are doing a wonderful job. However, to expand services, especially in rural areas, to provide for the future, and to bring abortion out of that grey area of medical practice and into mainstream medicine, we need to start training all students and junior doctors (and other health professionals) in the basics of abortion care.

Caroline de Costa

Out of the shadows: abortion in Queensland

On 16 October 2018 I climbed the elegant timber staircase that leads to the public gallery of Queensland's Parliament House in Brisbane, and seated myself in the front row. The House is a magnificent building that has aged gracefully; constructed of sandstone, with a copper roof, ornate ceilings and splendid painted friezes, it is surrounded by parklands that help keep it cool in Brisbane summers. Building began in 1864, and took 25 years. Throughout that time, Queensland was a colony, part of the British Empire, ruled by Queen Victoria.

Much of the criminal legislation of Queensland also dates back to the same Victorian era. The Queensland Criminal Code was written and promulgated in 1899, just prior to Australian Federation; sections 224–226 of the Code, however, were taken almost word-for-word from earlier legislation: the English

Offences Against the Person Act of 1861. These sections deal with the matter of abortion, and they contain none of the charm of the building in which they were conceived. Instead they are brusque, promising years of imprisonment with hard labour to any woman convicted of attempting to procure an abortion for herself, anyone attempting to perform an abortion, and anyone assisting. Note the word attempting – the abortion did not need to be successful. Nor did the woman need to be pregnant, she had only to fear that she might be, that fear leading to her action; these laws date from a time long before pregnancy could be confidently diagnosed by two blue lines glimpsed in the privacy of a woman's own bathroom. There was a defence for a doctor prosecuted for abortion in section 282 of the Code, if it could be shown that a 'surgical operation' was necessary 'for the preservation of the mother's life, if the performance of the operation (was) reasonable'; but what doctor would want to risk prosecution and a possible prison sentence to perform such an operation?

Unlike the building, these laws did not mature and grow more graceful with the passing years. Rather, they contributed mightily to the shame, stigma and secrecy surrounding abortion in Queensland, and to the deaths of hundreds and maybe thousands of Queensland women, as well as to the chronic ill-health and infertility of many others.

Ostensibly, the laws were intended to protect women from the hands of untrained 'backstreet' abortion providers, whose ministrations often led to severe bleeding or infection. But they were also designed to punish women who dared to stray outside the accepted 19th-century boundaries of female sexuality, when women were supposed to engage in sex only within marriage, for the purpose of procreation of any number of children. Never mind if a woman was single, or raped, or poor, or very young, or the victim of domestic violence, or forced into sex she did not want with a partner or husband, and had no wish for procreation.

The legislation did not work even for its stated purpose. My research in the state archives in outer Brisbane showed many death certificates in the period 1899–1970 for women who died from 'miscarriage' or 'peritonitis' that were probably from illegal and unsafe abortion; doctors wanted to spare families the shame of such a diagnosis. But some coronial reports speak the truth. In 1912 Alice A, aged 42, a farmer's wife and mother of seven children, died in Ingham hospital after swallowing toxic chemicals: savin and pennyroyal. In 1932 Lizzie H, a mother of five, died in Ipswich Hospital after a local chemist attempted an abortion with a syringe. In 1933, Rita L, a single woman of 23, died in Goondiwindi from sepsis after attempting abortion with 'a yellow knitting needle, broken in three pieces', which was produced in court. Doctors right across Queensland would have been very familiar with such scenarios, but although many of them would have been sympathetic towards the women concerned, there was little they could do to save or cure them, even after the introduction of antibiotics at the time of the Second World War. And with abortion in the Criminal Code, very few doctors ever contemplated openly performing an abortion in a hospital, even when section 282 might have protected them because the procedure would have been done in the interests of the woman's life.

So it was with great interest that I climbed those parliamentary stairs last October and sat watching the two days and one evening of the debate and vote on the Termination of Pregnancy Bill 2018, designed to end the laws that had been in force for 119 years.

The situation around abortion in Queensland began to change in the 1970s. In Victoria and New South Wales, where there was criminal legislation similar to Queensland's, the Menhennitt and Levine judgments, of 1969 and 1972 respectively, had provided case law which meant a registered medical practitioner could legally perform an abortion in certain circumstances. In Victoria Dr Davidson and in New South Wales Dr Wald had been acquitted of charges of abortion when the judges ruled that the doctors had acted in good faith to preserve the life or health of the woman. As a result, clinics providing surgical abortions (medical abortion had yet to be developed) were cautiously opened in both states, and Queensland women who were aware of the existence of these, and had the means to travel, began to avail themselves of their services. However, information for women about abortion, and even about contraception, was virtually non-existent in Queensland.

In 1971, Brisbane members of the Humanist League and others decided to establish a branch of the Abortion Law Reform Association. ALRA branches had been very successful in the movements to decriminalise or legalise abortion elsewhere in the English-speaking world. The aims of the original members – teacher Beryl Holmes, social worker Liz Pasmore, Dr Trevor Sauer, Dr Janet Irwin and others – were to press for sex education in schools, family planning services and women's right to choose abortion.

The founding members quickly discovered that there was an enormous unmet demand for the provision of information about abortion, quite apart from the provision of abortion services themselves. In 1972, ALRA members decided to set up an organisation to be called Children by Choice, which quickly became a referral service for women travelling interstate for safe abortion. Children by Choice exists to this day, and is a unique organisation that provides women experiencing unintended pregnancies with information about their options, as well as counselling and referral for abortion if that is their choice. Children by Choice staff and supporters have also taken on political roles and were very involved in recent campaigns for Queensland abortion law reform; by the time the vote was approaching in the House on the evening of 17 October, many were gathered in the Public Gallery, including some of the women who had been part of those early days.

In 1977, Dr Peter Bayliss moved to Queensland. He had worked in the first abortion clinic in Victoria, set up by Dr Bert Wainer and his wife Jo in Melbourne after the landmark Menhennitt decision, and he opened an abortion service at Greenslopes in suburban Brisbane, relying on the interstate cases for a defence should he be prosecuted under the Criminal Code. In 1983, Dr David Grundmann opened a similar clinic in Townsville.

Dr Bayliss's clinic went about its work openly for eight years up until 1985, although it was certainly the object of much polarised debate in Queensland, including among parliamentarians. There were numerous attempts by members of Queensland's Right to Life lobby group to shut it down; undoubtedly, these attempts were supported by Premier Joh Bjelke-Petersen. However, Bayliss was popular with the Queensland media who regarded him as a 'colourful' figure. He appeared often in television debates, defending the right of Queensland women to access abortion, and publicly challenging the Right to Life group to prosecute him. His nemesis was Right to Life Queensland secretary Winifred Egan, who called constantly for Bayliss's prosecution under the Criminal Code. Eventually the police did act – though not as a result of private pressure by Egan but following the directions of Justice minister Neville Harper, who was probably motivated by a belief that he had the approval of the Premier and therefore the prospect of furthering his political career.

On the morning of 20 May 1985, Peter Bayliss was calmly operating in his clinic when more than 50 police arrived in a bus and burst through the door, armed with search warrants. They were accompanied by 'specialist gynaecologists, anaesthetists, nurses, government medical officers, pathologists and forensic biologists' – their presence necessary, according to Assistant Police Commissioner Bill McArthur, 'to ensure the welfare of any patient requiring emergency attention.' The clinic was surrounded with crime scene tape, and police technicians with crowbars began to dig up the building's drains – fruitlessly, as it turned out. Other specialist police technical staff, said the Assistant Commissioner, included photographic and fingerprint experts. 'We were outnumbered four to one,' Bayliss later said. 'You could have robbed every bank in Brisbane at that moment.'

More than 45,000 case history cards, filed alphabetically in more than 300 boxes, were seized by police and taken away in trucks. Another smaller raid on Dr Grundmann's Townsville clinic netted 2000 further case records. The bearded Bayliss was driven away in a squad car – looking unruffled and smoking his pipe – when he refused to give an undertaking to police that he would not continue to conduct terminations of pregnancy in the clinic. He was charged under section 224 of the Criminal Code with having 'conspired with persons unknown to use force to procure an abortion' and released on bail. It appeared that police were planning to trawl through records to find a patient or patients with whom he might have 'conspired' in order to try to convict him. Dr Grundmann was similarly charged.

Initial public statements by police and the Justice minister were smug. 'The raids followed several months of secret investigation and planning by specially selected police officers,' said a police spokesman. Then as the reality of the clinic invasion and the seizure of personal records became clear, there was a huge outpouring of public concern and anger, and public opinion quickly turned against the government. Children by Choice organised a well-attended public meeting in City Hall. On May 24, a survey of Brisbane residents commissioned by the *Courier-Mail* and TV0 Eyewitness News showed that 78 per cent of Queenslanders disapproved of the police raids on the clinics, and a similar percentage believed that it was a woman's right to choose whether she should terminate a pregnancy. Parliamentarians were receiving hundreds of letters and phone calls from concerned citizens – particularly women who had been patients of the Brisbane and Townsville clinics and their partners and families, but also many others alarmed by the attack on civil rights.

Dr Bayliss himself was not idle. While Dr Bert Wainer organised colleagues to keep the clinic open, he and his lawyers filed a complaint with the Supreme Court of Queensland seeking the return of the files. Early in June, three senior judges of the Court ruled unanimously that the search warrants used to raid both the Brisbane and Townsville clinics were invalid, charges against the doctors were dropped, and costs of the court actions were ordered to be reimbursed to them. The Justice minister was also dropped – from the Cabinet.

The return of the records and the throwing out of the charges was, however, far from the end of the matter. In June of 1985 Des Sturgess QC, the state's Director of Public Prosecutions, took the unusual step of calling upon clients of the Greenslopes clinic to come forward with any complaints they might wish to make against Bayliss. This followed the surprising suggestion by the Justice minister, on the television program *60 Minutes*, that it would be appropriate for his department to initiate a criminal prosecution against one or more doctors in order to test the limits of existing legislation (that is, of sections 224–226 of the Criminal Code). Clearly such actions would have been a misuse of criminal proceedings.

It is noteworthy that not once throughout the public furore that surrounded the raids, nor indeed at any time previously, did even one of the 47,000 women whose records had been seized make a complaint against either of the doctors or suggest that their abortions had not been properly carried out. Now it was being reported on the radio that the Director of Public Prosecutions was seeking women willing to testify against Dr Bayliss, and at last one woman did so. This woman, Tracey T, who had undergone a procedure at the Greenslopes clinic in early 1985, later admitted in court that she had believed she would receive some financial reward from making such a complaint, and that this was the reason she brought her complaint to the DPP's office. (Unfortunately for her, there was no such financial incentive.)

So Dr Bayliss was again charged under section 224 with unlawfully using force to procure an abortion, and this time the prosecution had an actual patient: Tracey. Dr Bayliss's anaesthetist for the operation was Dr Dawn Cullen, who was also charged under section 224. The trial, which took place in late January of 1986, would become a landmark, although not in the way intended by Des Sturgess. Both doctors pleaded not guilty to the charges.

The trial took place in the District Court in Brisbane and the judge was Frederick McGuire, who at the age of 57 had been twelve years on the Bench. Sturgess himself led the prosecution. The public gallery overflowed with lawyers, doctors, pro- and anti-abortion supporters, members of Right to Life and of radical women's organisations. Those who couldn't fit into the court room stood outside under the trees around the Court complex.

From the beginning Sturgess sought to portray Bayliss, and to a lesser extent Dawn Cullen, as running 'an abortion factory' – there was no evidence, he said, to suggest that Mrs T's procedure was 'any attempt to be a lawful operation.' Referring to Mrs T's record cards from the clinic, he described her consultations with a counsellor, two doctors and a nurse as 'perfunctory and superficial.' She is, he said, 'a sturdy woman.'

But the 'sturdy woman' herself thought otherwise. Under cross-examination from the defence lawyers, Tracey said that she had told a counsellor at the clinic that at the age of twenty she could not cope physically, mentally, emotionally or financially with a fourth child. According to her lawyers, she met the criteria of the defence section, 282, of the Criminal Code.

Justice McGuire addressed the jury, and the subsequent 56-page document he wrote provided the McGuire ruling upon which, for the past 33 years, doctors performing abortions in Queensland have relied for support if prosecuted. Essentially, McGuire ruled that 'the doctor(s) held a belief on reasonable grounds that the operation was necessary to preserve the life and health of Mrs T.' McGuire referred to both the earlier Menhennitt and Levine judgments in reaching his conclusions. Following the judge's address, the jury of eight women and four men returned a unanimous verdict of 'not guilty' for both Bayliss and Cullen.

McGuire, in the introductory remarks of his written judgment, said: 'I think it fair and proper that there should be some authoritative guidance offered to the public and the medical profession, whether it comes from the Parliament or the Courts, or both, on the thorny problems to which the subject of abortion gives rise. The task before me is a responsible and formidable one. I approach it, as best I can, free of emotion and predilection.' By the time he reached the end of his deliberations, he was very clear on just one thing: 'This Ruling serves to illustrate the uncertainty of the present abortion laws of Queensland. It will require more imperative authority (either the Court of Appeal or Parliament) to effect changes if changes are thought to be desirable or necessary with a view to amending and clarifying the law.'

However, apart from some minor changes to section 282 in 2009, adding medical abortion using drugs to the wording of section 282, successive parliaments recoiled from every suggestion that the antiquated Victorian-era abortion laws be in any way updated or amended.

Nevertheless, abortion did gradually become more available to Queensland women. To understand how this happened it's first necessary to understand that there are big differences between the way abortion is practised in early and later pregnancy, why it may be requested in these two situations, and where and by whom it is provided, although practice in Queensland is very similar to that in all states and territories across Australia.

Around 95 per cent of all abortions are performed in the first trimester, the first fourteen weeks of pregnancy, for medical, psychological, financial or social reasons, or a combination of these. (As anyone concerned in the provision of abortion services can testify, 'social' often covers severe economic hardship, single motherhood, domestic violence, incest and sexual coercion, and in general women do not make the decision for abortion lightly.) Until 2006 these were always done surgically, in licensed clinics or hospitals, almost exclusively in the private sector. In 2006, legislation in the federal parliament brought as a private members' bill by four cross-party women senators overturned earlier legislation – the 'Harradine Amendment – that had prevented the import and use of the drug mifepristone (RU486) in Australia. In that same year, Dr Mike Carrette and I, working in Cairns, became the first doctors in Australia to use the drug for early medical abortion (EMA). Gradually, more doctors joined us and the drug was fully licensed by the Therapeutic Goods Administration in 2012. In many urban areas of Queensland women have for years now been able to choose between medical or surgical methods for an abortion in the early part of pregnancy, as private providers, particularly the Marie Stopes Australia organisation, have established clinics.

However, because of the spectre of the Criminal Code, only a small number of other doctors have been willing to provide early abortions, both surgical and medical, keeping the practice of abortion, and discussion around it, very much in the shadows. Early abortion, at the time of writing, is not available in the public hospital system in Queensland, apart from the unique service of early medical abortion set up by the Sexual Health Clinic in Cairns Hospital under the direction of Dr Darren Russell, who has worked closely with myself and Mike Carrette.

Many women in rural and remote areas of the state, and still quite a few in the larger towns, have had difficulties accessing both information about services, and the services themselves, particularly if the general practitioners in their area hold religious or other objections to abortion. However, even doctors who have provided abortions have needed to consult with the woman and determine that her physical and/or mental health will be at risk if she continues the pregnancy, in accordance with the dictates of the Criminal Code; the ever-present possibility of prosecution has kept abortion in a very grey area for many doctors.

The remaining 5 per cent or so of abortions take place later in pregnancy – that is, later than fourteen weeks; most are done by twenty weeks of pregnancy but a small number later than this. By far the most common reason for these late terminations is the discovery of a severe and often life-threatening abnormality in the foetus; sometimes a severe medical condition in the woman means termination is recommended.

There is now high quality, very sensitive screening for foetal abnormalities which is offered to all pregnant women having antenatal care in Australia, including in Queensland. This screening is offered from ten weeks of pregnancy onwards. If a woman is found to be at high risk of an abnormality she is then offered a diagnostic test – diagnostic tests are more invasive than screening tests but they can give a definite answer as to whether or not a foetus does have a particular abnormality. If such a diagnosis is made, the woman can then be offered termination of the pregnancy, although not all hospitals carrying out the diagnostic tests will also offer abortion: the Catholic Mater Hospital in Brisbane is an example of such a hospital that does the tests but not the terminations.

The decision to terminate what is mostly a planned and wanted pregnancy, because of the unexpected and shocking diagnosis of an abnormality at quite an advanced stage of that pregnancy, is a very different situation for the woman concerned from that facing the woman making her decision much earlier, for whatever reason. In Queensland, most later abortions are done in public hospitals, as part of antenatal care, and in many cases they are performed by Maternal Foetal Medicine specialists in just one or two Queensland hospitals. These specialists work with teams of midwives, nurses, psychologists, social workers and others to assist the woman, her partner and family through the challenging experience of late abortion, which is generally carried out as a medical abortion, using the same drugs (including mifepristone, RU486) as are used in EMA. This means that the woman goes through a process very similar to the labour preceding the birth of a full-term healthy baby, but without the same result.

Ultrasound and other tests of foetal wellbeing were unknown to the writers of the Queensland Criminal Code in 1899; in fact, there was barely any antenatal care provided to pregnant women. So the idea that women might be give a diagnosis of an abnormality in their yet-to-be-born infant and that this should be grounds for legally terminating the pregnancy, safely, in hospital, did not enter the heads of the founding fathers convening in Parliament House. To justify performing late abortions for severe foetal abnormality, Queensland doctors have often had to use the claim that the woman was at risk of psychiatric sequelae, even when that woman was simply making an informed and reasonable decision for herself. So the development of major new medical techniques and drugs, as well as improvements in the practice of surgery and anaesthesia, and the introduction of antibiotics, all meant that by the beginning of the 21st-century Queensland abortion law was way out of step with actual abortion practice.

In 2009, bizarre events began to unfold in Cairns. A young couple were charged with importing the drugs mifepristone and misoprostol from relatives in the Ukraine, and using these to bring about an apparently successful abortion in the woman. Police were searching the couple's home on an unrelated matter (for which no charges were ever laid) when they discovered the discarded packaging from the drugs. Quite why the police prosecutor decided to press charges under sections 225–226 of the Criminal Code has never been clear but press them he did, into the magistrate's court and eventually the District Court of Queensland. This took eighteen months and was accompanied by a huge wave of unwanted publicity for the couple, across all media and the internet. There was huge support for the couple from pro-choice organisations in Cairns, Brisbane, the rest of Queensland and across the country. The culmination was a three-day trial in front of a jury, who returned a unanimous decision of 'not guilty' – to much cheering from the many supporters in the public gallery.

Following the verdict, the couple returned to private life but the campaign to change the archaic Queensland law continued and grew stronger. In 2015 Rob Pyne, a former Cairns Council member, was elected as the Labor member for Cairns in the new government led by Annastacia Palaszczuk and containing a number of women – Jackie Trad, Shannon Fentiman, Nikki Boyd and others – who were prominent supporters of abortion law reform. Rob Pyne pressed for legislation to be drafted and presented to the new parliament – he was very conscious of the law having so recently been used against two of his own constituents. He was unsuccessful in this – it was, apparently, felt that the government did not have the numbers to pass what would be controversial legislation. Rob Pyne resigned from the ALP but continued as an independent member, and in that capacity, in 2016, he introduced two private member's bills. The first simply called for decriminalisation; the second went into some detail around matters such as the rights of conscientious objectors.

Parliament appointed a committee of inquiry who made in-depth studies of the legislation in other Australian jurisdictions, and sought the views of the Australian Medical Association, the Royal Australian and New Zealand College of Obstetricians and Gynaecologists, the Queensland Nurses' Union and many other relevant bodies, as well as such authorities as Professor Heather Douglas, professor of criminal law at the University of Queensland. All Queenslanders were also publicly invited to express an opinion, and thousands did so. Two detailed reports were produced but no formal recommendations were made by the committee, whose members were evenly split along party lines. Pyne withdrew the two bills in February 2017 and they were never discussed or voted on by the parliament.

However, the Premier promised to refer the matter of abortion law to the Queensland Law Reform Commission, and in June of 2017 she did just that, requesting the Commission to review sections 224–226 of the Criminal Code with a view to reforming and decriminalising, and to prepare draft legislation. In the interim there was another Queensland election and the Palaszczuk government was returned, now with a significant majority.

The QLRC took a year to examine the matter; they also conducted their own independent inquiry and sought the views of many experts. While the members of the Commission worked away, the need – or not – for reform was widely debated in Queensland media; the newspapers are almost all Murdoch-owned, and while some views in favour of reform were published there were many more pages opposing the idea. *BuzzFeed*, *The Guardian* and other independent media provided more balanced views, more reflective of the belief of most Queenslanders that women should have access to safe, legal abortion when that is their choice.

Eventually, on 30 June 2018, the QLRC released their report and the draft legislation they proposed to the government. In essence the legislation:
- removes sections 224–226 from the Criminal Code, decriminalising abortion;

- allows abortion to 22 weeks when a woman and her doctor agree to the procedure; after 22 weeks the full and considered approval of a second doctor is required;
- allows for conscientious objectors to opt out of abortion provision but requires such doctors to make an effective and timely referral of a woman requesting abortion to a service that will discuss all options including abortion;
- makes provision for exclusion zones of 150 metres around services providing abortions, to protect 'the safety and wellbeing' of women and staff entering and leaving the premises; harassment by anti-choice protesters has long been a problem in Queensland, as elsewhere.

The bill was presented to parliament by Attorney-General Yvette D'Ath and had its first reading on 22 August 2018. Essentially, it was as the draft legislation was written. After that reading it was allowed to lie on the table for six weeks while a further parliamentary committee inquiry was conducted. A further 1200 submissions were received by this committee. The opportunities for Queenslanders to record their views on this topic have been almost boundless.

The second reading and the debate took place on 16 and 17 October and for people like myself, involved for many years in campaigning for abortion law change, and seated behind glass in the public gallery, the spectacle of parliamentarians, respectfully and intelligently discussing and debating the legislation, was theatrical in its intensity. Acts 1 and 2 took place on the first and second days, as alternately members of the government and the Liberal National Party opposition rose to speak: the former in favour of, and the latter against the bill. It seemed that the numbers were there to pass the legislation, but there was at that stage no certainty of this. The two members of

Katter's Australian Party were opposed to the bill, but the one Greens member and the single independent spoke in favour.

Act 3 began mid-afternoon of Wednesday 17 October, when Steve Minnikin, LNP member for Chatsworth, rose and strongly stated his intention to vote in favour of the bill. He spoke with great conviction and had a clearly thought-out position. Not long afterwards, Tim Nicholls, formerly LNP leader, also showed his hand: he would be voting for the bill.

There was a series of amendments, eight in all, brought by the LNP's Mark McArdle; they included reducing the 22 week cutoff point to sixteen, the mandatory offer of counselling to women requesting abortion, and alterations to the plans around conscientious objection. As each was presented, the minister for Health, Steven Miles, rose in his seat and with Shakespearean gravitas provided cogent arguments against the amendment; all were voted down.

It had been expected that parliament would adjourn and return the following day for the bill's third reading and the final vote. Instead, Minister Miles rose again, and moved that the reading be held immediately and the vote taken. This was agreed; the tension in the public gallery reached fevered levels, albeit in the total silence demanded by the ushers.

The parliamentarians stood: Minnikin, Nicholls and Jann Stuckey of the LNP, Michael Berkman of the Greens and independent Sandy Bolton crossed to join the ALP members of the government, and the bill was passed 50 votes to 41. Cheering broke out in the gallery as the Speaker, Curtis Pitt, struggled to maintain order, but the elation was there in the members as well, especially the Cabinet members and the many women who had supported these changes for so long.

Subsequently, some in the media questioned the propriety of our celebrating something as serious as abortion. I believe that our feelings were not only entirely justified, they were well placed. Queensland women now have world-class legislation around abortion. We can begin installing new services, and improving existing ones, so that they are woman-centred, accessible, safe and *legal*. We can watch abortion become part of mainstream women's healthcare, part of discussion in regular society. We can see it come out of the shadows where it has been hidden for the past 119 years.

Melissa Lucashenko
Together we are powerful

1960s
A girl is four, or five, or six. She runs uphill, her legs scissoring faster and faster as she rounds the bend to the letterbox. She is intoxicated by her own speed. The girl has learned that her body is a vehicle for power and joy.

1970s
A girl is seven and lies on a single bed. Her relative touches her in ways that are first pleasurable, then bewildering. There is a gap in her brain, and then she is crying in the laundry while her mother asks her what's wrong. The tone of her mother's voice tells her that something very bad has happened. The girl has learned that her body does not belong to her and is a source of shame and trouble.

A girl is ten and a young boy she knows offers her twenty cents to pull her pants down for him in a park. She refuses and tells no one of his odd request. She has learned that her body and money are connected.

1980s
A girl is fifteen and has intercourse with a much older married man who has groomed her for half a year. It hurts. 'Try to relax,' he tells her. Afterwards, the man arranges to see her again in a month. When she asks why so long, he explains that it is to check that she isn't pregnant. She has learned that she is disposable.

A young woman comes back to Australia from an overseas trip, vomiting with stress and travel sickness. She has sex with her boyfriend that afternoon. Saying no is an option, but not worth his sulky displeasure. She has learned long ago to give in.

A teenager is pregnant in country New South Wales after a doctor prescribes her both The Pill, and antibiotics rendering The Pill useless, in the same visit. She is taken by a cousin for an abortion in the city. The train trip is long, shameful, frightening. The mother of the pregnant teenager has had several traumatic abortions of her own and can't face the reality of her daughter's. Nobody ever speaks about it again. The teenager has learned that reproductive accidents are her fault, and that abortion is a 'sin' she must carry for the rest of her life.

A woman is couch-surfing in Brisbane and her period is late. Neither she nor the potential father have money for food, let alone an abortion. She walks into a doctor's office anyway. An older woman behind the desk points up the road, sourly. 'It's that one up on the next block,' the older woman says, as though it's a phrase she utters many times a week. It turns out the woman isn't pregnant, after all. She has learned that she can be lucky, sometimes.

1990s

A Christian woman is at university in Brisbane. A single parent of two, she finds herself pregnant, yet again. She goes dirt-biking the next weekend, deliberately hitting the rutted road as hard as she possibly can, jolting her body over and over. She aborts at home and feels only massive relief. She has learned to find a way.

An older woman talks of helping pregnant Tasmanian women get to Melbourne for terminations. 'They talk about the grief and shame of abortion,' she says, 'but every woman I ever took across was just fucking relieved to have it done and dusted, full stop.' The older woman has long ago learned not to believe the patriarchal bullshit.

2000s

A woman walks past a male anti-abortion protestor in Brisbane city. 'When was the last time you were pregnant, shit for brains?' she asks him scornfully. The woman has learned to disbelieve the lies.

A Murri teenager in Brisbane is pregnant. She wants her baby to go to her older sister to be raised in the community, like her first baby, but DOCS gets there first. The baby is forcibly taken from her in the hospital over the frantic objections of her family and support workers. The girl is consumed with grief and rage. She has learned that the stolen generations never ended.

A woman is bashed and raped and deliberately kept pregnant in Logan by an abusive partner. With a superhuman effort, she manages to flee interstate, and later to gain custody of her five young kids. Two years on, she is struggling. The Gillard government slashes the parenting payment, and the exhausted woman is forced to labour cleaning white women's houses while she also parents her small kids alone. Hoping for love, and a partner to make her life easier, she falls pregnant. The man quickly disappears; she goes to the clinic in despair. She has learned that she has few good choices.

2016–17

A Goorie woman is using a variety of drugs to self-medicate after a lifetime of abuse. Pregnant with her fourth child, she seeks money for an abortion, but her family fears she will spend it on ice instead and refuse her request. The baby is eventually raised interstate by the father's family and has little or no contact with the woman.

A Murri woman is living in her hometown in remote northern Queensland. She finds herself pregnant. If her husband finds out, he will pressure her to keep it. She takes bush medicine, and the foetal cells are aborted that night. She feels enormous relief and tells her sisters, who support her decision. They have learned their grandmother's cultural way.

2018

Hundreds of us gather in the rain in Queen's Park, Brisbane. Black and brown and yellow and white, gay and straight and trans and queer, old and young, we cluster together around a statue of Queen Victoria, who towers over this stolen land. We listen to doctors, activists and community workers talk about the decades of struggle for women's control of our bodies. Two days later, the Queensland Parliament finally votes to make abortion legal. As in the millennia before Captain Cook, more Queensland women will once again control their own fertility. More of us will be able to make our own decisions about how many children to have, and when, and why.

We have remembered that together we are powerful.

Laura Jean
Day of

In early March 2017, I had some x-rays on my arthritic left hip and was told I needed a hip replacement. A week later I found out I was pregnant. My aunty Susan died within the short time I was pregnant, I went to her funeral a few days after my abortion. I was also in the middle of recording my fifth album, Devotion. *The following is what I wrote leading up to my abortion, some reflections on the day of the abortion, and how I felt. I was raised in a Christian household and I carry a lot of that conditioning – the idea that pregnancy and childbirth is spiritual and sacred. I think it is, but not in the sanitised, filtered, patronised way that is favoured in our society. Some of this writing is me trying to question and undo that conditioning. I don't mention my boyfriend much, because even though he was supportive, honest and loving throughout the experience, we decided the decision to have a baby* or *not ultimately lay with me because it was happening in my body.*

Week before
I googled what you look like, and all the writing and pictures I find are aimed at people keeping the foetus. They call it 'your baby' and they emphasise the humanness of the group of cells. It's highly sentimental, designed to start soon-to-be mothers bonding, obsessed, attaching. If they have to try that hard to make people feel something for the foetus at six weeks, there must be an element of manufacture. Why do we emotionalise pregnancy and make it out to be divine when it is not – just a physical act that can happen to almost any person with a womb. For me to become pregnant it did not require skill, commitment, devotion or any earned qualities. Yet pregnant is what I need to be to find support and validation in my culture.

I have sung my deepest feelings in front of a bunch of cruel surfies in Coffs Harbour, breaking down crying in front of them when an audience member tried to bully me. I have sung in front of thousands of people in a city after being harassed by the roadies about my torn jeans ('you can see right up her arse). I kept playing music when I was told by a critic that there was no need for me to exist as an artist. I have suffered breaches of my privacy by journalists. I have stared at a wall for two years night after night, working on a word, a line, a phrase, over and over until it rung true in my body. I have channelled any spare money into creating something that thousands of people are touched by daily, leaving me below the poverty line, and isolated from the people I'm making music for.

How is this life less heroic than allowing my body to make a baby? How is it more acceptable for me, as a woman, to devote my life to creating one more single human than to devote all my time and money to something that will benefit thousands? Why is it unusual for me to make that choice, as a 35 year old, after working my way, for seventeen years, to this fifth album, my strongest and most far-reaching yet? I am hitting my stride as an artist, a teacher, a mentor, a creator of culture. Yet it is odd for me to right this one mistake? I am made to feel like a murderer of a tiny, alien baby with 'blood running through its body' and a heart that beats 'much faster than mine'.

Where are the voices of the female career artists in their thirties, not having kids? Perhaps they are trying to be taken seriously, terrified that any mention of women's issues will relegate them to the 'dear diary' brigade. I don't blame them at all. I want respect from the mainstream community for my role. I am storyteller, translator of emotion into tangible words and music, and I will sing it back to you and release you. When I sing on stage, whether you listen to or ignore me, I am offering you my heart to take comfort in. I am choosing not to have a baby because I want to continue to channel my full energy into this act. I am not ready to give my body to another human being, just so they can experience this nonsensical, often boring, often painful, occasionally wonderful state called life.

Two days before
Today is the second-last day I will be pregnant. I have enjoyed the feeling. My body has wanted to be pregnant for a long time and got its wish for a little while. I wonder how my body will react when I lose the pregnancy. Sometimes I feel like my body wants different things to my brain, and I wonder if I am being foolish to not give in to my physicality. Maybe a life ruled by the mind is a waste – you don't get to experience the full sensation of the animal body. That said, what a tiny amount of years we have – surely we can't have every experience we desire. I don't

know if I desire to be a mother yet – I know that being pregnant and having a child is something I could cope with, even enjoy, but what about the lifetime of motherhood after that? I don't know if that's what I want.

The relationship between a woman and a foetus she will terminate is complicated. For me, it's like meeting someone you could possibly love just before you go overseas to start the job of your dreams. Either way, you win and you lose. You always wonder what the other life would have been. You always wonder what you missed out on.

Thus far I have dedicated myself to building an artistic and contemplative practice. This path has not provided for me materially. It hasn't earned much validation from the wider community, apart from the odd review and award nomination. I can't explain to most people what I do, and that makes me sad because I love people and want to connect with them. I want them to be able to relate to me, I want to make them feel good about themselves. Instead I often confuse and irritate them when they realise I have figured out a way to scrape by on daydreams and ideas. The shock is even bigger when they realise I am in my mid-thirties – in Australian culture, art and music is something you do in your twenties as a hobby. When you persist through your thirties and forties, you are relegated to outsider until finally, when you are no longer fertile, you are congratulated on your body of work.

My path does not attract familial financial support either – it's considered 'my thing' even though my body of work is likely to keep my family name in history and benefit far more people than if I was to give birth to a child. People who had practices in their twenties and now have kids tell me that having kids is the greatest thing in the world. To me, making music is the best thing in the world. I chose it yesterday and I choose it today.

I know I could continue making music and art if I was a mother, but I don't think I could dedicate as much time to it for several years, and I am peaking as an artist NOW.

I feel like I have failed the fairytales of my childhood. If I am not a princess, what character am I? The talking tree, the witch? The stories I was told keep pulling me into their intoxicating familiarity – marriage, settle down, children, peace. Suddenly the rest of the world gets you. I don't know if most people will ever GET me. I have always been an outsider and it has not changed in adulthood.

My dog lies stomach-down on a pile of clothes on my bed, growling at my neighbours. I look out the window and realise I prefer how the light and trees look from inside my room, filtered by window glass and white gauze. When Susan was dying she saw the sunlight from the street through the window in her loungeroom and asked to be taken out there to *be* in it. I knew she was disappointed when we got onto the street, the unfiltered light harsh, the UV bearing down.

Day before

Today is the last day I will be pregnant. Big deal, eh? Who cares. A tiny cluster of cells develop in my body. A potential human being, as much as a glance between two people is. I feel like a recluse. Nothing seems important anymore. I don't want to go to gigs or see my friends. I can't imagine wanting to ever again. I feel like being near my blood family. My flesh and bone. The people who share my gene pool and are forced to love me. The people who have known me since I was a kid. That have seen me go through multiple seven-year, complete-cell renewal cycles. And they can identify what has stayed the same in all those cell changeovers. My slouch and my gaze. I just want to go home to Sydney. But it's too expensive to live there. And I am almost unemployable. I have made life very, very difficult for myself. I have devoted my adult life to a fairytale that doesn't exist. Because I am stubborn and I don't give up. Maybe it's my time to give up. I want to. I am so close to finishing this album but I could so easily let it go now. If I burn out I will become bitter. This ridiculous game of faith I play – how will I survive these next few months? I am 35 and still going on and off the dole. I am on the verge of becoming very bitter and angry. I am becoming a recluse.

Day of
The lady said my foetus might be too small to abort. They decided they could do it. Lots of teenagers and girls in their early twenties in the waiting room with their boyfriends. Why didn't I ask my boyfriend to be here? I wanted to be alone. When I was going under they asked me what I did. I said I was a musician. As I drifted off, I heard them say 'sing us a song' and laugh at me mockingly.

Week later
I sit in my body like a nervous cat, wanting to jump and twist away. I am so terrified of being hurt, terrified of being in love, terrified of being alone, terrified of dying, terrified of living, terrified of hurting someone. I have always felt too weak for this life, like I can't handle the violence of this world. I can't deal with the aggression, the competitiveness, the anger, the hurt, the ignorance, the cruelty. I can't handle it. I am not made for this planet. I shouldn't have been born. I shouldn't have been born. I shouldn't have been born. I can't handle myself. I can't be my true self because people would think I was completely crazy. If I was my true self, I would be the person raging in the street, I would have pushed everyone away by now.

Laura's going to Sydney tomorrow for her aunty's funeral. All on her own. Just one girl, shouldering all this. I don't want to shoulder this anymore. I give up. I don't want to be a good daughter. I don't want to be a good girlfriend.

If you're in a long-term relationship why would you have an abortion, people might say. Why would we? I don't know. Maybe I told god to FUCK OFF. Maybe I told the natural way of things to get fucked. I am a robot, I am cyber, my brain rules my heart and my body, I don't follow my intuition, I don't follow my feelings, I follow my head.

Obviously, this last statement is untrue. It's just me saying fuck the sentimentalism around being a parent. Don't tell me having a kid is the most love I will ever feel. Don't tell me to follow my heart. Don't tell me to just have a kid and think about money later. That's your privilege talking. You aren't me. How do you know how love feels to me? How do you know the love I feel watching a leaf twist through the air down to the ground? You only know how YOU feel. Stop the fetishisation of parenthood. I know it's hard to be a parent but deal with your decision with humour and honesty, not making yourselves into heroes. You're not. Neither am I.

Clem Bastow

I dreamed I lost my reproductive rights in my Maidenform bra

At first glance, it was easy to miss the armed guard.

Split-level 'business centres' are a common sight around Los Angeles – those L-shaped terraces of shops and services overlooking a parking lot (or if you're lucky, some sort of nod in the direction of a garden) with a dozen or so unrelated businesses crammed next to each other like architectural non-sequiturs.

There might be a bubble cup shop next to a dry cleaner on ground level, up top maybe a script-printing business or a personal investigator, acrylic nails or an MMA McDojo, a vegan soul food cafe next to a wireless router repairer, a Subway underneath an abortion clinic.

I was sniffing around in a rear parking lot near Santa Monica and Vermont, trying to work out which dingy staircase to the upper level of a business centre was the one that would lead me to Planned Parenthood; you could see the sign, plain as day, from Vermont, but from the back of the building everything felt eerily nondescript.

It had been a year since I moved to Los Angeles and, having discovered that my Australian script for Yaz – The Pill – was next to useless on American soil, had made an appointment at my local Planned Parenthood – the evocatively named Hollywood Health Centre – to get checked out for a prescription. At least, that was the plan, which on that hot April morning felt dangerously close to being scuppered given I couldn't seem to get into the damn building.

After a few more minutes of hopeless pacing, I squinted into the shadows and noticed a security guard hovering near one of the staircases and thought, ah, this must be the place. And the armed security guard – despite the Hollywood Health Centre being in the heart of liberal-minded Los Angeles, in the predominantly Democrat state of California, where a relatively low 45 per cent of counties are without abortion providers, and where there are no mandatory ultrasound or counselling laws – was a reminder that there are still plenty of people in America who would like to see *Roe v. Wade* overturned – violently, if necessary.

Like improbably broad Strine-isms and Pizza Shapes tucked in our suitcases, Australians bring to America our unwavering – and perhaps cock-eyed – assumption that life across the Pacific continues as it does on our shores: that everybody votes, people indicate on the freeway, and that women's reproductive healthcare is a given.

This is especially true of Victorians, like me, where abortion is legal on request until up to 24 weeks of pregnancy, and with the agreement of two doctors after that point if the woman's current and future physical, psychological or social circumstances are in question. Abortion is, though we'd never be complacent about it, a given: just one of those things we know, solemnly, we'd be able to access if necessary.

Before I moved to L.A, the worst I'd had to deal with was walking by the Helpers of God's Precious Infants 'sidewalk counsellors' – inevitably white, usually male, and in their sixties or older – outside the East Melbourne clinic that I passed on the way to my therapist.

(My long-held vigilante daydream of kung-fu-kicking the pro-life/anti-choice 'protesters' in the temple while torching their ugly pamphlets was quietly laid to rest when Victoria introduced safe access zones around abortion clinics in 2015. Those laws have already been challenged by Kathleen Clubb, the first person fined for breaching a safe access zone; in her 2018 submission to the High Court, Clubb had the mind-boggling temerity to compare her 'political communication' to the 1998 Australian waterfront dispute, Eureka Stockade and the Freedom Ride of 1965.)

Once I passed the armed guard, I climbed the stairs to the upper level. Having conquered a slightly byzantine intercom system (another nod towards the presence of anti-choice 'activists'), I was welcomed into a reassuringly dull waiting room. Dotted about the plastic chairs were all sorts of people: young women, older ladies, new parents, couples, punks, workers. Who could ever want to bring a gun into this friendly, quiet space?

Planned Parenthood looms large in the American psyche, the name almost a code for 'abortion' in many circles, though it's not the only place one can, in Juno MacGuff's words, 'procure a hasty abortion' – nor is abortion (at around 3 per cent of the organisation's overall healthcare services) the only service Planned Parenthood provides. Indeed, it provides many other vital services including contraceptives, STI testing and treatment – and even prostate, colon and testicular cancer screenings vasectomies, male infertility screenings and sexual-health services for men.

L.A. – like California – is one of those places where you can almost pretend the rest of America doesn't exist. Not just because of the eucalyptus trees that make Melrose smell like Fitzroy when it rains, or because of its friendly Southern Californian people who are always up for a chat, but because like my Australia, women's reproductive rights are – relatively, at least – secure. It's one of the many reasons that L.A. feels like home to me even now that I've returned to Melbourne for the foreseeable future.

In order to get a sense of how bad it could be elsewhere, I'd travelled to Louisiana a few months earlier. I mean, I travelled to Louisiana to visit friends, not to suss out the state's mood on reproductive rights, but once I disembarked the Amtrak in Lafayette it was hard to avoid pro-life sentiment. The more I travelled through the state, the more the pro-life bumper stickers and billboards began to scream at me from across bayous and under graceful willow trees.

'IT'S NOT A CHOICE, IT'S A CHILD' was plastered across a passing truck. 'ABORTION: IT'S AGAINST THE HIPPOCRATIC OATH,' one billboard on the freeway trumpeted, '58 MILLION DEAD'. They were some of the more polite offerings.

Louisiana is one of a number of states with 'trigger laws' that would, as the name suggests, immediately come into play if *Roe v. Wade* were overturned. The state's law, which would outlaw abortion in all cases but those where a woman's life was immediately threatened by the pregnancy, would also allow the prosecution of any person who performed or aided in an abortion, with penalties including up to a decade in jail and maximum fines of $100,000. The possibility of *Roe v. Wade* being overturned, which once seemed like a flight of dystopian fancy, feels ever more real in the Trump era, especially with the ascendancy of Brett Kavanaugh to the Supreme Court – but back in 2012, with President Obama sworn in for a second term, it seemed a distant possibility at best.

In the first of many classic 'an Australian in Louisiana' experiences, I dragged my friend Burt to the local gun show; guns, like draconian reproductive rights laws, are one of those things that are so alien to Australians as to draw us like moths to a scary flame. What enthusiasm I initially had for this weird holdout of Americana soon dissipated as I moved about a hot and stuffy community hall crammed full of trestle tables heaving with firearms. The most sinister were the pink guns – pink for ladies, or breast cancer, or both – and I was not surprised to find a significant showing of pro-life sentiment on the bumper bars and rear windscreens that populated the parking lot. The right to bear arms and the belief that a woman's body is not her own might initially seem like disparate issues, but they're cut from a similar 'founding fathers' cloth.

Increasingly, as I spent more time in Lafayette, I became fascinated by the commonplace nature of so much pro-life propaganda; blood-curdling bumper stickers would nestle up against 'My Family' stickers and sparkly, love-heart daubed decals about jazz ballet or dog breeds. In much the same way I occasionally find myself drawn to stare at a traffic accident or click on a news article I know will haunt me, I felt compelled to attempt to fully engage with this alien notion. But how?

Happily, the Christian pro-life movie *October Baby* – tagline: 'Every Life Is Beautiful' – was showing at the cinema down the road. What better way to immerse myself in pro-life sentiment than with a giant cup of root beer as I thrilled to the story of an abortion survivor? *October Baby* concerned a young woman, Hannah (Rachel Hendrix) who discovers she survived an attempted abortion and was later adopted, experiences a crisis of faith, and so sets off on a road trip to find both her birth mother and herself.

The film was inspired in part by the story of Gianna Jessen, a pro-life and disability rights activist, who was born after an attempted late-term saline abortion, and consequently diagnosed with cerebral palsy. True 'abortion survivors' like Jessen are rare (according to a 1985 study, in '33,090 suction curettage abortions performed at less than or equal to twelve weeks' gestation, the rate of unrecognised failed abortions was 2.3 per 1000 abortions'), but many pro-life organisations confusingly also use the term to describe twins who survive 'selective reductions', and even children born into families where one or more pregnancies were terminated.

October Baby was, like many Christian movies, a surprise hit in 2012. (*Fireproof*, a film about a firefighter's marriage breakdown and crisis of faith, was 2008's highest-grossing independent film, taking in over $33 million.) With a budget of around $1 million, it made roughly five times that at the box office, going from a limited release to a relatively wide expansion of 500 screens nationally; when I went to the movie theatre that hot afternoon, *October Baby* was #8 in the box office rankings.

The film itself is typical of the ho-hum nature of many evangelical films – lots of padding, no frisson between nominally romantic leads, plenty of 'magic hour' shots – but its one effective scene is also its most chilling.

In it, Hannah finally tracks down the nurse (Jasmine Guy) who assisted in the abortion attempt. The kindly but rattled nurse – 'There were things that happened there, terrible things, things they had me do . . .' – explains that Hannah was a twin, and her late brother fared far worse than she did: 'His arm was missing, torn off during the attempt.' Of the scene, Roger Ebert generously wrote, 'Jasmine Guy's monologue here is so well-performed and effective that we almost forgive it for being such a contrivance that shoe-horns in all the film's necessary background detail.' (*The AV Club*'s Alison Willmore wrote, more in line with the general critical consensus, 'This isn't a movie; this is propaganda for the already converted.')

Even as *October Baby* trundled to its inevitably uplifting conclusion (Hannah finds a way to love herself, forgive her birth mother, and even – as a Baptist – find salvation in a conveniently located Catholic church), I found myself haunted by Guy's monologue.

Such descriptions of mutilated babies and callously discarded body parts are common to much pro-life propaganda; even the Helpers of God's Precious Infants are not above bewildering already upset women with graphic 'evidence' of the cruelties of abortion. In the minds of the militant pro-lifers, late-term abortions are commonplace, are carried out in subpar conditions by ethically dubious doctors ('AGAINST THE HIPPOCRATIC OATH', as the billboards put it) and ordered up willy nilly by women who don't care a jot for the precious life they are about to snuff out.

The women in question, I don't need to tell you, barely figure in the hair-raising fantasy. (Ironically enough, *October Baby* presents Hannah's birth mother's decision as wildly irresponsible and cruel, when in fact it seems an utterly mundane reason a woman might seek a termination: she's in law school, and concerned about the effect a child – much less one born after a one-night stand – might have on her studies and career.) Every abortion is a selfish act against God's will, no matter the circumstances of the pregnancy or the likelihood of the child in question having a happy and healthy life.

This is, of course, not something that needs to be told to anyone who is pro-choice; even writing the words feels like an exercise in futility. But being confronted with such unbridled anti-choice propaganda tends to spark in you an intense need to recite the obvious facts of abortion (even though, you quickly realise, most anti-choicers are impervious to things like 'facts' and 'rational thought').

October Baby, like the gun show, put a dead-end stop to my macabre fascination with the worst excesses of conservative sentiment. In that dull but disturbing tract, I'd seen and heard everything I needed to see and hear, and saw out the rest of my Louisiana holiday meditating intensely on beignets and Zydeco (all the better to ignore the billboards of dead foetuses) before fleeing back into the welcoming arms of California.

Which brings us back to the business centre on Vermont and Santa Monica.

I thought – briefly – of *October Baby* and those bumper stickers and billboards while I sat in the Planned Parenthood waiting room, but for the most part, the sheer boredom of the experience was intensely moving. It's impossible to know who, if any, of the people waiting there that afternoon were seeking an abortion (if we apply the aforementioned statistics, maybe a couple of them), but if so, they did it freely, without being yelled at, shown a horrible placard, or forced to undergo an ultrasound and 'counselling' session beforehand.

Eventually, I got called in for my appointment, and had a very matter of fact discussion about my reproductive health with a kind doctor, stood on one of *those* sets of American mechanical scales (just like in the movies!), and was dispatched with my prescription for drospirenone. I smiled at the armed guard on my way out; he either didn't see me, or chose not to acknowledge me.

In the years to come, as the dark cloud of the Trump era gathered, Planned Parenthood would once more become a flashpoint for debate about reproductive rights; I posted a photo of my Planned Parenthood card along with the hashtag #IStandWithPlannedParenthood when talk of defunding spread. But on that sunny afternoon, as I strolled to Rite Aid to fill my prescription, I thought: there's no place like home.

Meredith Burgmann
For the long haul

This will be a personal and episodic view of the (unfinished) fight for reproductive rights in New South Wales, and particularly the struggle of women within the Labor Party in that most Catholic of states.

My first memory of abortion as an issue is probably around 1969. I was a member of the women's liberation movement (WLM) which was just beginning to gain ground in Sydney. Apart from endless consciousness-raising sessions at women's liberation house at 67 Glebe Point Road, our other important activity was around abortion. This was before the crucial 'Heatherbrae' case of 1971 (also known as the Levine ruling) which provided for safer and semi-legal abortions in New South Wales but still retained abortion as a crime within the New South Wales *Crimes Act 1900* – the situation that remains until this day.

In a flurry of blue overalls, severe haircuts and excellent earrings (we never opposed interesting jewellery) we would march down Broadway to the CBD or gather at Martin Place or the Archibald Fountain and march on some strategic target. Our voices were raised in chants which were confident and, in retrospect, hopeful: 'Free abortion on demand.'

As I remember, we were not consciously using the term 'a woman's right to choose' at that early stage. We became more aware of the importance of terminology when our opponents started to use the term 'pro-life' instead of what we called them: 'anti-abortion'. So we became 'pro-choicers' – a good and fitting terminology.

As Women's Lib, we were an inchoate but large and rowdy grouping. We had a respectful relationship with the older abortion campaigners such as Biddy Gilling and Julia Freedbury (and later the Women's Electoral Lobby feminists) but we felt that more vocal and direct-action activity had to take place. My memories of this time are enthusiastic and chaotic marches led by Sue Bellamy, Joyce Stevens, Jozefa Sobski, and other fearsome leaders of the WLM.

We followed with great interest the heroic activity of Bertram and Jo Wainer in Victoria and of course were supportive of the legal war being waged by left-wing lawyers such as Jimmy Staples in New South Wales, but we believed the issue could and should be won in the streets (it was the seventies after all). The formation of WAAC (Women's Abortion Action Campaign) in 1972 and the establishment of the Leichhardt Women's Health Centre strengthened our forces immeasurably.

Although I never had any personal involvement with abortion, the books and films of the period often dealt with the issue – always tragically. I remember the sense of foreboding you would feel in the cinema as the heroine went off to some back lane with a wad of cash. It always made me shiver with anxiety.

By 1971 I had become peripherally involved with the Labor Party, which had a large and active Women's Conference that was involved with abortion as a priority issue.

Our problem in the Labor Party was that it was a very Catholic party in a very Catholic state. The leader of the Catholics was Johno Johnson, (my Labor predecessor as President of the New South Wales Legislative Council) who wore the tiny silver feet badge of the anti-abortionists proudly on his lapel for all the time I knew him.

The reasons for this religious imbalance can be traced back to the Labor Party split of the fifties when Cardinal Gilroy of New South Wales encouraged the Catholics to stay in the party and fight while his counterpart in Victoria, Archbishop Mannix, urged the Catholics to split from the party and form the DLP.

New South Wales is the most Catholic state (24.1 per cent Catholics) because of the patterns of early settlement – Irish convicts in the east and Protestant settlers in the west and south (South Australia is 17.9 per cent Catholic), compounded by later post-war immigration to New South Wales from Catholic communities in Europe and the Middle East. Interestingly, New South Wales is the most religious state generally with 65.3 per cent nominating a religion in the 2016 census as opposed to 60 per cent in Australia.

So the women abortion activists in the Labor Party, mainly but not exclusively from the Left faction, were hugely frowned on. It is one of the main reasons that the Right Wing of the party was eventually successful in abolishing the Women's Conference in 1986. They believed that shutting down the formal structure for women would shut down the fight for women's rights, and to some degree they were successful.

It was during this period in the late seventies and early eighties that a ludicrous situation developed. A big women's rights rally was planned in the city and the Labor women activists decided to march under the Labor Women's Conference banner. The party officers called it a 'pro-abortion rally' and made it known that any Labor woman who took part would be expelled from the party. This may sound like overreach and it certainly was but it was at a time when the fight between the Right and the Left was at its height. The old Right was fond of 'proscribing' organisations that Labor Party members were forbidden from joining or being involved with such as resident action groups or in this case abortion activists.

The order forbidding us to march began to attract press coverage and there were tense discussions among us as to what to do. I can remember Kate Butler, Chris Kibble, Pam Allan, Ann Symonds and Sandra Wall being part of these discussions.

Eventually we hit on the perfect media stunt of marching with our heads in paper bags behind a banner proclaiming '36 Faceless Women' – a pun on the famous Alan Reid quip about the ALP National Executive being '36 Faceless Men'.

If I did not have a press photograph of the occasion I would not have been able to convince later generations of ALP women that we had to resort to such tactics. I proudly point myself out as the fourth paper bag from the right.

Such was the media coverage of the protest that expulsions did not occur. Anyway, how could they prove who it was inside each paper bag? The argument at the Administrative Committee would have been hilarious.

The campaign dragged on. In 1991 I ended up in the New South Wales Parliament where the fight to decriminalise abortion took a more formal but just as heated form.

Shortly after my election, the Call to Australia Party MLC

(Member of the Legislative Council), the Reverend Fred Nile, a long-time morals and anti-abortion campaigner, introduced two bills to the parliament: the Unborn Child Protection Bill 1991 and the Procurement of Miscarriage Limitation Bill 1991.

By 12 September that year the bills were actually being debated in the Legislative Council. At that stage it was the most feminised chamber in Australia. We were exactly one-third of the 45-member Council.

During a long and extraordinary speech by Fred's colleague (his wife Elaine Nile), the women in the chamber became restless.

Eventually action was taken. The Liberal Party matriarch, Beryl Evans, started to round up the troops. We all liked Beryl. She was an old-fashioned bluestocking who had served in some military capacity during the Second World War. We always used to tell people that she had been a bomber pilot – it suited her 'born to rule' persona. Beryl persuaded thirteen of the fifteen women in the chamber to stage a walkout. We represented all parties and factions except Fred Nile's. There were women from the Liberals, Nationals, Democrats and the Right and Left of the Labor Party. Only one woman remained in the House with Elaine Nile. It was a stunning feat of organisation.

We stormed out of the chamber and returned to our offices. After about ten minutes I decided that the media should be told that the walkout had been organised by Beryl. I went down to the press gallery and said to the journos: 'you probably should know that the walkout was actually organised by Beryl Evans.' 'What walkout?' was their response. Thirteen of fifteen women in the chamber had staged a coordinated walkout and the (mostly) male press corps had not noticed!

They were pretty excited about the event and persuaded us to re-stage our walkout. We stormed down the exterior stairs and were duly photographed in the bright light of day. All thirteen of us. We always laughed about the fact that we had to do it twice before we were noticed.

Beryl was obviously chuffed with her achievement because she sent us photocopies of the letters of thanks and congratulations she had received.

Sometimes I am asked during debates about women's representation in parliament, whether 'women's issues' actually exist. I always list abortion, guns and swimming pool fences as quite specific issues where women cross party lines in temporary sisterhood.

Another interesting debate happened inside the party when we decided to oppose Fred Nile's Public Health (Conscientious Objection) Bill 1991 and a brace of similar bills such as the Nurses (Conscientious Objection) Bill 1991. These bills would have allowed workers in public hospitals to refuse services involving legal terminations. The ALP leadership had decided that these were public policy bills and as such not an 'abortion' bill which would have attracted a conscience vote within the party. Bob Carr and Health spokesman Andrew Refshauge managed to get our very Catholic caucus to support this view – even Johno Johnson.

Bob Carr commented to Ann Symonds and me later when we were unhappy about some other decision: 'how can you expect me to get Johno to toe the line on stuff he opposes if you won't toe the line on stuff you oppose?' He was right, and those words often came back to me during our endless tussles over 'law and order' and drug policy.

Strangely, there was quite a lot of co-operation between the party leaderships to avoid raising the abortion issue in Parliament at this stage. Both sides realised that there was no guarantee which side would win, so an uneasy truce existed between the pro and anti sides. Also, the Labor leadership was loath to have the divisions within the party on the issue exacerbated and publicised.

All of this surreptitious co-operation of course excluded Fred Nile whose whole reason for being in Parliament was to oppose abortion and homosexuality. Sometimes this informal and unspoken arrangement led to hilarious outcomes.

On 23 November 1995, I was fulfilling my obedient backbencher role and had risen to congratulate DanceSport Australia on being chosen as an exhibition sport for the Sydney 2000 Olympics. These 'stocking fillers' normally take three minutes and we get a few pointers sent to us from the powers that be to work with. I had come to the end of my three-minute speech when I was handed a note: 'Fred's wanting to bring his abortion bill on before lunch, keep talking.' Thus began the most incompetent filibuster in Legislative Council history. We knew that if I could talk for about twenty minutes until the lunch break then other business would take precedence after that.

The main problem with these occasional filibusters is that you have to stick to the given subject. Also, and this was uppermost in my mind, everything you say is meticulously recorded by Hansard for posterity. I have a real dislike of making long, boring speeches or of sounding like a goose. I staggered on blurting out inane observations. At last some comrades realised what was happening and started interjecting. What bliss. You can riff off a good interjection for some minutes. Ann asked me about Tonya Harding, and Michael Egan called out about line dancing. So I was able to ruminate about line dancing and correct-line dancing. Someone else mentioned Fred Astaire – so I was able to riff on the feminist joke about Ginger Rogers doing everything he did, except backwards and in high heels. And so it went on. Even Fred, realising his bill was doomed, got into the spirit of the thing and started to call out about the need for the contestants to wear 'neck to ankle gear'. I have never had the guts to google 'DanceSport Australia' and check my speech but it's lying there somewhere as part of the great Fred Nile abortion war of attrition.

So why is abortion still there in the New South Wales *Crimes Act*? Fifty years after we first started our public demonstrations and 120 years since it was included in the Act?

I realise, when I talk to young women about our abortion marches of fifty years ago, that it's exactly like older women talking to me as a young student about the Suffragettes and their struggle for the vote – except that the Suffragettes won the vote much quicker than we have won legal abortions. Did we really think that it would take another fifty years before we would succeed?

Twice, Ann Symonds and I went through the process of straw polling the MPs and MLCs in the New South Wales Parliament. There is no point putting up a decriminalisation bill unless you know it can win. Otherwise you run the risk that the majority group can make things worse, as has been threatened in other states. Each time we started the straw poll we stopped before we had gone very far. It was too obvious; we didn't have the numbers. The preponderance of Catholics in the ALP has certainly fallen over the years but it has been supplemented by a proportional rise in Catholics and fundamentalist or Pentecostal adherents in the Coalition.

Cross your fingers for the 2019 election but I hope the women of the new New South Wales Parliament know how to do a good straw poll.

With Queensland's historic Termination of Pregnancy Bill 2018 having just been passed it now leaves only New South Wales with abortion still listed as a crime.

The Stop Press announcement on 23 October 2018 that a New South Wales Labor government would move to decriminalise abortion if elected has left me gobsmacked. Perhaps our efforts were not in vain after all.

Ellena Savage

Unwed teen mum Mary

I'm trying to get work taste-testing new snacks for 7-Eleven at their head office. They pay $40 per taste-test in the form of a prepaid credit card, which will be handy for buying groceries or topping up my Myki. To apply to be a person whom 7-Eleven advertises such precious opportunities to, I must fill out a questionnaire in such a way as to convince the marketing people that I am a frantic consumer of overpriced snacks.

In the questionnaire, I select the statement 'I work to live,' which is *true*, but only in the sense that to pay for the debt of living, a person is required to work. This is not a 'choice' so much as a banality.

'How often do you make impulse purchases at 7-Eleven stores?' the questionnaire asks. 'Frequently,' I lie. In fact, I hate 7-Eleven and everything in it; in fact, I almost never impulse-buy convenience store products.

Yesterday, I applied for work running heavy platters of canapés at the catering company I worked at when I was twenty. Yesterday, I signed on to a mailing list for market research opportunities. Yesterday, I asked my friends with kids to pass my number on to any wealthy parents they know who are looking for help with childcare or cleaning. Yesterday, I applied for work counting votes at the upcoming state election.

An editor emailed the other day asking if I would contribute to her anthology on abortion, something with the word 'choice' in the title, that would raise funds for a national non-profit abortion provider. She said I'd get paid for my contribution. I thought about the kind of anthology this would be and how the kind of anthology this would be would probably be the kind of anthology I would probably pay little attention to, because I am a snob, and because I don't think that what governments who are intent on restricting or criminalising abortion need is a nuanced anthology on abortion written by mostly white, mostly middle-class women like me as much as they need to be taken out one scumbag at a time. A joke! That's a joke. And then I thought about the number of 7-Eleven taste-tests I'd have to do for the same amount of money, how many hours of running heavy platters of canapés to hotel corporation stakeholders on Cup weekend, how many lies I'd have to tell to market researchers. And then I chose the money.

When I think about the word choice I think about how, largely, this word represents a fantasy. An important fantasy and one, perhaps, worth protecting. But an unreal circumstance, really. 'Circumstance,' writes Anne Boyer, 'is the stage upon which agency plays.' Agency as opposed to autonomy, which requires some degree of control over circumstances. For example, I didn't choose to be alive and I didn't choose to be settled in an overpriced city and I didn't choose to be lying about my love of slurpees aged thirty to pay for groceries from one of the two price-fixing supermarkets of the duopoly, groceries I cook up at my house that serves also as my primary workspace where I work at my several not-really real jobs, and I didn't choose to carry around a small robot that exposes me to radiation and listens to all of my words and bodily excretions – well perhaps I did choose that purchase, naïve consumer me, but without it my several not-really real jobs would fast become unviable.

Siri, do I have a choice?

I really couldn't say, Ellena.

I didn't choose my parents and they didn't choose me – they didn't choose my particular genetic code nor my penchant for feeling hard-done-by nor my rather negative attitude towards the hegemony of biological family-making. I didn't choose to be a person who finds intolerable things that other people, most people – normal people – tolerate seemingly with pleasure and with ease. Things like handing over personal data to corporations in exchange for small product bonuses. Things like wedding registries. Things like the legal enforcement of helmet-wearing.

I didn't choose to get pregnant when I did, though I was complicit in the choice in that I chose to have sex that night, I suppose, in the mangled way that sometimes happens with a person you have not planned to have sex with and probably won't again, and I chose to have it in such a way that made possible a slippage of fecund biological material from one place to another, though in all honesty I thought that the person I was with would not be so careless or cruel as to endanger me in that way, and I chose to imbibe the several drinks that led me to this somewhat unglamorous affair. I did not choose the patriarchal condition of normative heterosexual hook-ups whereby the primary form of eroticism is the careless penile penetration of women and woman-shaped people in pursuit of male orgasm regardless of the risk of disease or pregnancy, but I did choose to exercise in my warped way my puny young girl agency to objectify and 'fuck' guys with the aim of reversing the ways in which I had been fucked and fucked over by them.

I didn't choose to be too broke to pay the out-of-pocket for the abortion anaesthetic, which at the Royal Women's was $140, and I didn't choose the character of the girl I was seeing at the time though the character of the girl I was seeing at the time was what had endeared her to me, and while I did not choose for her to pay for the anaesthetic, she did it anyway, because that was her character, and while I was getting my guts pried open the girl napped on her rolled up leather jacket like a sweet punk-rock baby in the barren chamber of the hospital and for this she is due my eternal gratitude.

I didn't choose to have zero emotional after-effects of that abortion, though I felt as though I couldn't mention this too often or too loudly in case it seemed in some way to trivialise the emotional after-effects some others experienced after their abortions. More trivialising is the dominant cultural narrative I choose now not to abide by, the narrative of inevitable future shame and regret pre-post abortion, as though a feeling of regret is worse than a lifetime of poverty or being eternally tethered to a man you hate or being dependent for years on a biological family you wish to be separate from, or simply being forced to do something you instinctively don't want to do, well. I regret a lot, believe me: I regret my poor food choices and my poor work choices and I regret being born with the biological equipment that bears the burden of poor sexual choice-making under the influence of alcohol at age twenty. But in no chamber of my soul is there an inkling of regret at ending a pregnancy I did not want and if I hadn't had the legal choice to end it at the Royal Women's I'd have done it anyway, I'd have rolled down a flight of stairs, I'd have seen a dodgy doctor, I'd have drunk poison, I'd have done it all, and I might have died trying.

Because this is what agency is; it is doing what you can do with the circumstances you are dealt. It is choosing to do what you need to do even and especially when your mother or your superego disapproves. In my opinion sex is not a sacred jewel and poor erotic decisions are not something I need protection from and motherhood is not holy. In my view, motherhood is a practical economic matter and any effort to pair femininity with maternity with biological destiny with virgin births with earthy crystal-lovemaking is an effort to relegate the female form to a position of inferiority, to a state of constant need and gratitude and dependence.

Julia Kristeva writes that the 'virgin' of the Virgin Mary was in fact a mistranslation of an ancient Semitic word for unmarried young woman. Conflating 'virgin' with 'unmarried young woman', she says, erases the young mother's extra-patriarchal *jouissance*, evidence of her bodily joy and her sensual desires, and subsumes it under the sign of the male-controlled 'virgin'. The mistranslation is said to strip pre-Christian societies of their matrilineal inheritance rites and it strips Mary of her agency, too – her scampish, light-filled, unwed spirit – and replaces it with the sign of the father.

In other words, if the Virgin Mary had more correctly been named the Unwed Teen Mum Mary, we who inherit the moral framework of the Christian tradition might not feel compelled to trot out evidence that our access to abortion is a moral good in that it is a material good in that there can be no moral good without humans exercising their agency in whatever puny ways they can, like having a son named Jesus. Or just not.

Sexuality and impurity might not be coupled. Maternity might be understood as just one of the many ways a person can choose to belong to time rather than a duty women with wombs have, to tip themselves completely into the service of others.

It is true too, however, that we who have inherited the moral framework of the Christian tradition have inherited a limited set of tropes through which we understand what a body is and what a gender does, and from within this fog we find it challenging or perhaps inconvenient to look upon the full force of the animal urges that course through us all. The animal spirit that offers recourse to say no, to say I will not abide, to say I will choose the smallest thing that has been offered to me, to protect me, to protect the others whose tender red organs have been taken, in name and in law, from them.

At twenty, I did not want to be someone's mother. At thirty, I have been all kinds of mother: I have paid the rent for rockdogs, I have made more meals than have been made for me, I have poured out more love than has been poured into me, I am practically a saint – but no one tells me that, not enough anyway – and I am trying again to choose to not do that, to not be a mother.

Instead I'm trying to see that my tender red organs and the few dollars I earn and the words that I say and write are truly mine and that I'm therefore responsible for what I do with them. Sheila Heti writes that the hardest thing for a woman to do is to choose to not become a mother and while the hardest thing is not always the best thing, I am curious about a life where choice is more rigorously available to me and perhaps the first choice to make is the choice to take my agency, take it, make it mine.

'What do you love most about 7-Eleven stores?' the questionnaire asks me.

'The convenience,' I reply. 'And the charming service I always receive! :)'

Gideon Haigh
The racket

The Fourth Court in Victoria's Supreme Court complex would intimidate the sturdiest accused. It is poorly ventilated, dimly lit, high ceilinged and ornately decorated. The public gallery is supported by Doric columns; the judge presides from an elevated bench canopied in cedar; the witness stand is exposed on all sides. Nearest of all courts to the cells, it traditionally hosted the most lurid of cases. It was here that Ronald Ryan, awaiting the verdict in his murder trial on 30 March 1966, muttered to co-accused Peter John Walker: 'I think we're in deep shit.'

On 22 May 1969, the atmosphere was likewise tense, but less obviously dramatic. There were a scattering of watchers in the gallery; there were no journalists present; there was no cut and thrust of cross-examination. Instead, a single unamplified voice commenced to read into the court record a 3000-word ruling soporific with precedent: 'In *R v. MacKay* [1957] VicRp 79;

[1957] VR 560; [1957] ALR 648, Lowe, J, stated these two elements in his propositions numbered 3 and 6 set out at (VR) pp. 562–3; (ALR) p. 649. Smith, J, decided, at (VR) pp. 571–3; (ALR) pp. 654–6 . . .' and so forth.

Justice Clifford Menhennitt, 56 years old, enrobed, bewigged, heavy-set, looked and sounded nothing like a great reformer. He was sober, fussy, pedantic, slow. He had been an equity lawyer, best known at the bar for his expertise in section 92 ('Free Trade Between The States'), and most distinguished in his role as H.V. Evatt's junior in the bank nationalisation case. He had been on the Bench three years, and had peaked; when he was mentioned as potential High Court material, Garfield Barwick is said to have retorted: 'Heavens no, we don't have time.'

His Honour was the unlikeliest jurist to be presiding in the case before him, involving an East Melbourne gynaecologist facing four counts of 'unlawfully using an instrument or other means with intent to procure the miscarriage of a woman' and one count of 'conspiring unlawfully to procure the miscarriage of a woman'. His own marriage was childless; a former colleague would tell me: 'What Cliff would have known about abortion was precisely nothing.' The matter had come before him merely because he and his colleagues took turns in 'crime'; a ruling was now necessary on the admissibility of medical evidence. He had gone away for a few days to think about it; now he was back. When Menhennitt sat down, abortion was a crime tantamount to murder and nigh unspeakable, in a state where an entrenched conservative premier was shored up by a rusted on Catholic vote. When he stood up, abortion was, under simple and certain strikingly flexible criteria, lawful, and his standard became the basis of evaluation for the next half century.

———

I was introduced to the story by an ex-girlfriend whose work as an obstetrician we were discussing over lunch. When she deployed the word 'Menhennitt' several times in the context of how she and colleagues evaluated late-term abortion, I asked her to explain. The test asked, she said, whether the prolongation of the pregnancy would endanger a woman's physical or mental wellbeing, and whether the danger of the termination outweighed the danger it was designed to prevent. A useful and elegant standard, she agreed, although she was unable to elaborate on its provenance, beyond repeating that curious name. Note to self: find out more. Not because I had either a passionate view or a personal experience of abortion; more because of the opposite, that it was something of which I knew next to nothing, and ignorance is not to be feared but remedied.

Remedy was elusive. There existed a huge library about the ethics of abortion, its symbolic resonances, its partisan politics. Yet there was comparatively little to be found in the nature of basic information – that is, the origins of the regime of its accessibility. It was disappointing, and enticing. Clearly a book needed to be written. Why should I not write it? Actually there were a few reasons. I had no cause. I had no background. I was arguably the wrong gender. But I have always aspired to a journalism that is, above all, of use. Something that competently retold the past of this complex medico-legal story might be efficacious in its future. Subconsciously, I suspect, I applied a version of Menhennitt's standard – that a book's potential helpfulness outweighed its potential harm. I began work on my book about abortion, *The Racket* (2008).

I'm bound to say that this perspective changed as I charted the history of illegal abortion in this country, the scale of the demand, the fragmented, ruinous and frankly sadistic state of supply, and, perhaps above all, the pragmatism and stoicism with which women withstood both. This was not a subject for polite society; not even for impolite society; it was an urgent need for confused and fearful individuals, the livelihood of ambiguously motivated providers. The scale must be understood, too, in terms of immense sexual ignorance, high levels of female fertility, poor education about birth control, taboo on unwed motherhood, and prolonged phases of economic hardship for sizeable proportions of society. For most of Australian history, abortion has not been a lifestyle choice; it has been an alternative to worsening poverty.

Yet it has not been, in Australia at least, a forefront feminist issue, in the same way as women's suffrage, or property ownership, or equal pay, or educational availability. Abortion breaks cover quite regularly in female fiction in the first half of last century: in Jean Devanny's *Riven* (1929), Fay is counselled to 'put up with it and be quiet'; in Kylie Tennant's *Tiburon* (1935), Mrs Mulvey refers breezily to 'me operation'; in Eleanor Dark's *Waterway* (1938), Aggie Trugg counts herself as mother of six 'not counting odds and ends'; in Dymphna Cusack's *Jungfrau* (1936), free-spirited Marc Roberts describes the procedure as 'messy but no different to having your appendix out'; in Ruth Park's *The Harp in the South* (1948), the heroine's neighbour openly boasts of her 'fifteen misses'; most memorable of all, perhaps, is Catherine Edmonds' memoir *Caddie* (1953), where the procedure is the preserve of 'a dirty old hag with filthy fingernails' working in something 'like a morgue'. But it is treated as a woman's biological lot, something to deal with, to be endured, like a station of the cross. This is despite its pre-penicillin toll where women's hospitals had whole wards allocated to the treatment of post-abortion sepsis.

Illegality and shame cloak the historic record of these times. In the course of my research, I perused inquest files for about

150 abortion-related deaths at Victoria's Public Record Office, and ended up quoting from about fifty. The records are fragmentary, obfuscatory and far from comprehensive, but also suggestive. Abortion's demonology accentuates the influence of the 'backyard abortion'. The expression is more recent than it seems: the earliest reference Trove throws up is from the *Canberra Times* in 1968. What was meant varied. Providers always included the ranks of the greedy, the creepy, the cranky. But it was more often a lucrative business for entrepreneurial midwives, like the one who South Melbourne woman Jean Brett visited in the 1930s while her husband waited, impatiently and uncomprehendingly:

> I'm telling you, it's damned agony. You'd have no anaesthetic or nothing, all they would do is clean out your womb and you would be conscious. At any stage they would do it. They weren't doctors they were midwives. They were supposed to be midwives. I can't remember how much you'd pay ... but I do remember my husband was waiting for me in the car when I came out. I was half damn dead, I might tell you. He said: 'Christ I'm sick and tired of bloody waiting, I was nearly going to go home.'
>
> How can they possibly ... how can he ... because I had no idea either, I don't know what I expected. But you do think they're going to do something ... something gentle, don't you? No they don't. They just scrape it out as though it's a ... scraping up mud out of a gutter. That's the truth. They had no feelings whatsoever. You paid whatever sum it was, it was far more than a man's weekly wage would be. Some women couldn't have any more kids after that. As I said they just scraped you out, like scraping out the inside of a marrow.

My impression, however, was that abortion was more profuse, and riskier, when it was self-procured. There existed a prodigious variety of folk remedies such as castor oil, baking soda, eating matches, drinking turpentine, pills from lead-plaster, liquor in which copper coins had been boiled, riding bicycles, reclining in hot mustard baths, jumping off high places, driving on bumpy roads or riding the big dipper at Luna Park. In April 1929, the Coroner took evidence in the death of 32-year-old Elizabeth Bren, who had used a trusty piece of elmbark kept in a jar on the mantelpiece – inserted in the cervix, elmbark tended to swell from the moisture until it precipitated contractions. Bren, a friend revealed, was a serial offender: 'I said she was a foolish woman to do it. She said: "What else could I do with four hungry children around me? I could not possibly bring any more into the world." She did happen to mention she had done it eighteen times previously in the last four years.'

A sizeable proportion of houses also featured a Higginson's Syringe, a device devised in the 1850s to irrigate body cavities. It became a rite of reaching reproductive age to be instructed in inducing a miscarriage by administering a solution of Lifebuoy soap or Lysol disinfectant – hugely perilous in a non-sterile environment but also convenient for being minimally disruptive. Some of the inquest files I remember vividly. 33-year-old Doris Sanderson died after syringing a three-month pregnancy with Lifebuoy on 17 August 1946 while her husband was at the football and her sister listened to the radio in the kitchen. 33-year-old Janie Harrington suffered a fatal embolism on 16 January 1948 using Lysol, having told a friend over morning tea: 'I think I will fix myself up before the boys come home.' Admitted to Wangaratta Base Hospital in October 1956, 35-year-old Benalla waitress Muriel Swindle confessed to attempting to abort herself with Dettol, administered by a bicycle pump hidden in the cabinet of an old wireless set. The valve, sealed in a plastic pocket, is still in her inquest file at Victoria's Public Records Office.

All things considered, however, prosecutions were few, and convictions fewer. The prohibition on abortion in Victoria was carried from the old *Offences Against the Person Act* into the new *Crimes Act*, but the Homicide Squad, who had carriage of the law, enforced it spasmodically. Why? In the period from the 1930s to the 1960s, it would seem, the midwives were steadily replaced by doctors. Patients now slightly better off and growingly conscious of safety felt more comfortable about a *sotto voce* referral at a GP's surgery than disappearing down an alleyway in Collingwood. Doctors had waiting rooms. Doctors could offer antibiotics and anaesthetics. They charged exorbitant fees, in cash, on the nail. They set limits on term. But as the narrator observes in Katharine Susannah Prichard's *Winged Seeds* (1950): 'A lot of girls take this abortion business quite easily Bill. Of course, sometimes it ends in a dirty tragedy; but there are doctors and nurses who do the job skilfully, I know. Costs a lot – but at least you get hygienic surroundings.'

For police, doctors were also a great deal easier to shake down. They were wealthy, soft, protective of their good names. Police knew that there was a demand for abortion, that it would somehow be met. So rather than enforce a more or less unenforceable law, they decided to take a cut – or at least, in Victoria, the protestant police did. The Catholics were a different matter. The route to the Menhennit ruling was opened not by an act of democratic dissidence, or civil disobedience, or empassioned advocacy, but by the opposite – the law of unintended consequences.

In mid-1965, an ambitious new head of Homicide, Frank Holland, long-time secretary of the Order of St Christopher, the Catholic policeman's club, decided that once and for all he would put abortionists in Melbourne out of business. 'The law says abortion is illegal and that is enough for me,' he explained tersely. Over the course of the next five years, ten Melbourne abortionists went on trial. One was Ken Davidson. One night in 2007 I walked home from the football through East Melbourne to check on what now occupied his last known address. To my surprise, he did – his name was on a brass plate on the door. Journalism is full of serendipitous discoveries.

Holland's campaign inadvertently revealed a long and tangled relationship between doctors and the Homicide Squad, resulting in a headline-hogging Royal Commission, in which a prominent presence was a flamboyant and volatile GP, Bertram Wainer, who claimed that 100,000 abortions were performed in Australia annually. But here's a strange thing. The commission's interest was not in the procedure, or the legislation, or the ethics; its focus was police corruption, which was in the end a mere symptom of the hypocrisies of the age. The truly momentous development, Menhennitt's ruling, went completely unreported. On the day in question, according to *The Age*, the most pressing question in feminism was: 'Are Ladies in Trousers Respectable?' It was only when Wainer put the standard to the test by publicising an abortion and police took no action that it became clear something had shifted. The ruling underpinned the 1972 foundation of his controversial clinic, the first of its kind in Australia.

Nothing is inevitable, as they say, until it happens. What has often struck me about the story of abortion's stumbling progression to lawfulness and Menhennitt's judicial activism *avant la lettre* is its evitability. Australia was not exactly in feminist upheaval: Germaine Greer's *The Female Eunuch* (1970) and Kate Millett's *Sexual Politics* (1970) were still to come. Nor was Victoria a bastion of liberalism. The stick-in-the-mud Bolte government was underpinned by Catholic conservatives through the preference support of the Democratic Labor Party. What would have happened had Frank Holland not thrown the Homicide Squad into an anti-abortion crusade? What would have been the outcome had *R v. Davidson* come before a Catholic member of the Supreme Court Bench, of which there were several, and very distinguished at that? The story caused me to rethink my conception of Australia, which suddenly seemed a country luxuriating in great freedoms, little understood and tenuously grounded, that it tends to take for granted.

Those freedoms are important, however, precisely because, beneath the economic blessings and sun-kissed surfaces, lived experience in Australia has been harsher and nastier than we're comfortable acknowledging, that it's involved the sucking up of a lot of suffering by those on its margins, that there are many, many things we'd rather not think about. My experience with *The Racket* has been modestly instructive. It was rejected by the publisher with whom I had originally discussed it; it appeared eventually in cheap and tatty form; it went unpublicised and unreviewed; it sold miserably and was pulped. Yet in the decade since, I have received more correspondence about it than almost anything else I've ever published, including personal tales all deserving of their own tellers. If we forget what the reality of illegal abortion was like, then we are, to use Ronald Ryan's expression, in deep shit.

Anne Summers
A slice of life, 1965

It seemed doubly unfair to me that the sex that had resulted in my becoming pregnant had been forced, but I was far more worried about the calamitous consequences than about the event itself; far too preoccupied with the two goals that had suddenly become the focus of my life: how to get an abortion, and how to make sure my parents did not discover that I was pregnant. As it turned out, the second was a lot easier to achieve than the first.

It was extraordinarily difficult to get information. Everyone knew you went to Melbourne, but where in Melbourne? My friend Diana made discreet inquiries. Then someone suggested looking in the Pink Pages of the Melbourne telephone directory in the Barr Smith Library. I turned to the listing of medical practitioners and saw that someone had carefully placed asterisks beside several of the names. As I copied them down with the phone numbers, I wondered how I was going to begin the long-distance telephone conversation necessary to get an appointment. The word 'abortion' scarcely existed. Occasionally there was a reference in the newspapers – most likely in sensational rags such as *Truth* – to an 'illegal operation' that had resulted in a woman's death or the arrest of a doctor, or both. It was a long time before I had even vaguely understood what such an operation was since my mother was not willing to enlighten me, and even when I did I knew no one who had ever had one. Later, of course, women would talk openly of their abortions (or 'scrapes' as some ironically labelled them) when they pressed for the laws to change to remove the fear and the risks and the financial exploitation that in 1965 were still attached to terminating a pregnancy. If they could not find a doctor willing to risk his licence (in return for an exorbitant fee), many frantic women felt they had no choice but to try to 'get rid of it' themselves. Countless women resorted to potions and tablets or, in absolute desperation, tried to induce a miscarriage using a coat-hanger or similar sharp instrument. Each year in Australia in the 1960s as many as ten women died as a result. I did not know this at the time, but I doubt that it would have lessened my resolve. I had already tried all the so-called old wives' remedies. I had sat in a scalding-hot bath and tried to force down a bottle of gin. I had been on energetic walks. I had jumped off tables. I had even resorted to that usually foolproof means of bringing on your period: putting on a pair of snowy white slacks. Nothing worked. I went back to my doctor. He was willing to prescribe contraceptives for single girls, which made him an out and out radical; however, he drew the line at abortion. He confirmed I was pregnant but said there was nothing he could do to help if I planned to do something illegal.

I armed myself with a stack of two-shilling coins and went to a public phone box just outside the university gates near the River Torrens to make the trunk call to Melbourne. The woman who answered was reassuringly friendly as I stumbled through my request for an appointment. She gave me a date and time and then told me I had to bring cash on the day: the operation would cost £120. I was thunderstruck. This was far, far more than I had anticipated. There was no way I could raise that kind of money, my salary at the library was only £15 a week. I told the receptionist I would need to look for someone cheaper. Kindly she gave me a name. 'I think he charges about £60,' she said.

A few weeks later, I was standing early one evening on the corner of Collins and Russell streets in Melbourne; it had been prearranged that the doctor would pick me up there in his car. We drove for what seemed a long time to a surgery somewhere in the suburbs. I think I was blindfolded, though perhaps this is just a trick of memory, part of me wanting to block out what happened. Another doctor was waiting for us, but no one else was around. I should have been frightened: no one in the world knew where I was. I did not let myself think about what could happen if something went wrong. I just wanted it to be over, the nausea and the pregnancy, the feeling of shame and the guilt about what was about to happen.

I undressed and climbed onto the table, noticing with horror a plastic bucket on the floor near my legs. Suddenly the reality of what was happening hit me. I was about fourteen weeks pregnant, but not so 'far gone', I would later learn, as to make it dangerous. I was to have an anaesthetic and that was why the operation was still expensive. I did not know at the time that there were other, cheaper options – and I am glad I didn't because I worry even today about what I might have done. As I started to go under the anaesthetic, I heard the two men discussing my body; they were speculating about what I would look like in a bikini.

After I woke up, one of the doctors drove me to a St Kilda flat rented by a girl I had known when I lived at Tay Creggan. She was a strict Catholic, and while she was willing to let me stay she didn't want to know anything about why I was there. The flat was on the third floor and there was no lift. I was so groggy the doctor practically had to carry me up the stairs. He then went away and came back with six large bottles of lemonade, telling my friend I would be very thirsty when I came to fully. I remember being impressed by his kindness. He also left the name and phone number of a Collins Street specialist in case anything 'went wrong'.

Two days later I began to haemorrhage and to suffer bad cramplike pains. I went for a long walk through the gardens near the Shrine of Remembrance on St Kilda Road, hoping the exercise might help. It didn't. I felt absolutely alone. And scared. I rang the Collins Street doctor and he told me to come in the next day. It was a public holiday. There had been practically no one on the streets, and his rooms, and in fact the whole building, were deserted. He was a horrible old man with a fat belly and heavy breathing that suggested catarrh. I felt inexplicably nervous about being alone with him. He had not been present at the abortion, but he acted as if he were the person who had organised things. He gave me some tablets that he said would stop the bleeding. He also told me he would pay me commission if I sent other Adelaide girls to him. As I was leaving he grabbed me and tried to kiss me. I was very pleased a few years later to read in the papers that he had been charged by the police when the Victorian abortion rackets were exposed.

I returned to Adelaide and started university. Two weeks later I turned twenty. For the first few weeks of my student life I walked around the sun-filled grounds haemorrhaging. Instead of the excitement of enrolling in classes and starting a new phase of my life, I felt miserable and tainted, envious of all the other girls, who seemed so carefree and full of life. It was hard to recall when I had ever felt that way. I told no one, but I grew increasingly frightened by what was happening to me. Eventually the bleeding forced me back to the doctor who had refused to help me get an abortion. He looked at me with increasing horror as I told my story.

'*How* long have you been bleeding?' he exclaimed. He immediately picked up the phone.

'I've got a girl here who's been mucked up in Melbourne,' he told the North Terrace gynaecologist. 'Can you see her?'

A few days later I was in the gynaecologist's rooms hearing him tell me I had had what was known as 'an incomplete abortion'. In other words, despite the pain and the trauma and despite the huge amount of money, the abortion had not been done properly. I needed to go into hospital for a dilatation and curettage. No wonder, I thought, shaking with rage, no wonder the Collins Street doctor was trying to buy me off. He knew. That old bastard, he knew.

The straightforward – and legal – medical solution to my problem was not as easy to pursue as it sounded. I had no money, I explained to the doctor, because every penny I could lay my hands on had gone to pay for the abortion and the trip interstate. Nor, those pre-Medicare days, did I have any separate health insurance; as a student who lived at home I was covered by my parents' medical benefits, and to make a claim I would need one of their signatures. I did not know what I was going to do. But then my luck changed. With a generosity that was startling and unexpected, this man whom I had met for the first time less than half an hour earlier arranged for me to be admitted to a large public hospital as a teaching patient – which meant there would be no charge for the operation. He also organised for it to be over Easter when there would be no students – and when my family was planning a trip away so they would not know I was in hospital. He gave up several hours of his Easter holiday weekend to come in and do the curette. He never sent me a bill.

I have often wondered why this man did this for me. Perhaps he and some of his more enlightened colleagues recognised the damage being done to women by the outlawing of abortion. As my experience and that of countless others in those years demonstrated, making abortion illegal did not prevent women from seeking to end unwanted pregnancies. All it did was make abortions dangerous and expensive – and turned otherwise law-abiding people into criminals. If the law had permitted this doctor to do the D and C in a hospital in the first place, there would have been minimal if any medical risk. As it was, he performed exactly the same operation that I had paid £60 for in a backroom in Melbourne. He completed legally the abortion the *Crimes Act* said I was not allowed to have.

My experience paled beside what some women endured. In the Queen Victoria Hospital, where I had my curette, I shared a room with a girl of about fifteen who was also suffering from an incomplete abortion. She talked very tough, this young woman. She told me that when she came home at night her mother would demand she hand over her panties so she could sniff them for signs of sex. 'That was easy to get around,' the girl said. 'I'd take two pairs with me.' The vigilance of her mother and mine had not prevented either of us from having sex, though at least I had been able to spare my mother from having to cope with the consequences. This girl's mother had been less lucky, and so had her daughter. Her abortion had been done by her boyfriend. He had punched her in the jaw to knock her unconscious and had then used a coat-hanger.

The cruel absurdity of the law was further evinced about a year later when a young New Zealand woman who answered an advertisement to share the all-girl student house I lived in told the household her harrowing story. Katrina was a frail, blonde-haired musician. She had arrived in Adelaide to take up a job with the orchestra, not knowing a soul. She was also pregnant. Somehow she had discovered a local abortionist. Listening around the kitchen table, we were amazed. How could someone new to town find a facility that those of us who had grown up there knew nothing about? Tell us, we urged, it will save other girls having to go to Melbourne. So she did. She had found her way, with that instinct that belongs to the desperate, to a doctor in a seedy suburban area, who in his surgery and without using any form of anaesthetic had dilated her cervix and then sent her home in agony, telling her to present herself at the nearest hospital when the bleeding started. They'll have to take you in, he said. And he was right. No hospital would perform a termination, but no hospital would turn away a woman who was haemorrhaging from a botched abortion. The doctor had charged Katrina about £30. The public hospital system would fix her up for nothing. That is, if she had not already died from septicaemia or bleeding.

Years later in Brooklyn, New York, I visited an abortion clinic – a place that could perhaps best be described by the derogatory term 'mill'. Choices, as it was called, was owned and operated by Merle Hoffman, a feminist entrepreneur who had taken advantage of the liberalising of New York's abortion laws in 1970 to establish a facility where women could have safe and affordable abortions. About a hundred girls were 'done' each day in a suite of rooms in a modern office building on one of Brooklyn's main boulevards. I walked through the crowded waiting and counselling rooms, peeked into the operating area and proceeded through to the recovery ward, where every few moments another groggy young girl would be wheeled in. Ninety per cent of them were African-American and most looked under twenty – certainly I did not spot anyone who looked more than thirty. All the younger ones seemed to be there with their mothers. It was a confusing sight and I found myself shrinking from it. I almost felt a sense of revulsion. But then I remembered what it used to be like. Give me safe abortion en masse any day, I resolved, however squeamish my reaction to the reality; give me that any day over teenagers waiting on street corners in strange cities for predatory doctors to take their money and endanger their lives with botched abortions.

I felt nothing after my abortion. Now when I think back, I realise I simply would not allow myself to feel anything. I must have felt relieved, although because of the medical aftermath I was denied even that cathartic emotion for another couple of months. Eleven years later I would admire the courage of Italian journalist Oriana Fallaci for writing the book *Letter to a Child Never Born*. By then I, too, was a journalist and understood completely her decision to get up from the bed to which, her doctor warned, she needed to be confined for her entire pregnancy if the baby were to survive. She had rejected the advice of her friends and her boss to have an abortion, deciding that she would have the child. But she had not bargained on the fact that in order to have it, she would have to give up her life, her job, her passionate nature (the doctor said the slightest emotional upset could be fatal to the foetus), everything in fact that made her who she was. With great guilt, but in the knowledge that this was too large a sacrifice for her to make, Fallaci left her bed and went on a gruelling assignment in a developing country. The experience cost her her baby. Her rumination on the physical and emotional steps of a pregnancy that will not be completed, so familiar to so many thousands of women, is one that does not shirk from self-recrimination. It is a remarkable and brave book because it is so unblinkingly honest, so unsentimental and yet so sad.

I was driven by fear as much as anything, fear that my parents would find out, although I was also very aware that it would be my university studies that would be aborted if I had the child. It had taken several years for me finally to get there, and like Fallaci I made the decision that I was not yet ready to surrender my life to being a mother; there was certainly no way then that I could have done both. I loathed the man who against my protests had forced himself on me on a beach one night and with a couple of quick, unsatisfying thrusts left me pregnant. I would not even consider the idea of marrying him. Nor did I want to go through what my friend Jacinta had endured: carrying a baby to term only to have it snatched away.

Women are often accused, especially by so-called 'pro-lifers', of having abortions lightly and unthinkingly. But for every woman I know who has had an abortion, and most women I know have had at least one, the decision has involved a great deal of anguish and often intense feelings of guilt or remorse. I buried these feelings deep within myself because I had to. Inevitably in time they forced their way to the surface, and I found myself a year later telling John Summers, with whom I was very much in love, all about it. The emotions I had repressed for so long spilled over because finally here was someone I could trust enough to tell. We were sitting on my bed, which was the only place in my group house where we could be assured of privacy, and as I told him I started to cry. First I sniffled and dabbed at my cheeks, then my tears turned into sobs until finally I broke down completely and, letting it all go, I howled.

GIVEN the OPTIONS

by SARAH FIRTH

18th Sept 1998

I'm so hungry and scared. Not allowed to eat till after the operation.

We waited for so long. Then Mum had to go off to Sydney for work. I had to wear a gown with nothing else on. I lay down in the operating theatre then freaked out when they put my drip in and mask on. I pushed the nurse off me and tried to kick the doctor. I was in panic and crying but then I just passed out.

Woke up in the small recovery room in a weird nappy with orange brown iodine all over my crotch and legs. The nurse gave me a cup of milky tea and an anzac biccie.

Resting at Tomek's house now. Waiting for AJ to finish school. I'm so tired. Zonked.

Mum finally came back and brought me home. I've been crying and crying. When AJ came to visit me after school he lay down and cuddled me but then said he was horny. I said no. We have to wait two weeks for sex and that I was bleeding. He kept kissing me then started fucking me. I said no but was so tired and sad I just let him finish. I fucking hate him. I am crying again. I can't wait for this to be OVER.

"WOAH. THIS is HORRIBLE."

"YEAH he WAS. WE BROKE UP AFTER that AND HE went on to SPREAD RUMOURS ABOUT ME BEING A MEGA SLUT. WHILE HE SOLD VIDEOS of US HAVING SEX to GUYS at SCHOOL. THE VIDEO was filmed WITHOUT MY CONSENT ON SCHOOL EQUIPMENT!"

SHE USED TO HIDE UNDER THE TABLE and EAVESDROP on HER MOTHER'S LADIES AFTERNOON tea GATHERINGS.

AMONGST the FLOWERS, LACE and CAKE she HEARD GNARLY STORIES of MISCARRIAGE, DEATH in CHILDBIRTH, AFFAIRS, ILLEGITIMATE CHILDREN, UNSAFE ABORTIONS and DEATHS from SEPTICAEMIA and other TERMINATION-RELATED COMPLICATIONS.

THE BLEEDING won't STOP.

MUM even LEARNED that HER MOTHER HAD a BOTCHED abortion IN THE LATE 1940s and HAD to BE RUSHED TO HOSPITAL. SHE WAS LUCKY TO SURVIVE.

AT MUM'S HIGH SCHOOL SHE REMEMBERED HOW A FEW GIRLS DISAPPEARED with VAGUE STORIES LIKE "JENNY IS VISITING HER SICK GRANDMOTHER for a WHILE." SHE THINKS THEY WERE DISCREETLY TAKEN away TO GIVE BIRTH and the BABIES were MAYBE TAKEN IN by OTHER FAMILY MEMBERS OR FORCEABLY ADOPTED TO STRANGERS.

SHE SAID a few GIRLS WHO RETURNED from NEAR SIX MONTH ABSENCES were CLEARLY TRAUMATISED by WHAT HAPPENED.

THERE was SUCH A CULTURE of SECRECY, SHAME and GUILT with ANY REPRODUCTIVE CHOICE OTHER THAN the "GOOD CHRISTIAN" MODEL of ABSTINENCE, MARRIAGE and ONLY then, CHILDREN. THAT was THE RIGHT and MORAL WAY. WHO CAN LIVE UP TO THAT STANDARD?

YEP. DOGMA RARELY fits WELL WITH REAL LIVED EXPERIENCE and the COMPLEX realities and DECISIONS we HAVE to MAKE in OUR LIVES.

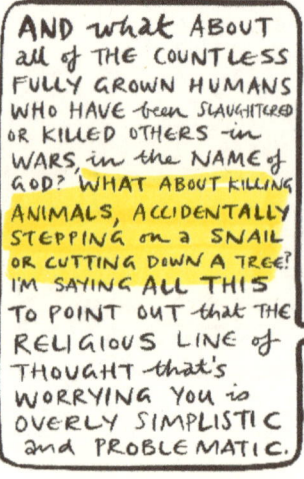

Gabrielle Stanley Blair

A Twitter thread: abortion, unwanted pregnancies and irresponsible ejaculation

I'm a mother of six, and a Mormon, so I have a good understanding of arguments surrounding abortion, religious and otherwise. I've been listening to men grandstand about women's reproductive rights, and I'm convinced that men actually have zero interest in stopping abortion.

Here's why: if you want to stop abortion, you need to prevent unwanted pregnancies. And men cause 100 per cent of unwanted pregnancies.

No, for real, they do.

Perhaps you are thinking: IT TAKES TWO TO TANGO! And yes, it does take two for *intentional* pregnancies. But ALL unwanted pregnancies are caused by the irresponsible ejaculations of men. Period.

Don't believe me? Let me walk you through it. Let's start with this: with rare exceptions, a woman's eggs are only fertile about two days each month. And that's for a limited number of years. That makes twenty-four days a year a woman is fertile.

But men are fertile, and can *cause* pregnancy, 365 days a year. In fact, if you're a man who ejaculates multiple times a day, you could cause multiple pregnancies daily. In theory a man could cause 1000+ unwanted pregnancies in just one year. And though their sperm gets crappier as they age, men can cause unwanted pregnancies from puberty till death.

So just starting with basic biology plus the calendar it's easy to see that men are the real issue here.

But what about birth control? If a woman doesn't want to risk an unwanted pregnancy, why wouldn't she just use birth control? If a woman can manage to figure out how to get an abortion, surely she can get birth control, right?

Great questions.

Modern birth control is possibly the greatest invention of the last century, and I am very grateful for it. It's also brutal. The side effects for many women are ridiculously harmful. So ridiculous, that when an oral contraception for men was created, it wasn't approved . . . because of the side effects. And the list of side effects was about one-third as long as the known side effects for women's oral contraception.

There's a lot to be unpacked just in that story, but I'll simply point out that as a society, we really don't mind if women suffer, physically or mentally, as long as it makes things easier for men.

But good news, men: even with the horrible side effects, women are still very willing to use birth control. Unfortunately, it's harder to get than it should be. Birth control options for women require a doctor's appointment and a prescription. It's not free, and often not cheap. In fact, there are many people trying to make it more expensive by fighting to make sure insurance companies refuse to cover it.

Oral contraceptives for women can't be acquired easily, or at the last minute. And they don't work instantly. If we're talking about The Pill, it requires consistent daily use and doesn't leave much room for mistakes, forgetfulness, or unexpected disruptions to daily schedules. And again, the side effects can be brutal.

I'M STILL GRATEFUL FOR IT PLEASE DON'T TAKE IT AWAY. I'm just saying women's birth control isn't simple or easy.

In contrast, let's look at birth control for men – meaning condoms. Condoms are readily available at all hours, inexpensive, convenient and don't require a prescription. They're effective, and work on demand, instantly. Men can keep them stocked up just in case, so they're always prepared. *Amazing!* They are so much easier than birth control options for women.

As a bonus, in general, women *love* when men use condoms. They keep us from getting STDs, they don't lessen our pleasure during sex or prevent us from climaxing. And the best part? Clean up is so much easier – no waddling to the toilet as your jizz drips down our legs.

So why in the world are there ever unwanted pregnancies? Why don't men just use condoms every time they have sex? Seems so simple, right?

Oh. I remember. Men *don't* love condoms. In fact, men frequently pressure women to have sex without a condom. And it's not unheard of for men to remove the condom during sex, without the woman's permission or knowledge. (Pro-tip: that's assault.)

Why would men want to have sex without a condom? Good question. Apparently it's because for the minutes they are penetrating their partner, having no condom on gives the experience more pleasure.

So ... there are men willing to risk getting a woman pregnant – which means literally risking her life, her health, her social status, her relationships, and her career – so that they can experience a few minutes of *slightly* more pleasure? Is that for real? Yes. Yes it is.

What are we talking about here, pleasure-wise? If there's a pleasure scale, with pain beginning at zero and going down into the negatives, a back-scratch falling at five, and an orgasm without a condom being a ten, where would sex with a condom fall? Like a seven or eight? So it's not like sex with a condom is *not* pleasurable, it's just not *as* pleasurable. An eight instead of a ten.

Let me emphasise that again: men regularly choose to put women at massive risk by having non-condom sex, in order to experience a few minutes of *slightly* more pleasure.

Now keep in mind, for the truly condom-averse, men also have a non-condom, always-ready birth control built right in, called the pull-out. It's not perfect, and it's a favourite joke, but according to Planned Parenthood it is 96 per cent effective when used correctly, and 78 per cent effective in practice (perhaps we should teach people to do it correctly?).

So, surely, we can expect men who aren't wearing a condom to *at least* pull out every time they have sex, right?

Nope.

And why not?

Well, again, apparently it's *slightly* more pleasurable to climax inside a vagina than, say, on their partner's stomach.

So men are willing to risk the life, health and wellbeing of women, in order to experience a tiny bit more pleasure for like five seconds during orgasm.

It's mind-boggling and disturbing when you realise that's the choice men are making. And honestly, I'm not as mad as I should be about this, because we've trained men from birth that their pleasure is of utmost importance in the world. (And to disassociate sex and pregnancy.)

While we're here, let's talk a bit more about pleasure and biology. Did you know that as a general rule a man CAN'T get a woman pregnant without having an orgasm? Yes, there are exceptions – it's possible for sperm to show up in pre-ejaculate – but in most cases, a man has an orgasm in order to impregnate a woman. Which means that we can conclude getting a woman pregnant is a pleasurable act for men.

But did you further know that men CAN get a woman pregnant without HER feeling any pleasure at all? In fact, it's totally possible for a man to impregnate a woman even while causing her excruciating pain, trauma or horror.

In contrast, a woman can have non-stop orgasms with or without a partner and never once get herself pregnant. A woman's orgasm has literally nothing to do with pregnancy or fertility – her clitoris exists not for creating new babies, but simply for pleasure.

No matter how many orgasms she has, they won't make her pregnant. Pregnancies can only happen when men have an orgasm. Unwanted pregnancies can only happen when men orgasm irresponsibly.

What this means is that a woman can be the sluttiest slut in the entire world who loves having orgasms all day long and all night long and she will never find herself with an unwanted pregnancy unless a man shows up and ejaculates irresponsibly.

Women enjoying sex does not equal unwanted pregnancy and abortion.

Men enjoying sex and having irresponsible ejaculations is what causes unwanted pregnancies and abortion.

Let's talk more about responsibility. Men often don't know, and don't ask, and don't think to ask, if they've caused a pregnancy. They may never think of it, or associate sex with making babies at all. Why?

Because there are *zero* consequences for men who cause unwanted pregnancies.

If the woman decides to have an abortion, the man may never know he caused an unwanted pregnancy with his irresponsible ejaculation.

If the woman decides to have the baby, or put the baby up for adoption, the man may never know that there's now a child walking around with 50 per cent of his DNA.

If the woman does tell him that he caused an unwanted pregnancy and that she's having the baby, the closest thing to a consequence for him, is that he may need to pay child support. But our current child support system is well-known to be a joke. Only 61 per cent of men (or women) who are legally required to pay it, do. There are little to no repercussions for skipping out. In some US states, their credit isn't even affected. So, many men keep going as is, causing unwanted pregnancies with irresponsible ejaculations and never giving it thought.

When the topic of abortion comes up, they might think: *Abortion is horrible; women should not have abortions.* And never once consider the man who CAUSED the unwanted pregnancy.

If you're not holding men responsible for unwanted pregnancies, then you are wasting your time.

Stop protesting at clinics. Stop shaming women. Stop trying to overturn abortion laws. If you actually care about reducing or eliminating the number of abortions, simply HOLD MEN RESPONSIBLE FOR THEIR ACTIONS.

What would that look like? What if there was a real and immediate consequence for men who cause an unwanted pregnancy? What kind of consequence would make sense? Should it be as harsh, painful, nauseating, scarring, expensive, risky and life-altering, as forcing a woman to go through a nine-month unwanted pregnancy?

In my experience, men really like their testicles. If irresponsible ejaculations were putting their balls at risk, they would stop being irresponsible. Does castration seem like a cruel and unusual punishment? Maybe. But is it worse than forcing 500,000 women a year to puke daily for three months, gain 40 pounds, and then rip their bodies apart in childbirth? Is a handful of castrations worse than women dying during forced pregnancy and childbirth?

Put a castration law on the books, implement the law, let the media tell the story, and in three months or less, *tada!* abortions will have virtually disappeared. Can you picture it? No more abortions in less than three months, without ever trying to outlaw them. Amazing.

For those of you who consider abortion to be murder, wouldn't you be on board with having a handful of men castrated, if it prevented 500,000 murders each year? And if not, is that because you actually care more about policing women's bodies, morality and sexuality than you do about reducing or eliminating abortions?

Hey, you can even have the men who will be castrated bank their sperm before it happens – just in case they want to responsibly have kids some day.

Can't wrap your head around a physical punishment for men? Even though you seem to be more than fine with physical punishments for women? Okay. Then how about this prevention idea: at the onset of puberty, all males could be required by law to get a vasectomy.

Vasectomies are very safe, highly reversible, and about as invasive as getting an IUD implanted. There is some soreness afterwards for about twenty-four hours, but that's pretty much it for side effects – so much better than The Pill, which is taken by millions of women, the side effects of which are well known and can be brutal.

If/when the male becomes a responsible adult, and perhaps finds a mate, if they want to have a baby, the vasectomy can be reversed, and then redone once the childbearing stage is over. And each male can bank their sperm before the vasectomy, just in case. It's not that wild of an idea. 80 per cent of males in the US are circumcised, most as babies. And circumcision is not reversible.

Don't like my ideas? That's fine. I'm sure there are better ones. Go ahead and suggest your own ideas. My point is that it's nonsense to focus on women if you're trying to get rid of abortions. Abortion is the 'treatment' for an unwanted pregnancy. If you want to stop abortions, you need to prevent the 'disease' – unwanted pregnancies. And the only way to do that, is by focusing on men, because:

MEN CAUSE 100 PER CENT OF UNWANTED PREGNANCIES. Or in other words: IRRESPONSIBLE EJACULATIONS BY MEN CAUSE 100 PER CENT OF UNWANTED PREGNANCIES.

If you're a man, what would the consequence need to be for you to never again ejaculate irresponsibly? Would it be money related? Maybe a loss of rights or freedoms? Physical pain? Ask yourselves: what would it take for you to value the life of your sexual partner more than your own temporary pleasure or convenience?

Are you someone who learns better with analogies? Let's try this one: think of another great pleasure in life, let's say food. Think of your favourite meal, dessert or drink. What if you found out that every time you indulge in that favourite food you risk causing great physical and mental pain for someone you know intimately. You might not cause *any* pain, but it's a real risk.

Well, you'd probably be sad, but never indulge in that food again, right? Not worth the risk!

And then, what if you further found out, there was a simple thing you could do before you ate that favourite food, and it would eliminate the risk of causing pain to someone else. Which is great news! BUT the simple thing you need to do makes the experience of eating the food slightly less pleasurable. To be clear, still VERY pleasurable, but slightly less so. Like maybe you have to eat the food with a fork or spoon that you don't particularly like.

Would you be willing to do that simple thing, and eliminate the risk of causing pain to someone you know, every single time you ate your favourite food? OF COURSE YOU WOULD.

Condoms (or even pulling out) is that simple thing. Don't put women at risk. Don't choose to maximise your own pleasure if it risks causing women pain.

Men mostly run our government. Men mostly make the laws. And men could eliminate abortions in three months or less without ever touching an abortion law or even mentioning women.

In summary: STOP TRYING TO CONTROL WOMEN'S BODIES AND SEXUALITY. UNWANTED PREGNANCIES ARE CAUSED BY MEN.

Brooke Davis
Snorkel

The penis, naturally, has been studied in exhaustive detail and there is no dissension about which parts belong to it. In fact, anatomists typically agree on the definitions of all other bodily structures and organs: a knee is a knee, an eye is an eye, and so forth, they have yet to agree on the definition of women's pleasure system.

Rebecca Chalker (*The Clitoral Truth*, 2018)

We have been raised to fear the yes within ourselves, our deepest cravings.

Audre Lorde

Women want sex, they just don't want the sex they can have.

Esther Perel

On Valentine's Day I visit a sex worker and it's not what I expect. Having said that, my understanding of the industry till now comes from *Friday Night Lights*, those photos of Hugh Grant in the nineties, and watching a sex show in Amsterdam that was set to the music from Batman, so my expectations may be skewed. I knock on the apartment door and she greets me warmly, shaking my hand and smiling.

'I'm Robyn,' she says.

Robyn is small, with red hair tied back in a ponytail. She's dressed comfortably in a black top and black pants, like she's working backstage at the theatre.

While I unravel myself from a coat, scarf and boots, I become this absurd babbling person, exclaiming about weather and the Winter Olympics, and complimenting her on anything that comes to mind. 'That winter sun is so lovely!' 'How lovely are Tess & Scott? That ice-skating couple?' 'This is *such* a lovely space!' I say 'lovely' about twenty-seven times in the space of three minutes.

If Robyn notices she doesn't let on and instead sits me down at the kitchenette table and boils the kettle. It's a small studio apartment, filled with the friendly clutter of a life. The kitchen and living area is one room, there's a closed door I assume is a bedroom, and a bathroom off to the left. A massage table looms in the centre of the living space. It's covered in white sheets, with a yoni egg and crystal placed neatly on top. It feels sacrificial, or reverential.

It's a crisp, bright day, and Toronto's winter sun *is* lovely, dammit. I've just walked for two hours, through dirty puddles, past mounds of snow, past school playgrounds with kids throwing actual snowballs, like I've only really seen on *The Simpsons*.

Robyn hands me a steaming mug of tea and pulls up a chair. I'm so curious about this woman, who I read about in *Closer*:

Notes from the Orgasmic Frontier of Female Sexuality by Sarah Barmak. Robyn has a degree in English literature and sexuality studies, has worked for years as an escort, and now works in the field of Sensual Bodywork, a field that focuses on the way touch and sex can heal. I already love her calm movements, the way she seems to be taking everything in, the spark and readiness in her eyes.

'Why are you here, Brooke?' she says, blowing on the top of her tea and leaning back in her chair. 'What do you want out of today?'

The thing is, I've been knocking around in this body of mine for close to forty years and for a lot of that time I've known where the baby grows, where the penis goes, and what parts the heterosexual men will look at, but I haven't always known the way it could be played with for my own joy. I've understood my reproductive system as this clean-lined diagram, this sea-creature thing, something you might find in a long white robe in the Cantina Bar in *Star Wars*. I've always liked the dancer's posture of it, the open arms, the arching back, as if it's breathing in, readying itself for war, for love, for both, maybe. Something like fireballs in each hand, winding up to throw. I've always liked knowing it's inside of me. How surprised I was when I saw bodies cut open on educational videos and hospital shows – when I discovered the brutal inelegance of our insides, the honest mess of what we are.

But before my thirties, I barely even heard a human being say 'clitoris', except perhaps in that dopey dad sitcom way ('Your keys are harder to find than the clitoris! Ha ha! Womens don't even like the sex anyway! So! Let's just not worry about it! Amirite! Beer! Etc!'). It wasn't till my thirties that I found out that the bean on the outside of my body is only a small part of the clitoris, that it's a bit like the tip of a snorkel rising up out of the ocean. That there's at least eighteen distinct parts to it that are hiding out under my skin. I now know the language of it: glans, hood, shaft, arms, bulbs. I now know it's a whole network of pleasure, that nerves branch out from it in unique ways and connect to the brain. I now know it engorges with blood when aroused. I now know it is the only human organ that exists purely for pleasure. I now know I can pleasure the shit out of it, and that I love doing that very much, whether someone else is there or not.

I believe I'm the kind of person who is uncomfortable talking about herself and yet, it turns out that I love talking about myself to Robyn. Turns out I can't get enough of talking about myself to Robyn, that I should be in the Winter Olympics for talking about myself to Robyn. We sit with our tea in the gentle afternoon light. We laugh a lot – she has this gorgeous dorky laugh that reminds me of a friend back home – and she is challenging, hopeful, encouraging, sharp, non-judgemental. I tell her things I've not told anybody, things I don't even really know about myself. I share a pretty ungraceful story about me having sex in a hostel shower. My mum had just died, I was in Europe, and I was drinking with a much younger person whose idea of seduction was to go into great detail about every single drinking-induced vomit he'd experienced (a particular favourite of his being a 'helicopter spew'). By 3 a.m. we were cohabiting the shower and at one point he said, 'What do you like?' and because it took me a few moments to realise what he meant, he repeated it: 'Tell me what you like.'

'It was the most simple thing to say to someone when you're naked with them,' I say to Robyn. 'The most common of courtesies. But it was the first time anybody had ever said that to me.' I pause. 'And it was genuinely the first time I'd thought to ask that of myself.'

I tell her I want to know what ego-less attention to my body feels like. I want to feel free to prioritise my own pleasure. I don't know how to do that, I say. I add that I'm not convinced the script of heterosexual sex is truly satisfying for people with vaginas. That I find the whole *linear, goal-oriented, prioritising his pleasure, centring of penetration, ending at his orgasm* script a bit boring. I tell her about some disconnected, unkind sex I've had, and some connected, kind sex I've also had.

'I'm asking myself why I have sex,' I say.

'That's a good question,' she says. 'Why do you?'

'I don't know,' I say. 'A hope for connection, I think. I want it to be about really knowing someone, and inviting them to really know me.' I check myself. 'I sound like a bit of a dick, don't I?'

She laughs, shakes her head, *no*, so I add: 'People often think I mean I need emotionality and deep love to enjoy sex – in that way women are told is "natural" for them. But I don't mean that. I mean something like tenderness and mutual respect while with another human being. Even if I only know them for one night.'

She nods. 'Do you masturbate?' she asks.

I tell her I come easily alone, that I find it distracting when there's someone else's brain in the room. 'I'm in their heads, wondering what they want.' I look over at the massage table. 'You must have so many people cry as soon as they get on that table,' I say, feeling a new, unrecognisable grief rising in me.

'So many people cry as soon as they sit in that chair,' Robyn nods. 'As soon as they walk in the door. They've spent all that energy making the appointment and now they're here and they're just like—' she breathes out. 'Everyone thinks they're abnormal. I want to scream at them on the street: *you're all normal!*'

Here's a question: why the fuck didn't I know anything about the clitoris till I was in my thirties?

It has to have something to do with not ever seeing a picture of a clitoris, or hearing the word in the mainstream. Nothing from my doctor, or gynaecologist or health teacher. Nothing from my parents, or partners or friends. Maybe – *maybe* – the magazines mentioned it (*Dolly* was all we really had back then), but my memory is of being rallied for when sex happened at our bodies – all the plucking and ab-curling and spots for perfume, all the witty ways to combat a claim of 'blue balls'.

Also, it probably has something to do with the whole of (western) history, which has a confusing relationship to the clitoris. Dr Laurie Mintz in *Becoming Cliterate* and Rebecca Chalker in *The Clitoral Truth* make it clear that this is because the people writing and drawing and studying the clitoris have historically not been the people who actually have clitorises, and so clitoral history becomes like the shittiest most drawn-out game of hide and seek you can think of.

A very, very, very short history would go something like this: the Greeks and Romans know about the external and internal parts of the clitoris but see it as a 'failed attempt at a penis', and in the Dark and Middle Ages it is 'the Devil's teat'.[19] The clitoris makes a comeback in the Renaissance era when anatomists start including the full clitoris on drawings of the female body, but we lose it again in the Victorian era, on account of doctors working out that it has nothing to do with pregnancy.[20] This is around the time that the clitoris goes from 'being depicted as an extensive organ system to a meaningless bump' and 'female orgasms [are] considered unnecessary, inappropriate and unhealthy'.[21] This is also around the time that the vibrator is invented (for doctors to use on 'hysterical' women), and the time Freud fucks us all up by declaring that 'clitoral orgasms' are for babies and 'vaginal orgasms' are for grown-ups (current research states that all orgasms are from the clitoral network). 'In essence,' Mintz says, 'he said that grown women who need clitoral stimulation to reach orgasm are defective'.[22] This probably leads to Princess Marie Bonaparte, a psychoanalyst and grand-niece of Napoleon, studying the relationship between female orgasm and penetration, discovering that women whose clitorises are further from their vagina find it more difficult to orgasm during vaginal penetration, and having an operation to move her clitoris closer to her vagina (it doesn't work). In 1947, we lose the clitoris again, because Dr Charles Mayo Goss, the editor of the 25th edition of *Gray's Anatomy*, widely considered to be the authority on anatomy, erases the clitoris entirely. In 1953 Alfred Kinsey finds it again, publishing a book that reminds us that the clitoris is the centre of female orgasm, and that 'intercourse is not the best means of pleasure for women'.[23]

In 1998 – I was nineteen – Australian urologist Dr Helen O'Connell 'discovers' the full clitoris, publishing a paper about the 'clitoral complex' that is often larger than the penis. In 2005 – I was 26 – Dr O'Connell and her colleagues 'did the first mapping of women's genitals using MRIs',[24] and in 2009 – I was thirty – French surgeons Pierre Foldès and Odile Buisson publish the first 3D ultrasound of the clitoris (Foldès also invents the first successful Female Genital Mutilation reversal surgery).[25] 'With perhaps up to or more than eight thousand nerve endings,' Chalker writes in 2018, 'it is the most densely innervated and, hence, most sensitive part of the human body, female or male. Almost no research has been done on the innervation of this extremely key anatomical feature, so this figure is only a guestimation'.[26]

It's clear that throughout the whole of western history, the clitoris gets lost and found, erased and discovered, revered and despised.

You guys: it's not fucking *Where's Wally*. IT'S BEEN HERE THE WHOLE TIME. You just had to ask.

As a vagina-owner, I'm accustomed to having the hands of strangers in and on my body – doctors and their metal scrapers, beauticians, strange men. But I do love (consensual) touch, and I cannot wait for this session with Robyn. As I lay myself down on the massage table, that thrilling winter sun on my skin through the curtains, Robyn says, 'Would you like to focus on presence of mind today, Brooke?' I don't really know how to do that but I say yes, and she starts slowly on my feet, and I think about a James Baldwin quote I found in Robert Jensen's *The End of Patriarchy*: 'If you can't be touched, you can't be changed. And if you can't be changed, you can't be alive.'

I loved the feel of things when I was a kid. The feeling of getting dirty and then clean again. Of getting cold and then hot. Hot and then cold. When I was six years old on sports day I took off my shoes at the last minute to run my race – even though we were specifically told not to – because I loved the feeling of the cool grass under my hot feet, and the way moving my body in this way turned air into wind. I was always so surprised by my own body. That I could use it to somersault in water, climb up sand dunes, lie on long grass, flip on trampolines. That I could close my eyelids and make it dark in my brain and my body would knock itself unconscious, for hours. That I could cut my hair and it would grow right back or nick my skin and it would heal itself. That the circles on my fingertips had their own art, that my eyelashes could grant a wish, that the lines on my palms knew my future.

For two hours Robyn touches me. It's calming, and peaceful, and safe. Fun. I don't have to perform for anybody else, and it's slow, unexplosive, and just, well. *Lovely*. It's lovely.

Later, after I've showered and we've chatted a bit, I'm piling on my winter clothes in whirls around me, and I say, 'I want sex to be like *that*. Not all the time. But more often than not, I want *that* to be how sex happens with my body.'

Robyn smiles, nodding patiently. 'It can be,' she says.

'Okay,' I say. 'Okay.' As I tie up my shoelaces I say, 'I want to live in your utopia. I want you to be the president of this utopia, and I'm living there.'

'I'm working on it,' she says.

I say goodbye to Robyn and on my way back to the Airbnb I wander into a secondhand bookshop. I start talking to the lady working there – Joan, she tells me eventually – small, short grey hair, eager to please. She says she's always wanted to write but life has gotten in the way.

'A lot of women do that, don't they?' I say. 'Put everyone else first and never do the thing they really want to do.'

'Oh, yes, hon,' she nods emphatically. 'It's what we do.' I think about my mum, how I didn't know till she was dead that she'd always wanted to do aid work in far-away countries. I never once heard her say that and only found out through a friend of hers. She had us instead, myself and my two brothers, while my dad got his doctorate and practised as a sports psychologist with some of the best athletes in the country.

I ask Joan what she likes to read and she says she once loved Mills and Boon, then moved onto crime, and now reads whatever catches her eye. 'I tried to read a Mills and Boon recently,' she says, 'And I thought, what a load of garbage!'

I smile. I've always wondered what they're like. 'It's funny how your tastes change,' I say.

'I now buy them for my mum,' she says. 'She's eighty-nine years old.'

'Oh, I love that!' I say. 'So your mum likes them?'

'Honey, she loves them. Calls them her "old lady pornography".' Joan winks, I laugh, and we chat a bit more.

Eventually, I head back out into the night. As I walk under neon lights, breathing in cold air, I think: *There is a part of my body that is there to make me feel good.*

I think about how I'm probably not going to use my body in the way I was told I would. That fire-ball-throwing, breathing-in Uterus Queen built for baby-housing. I probably won't ever know if she truly works, what noises I make during childbirth, what it feels like to grow a human from scratch in there.

I think about the diagrams I now know of the clitoris: huggable, sometimes swan-like, or even ferocious – a little like those terrifying Wheelers from *Return to Oz*. I think about the easy joy I had for and in my body as a kid. I think about all the people who have clitorises, and those who feel like they should – the complexity of experiences with this organ, particularly those outside of my own white-cis, able-bodied experience.

There is a part of my body that is there to make me feel good. That's the point of it. It doesn't make a baby. It's not a sheath for a penis. We don't bleed out of it. It's not the thing men are looking at. No one's really looking at it – including us. But it is just for us, if we want it to be.

I think: *It's mine, if I want it to be.*

Michelle Law
Choosing

I'm capable of conceiving frightful things:
irrational thoughts and impulses that frightened me
before I learned to diminish their power. Therapy
helps. What I fear now is conceiving a child.

In my apartment building there are young families,
toddlers with loose teeth, prams parked beside
piles of shoes, all mothers my age. I walk my cat
past their doors and he stops to smell them, to listen.

It's not pregnancy that frightens me, not the
bulging of stomach and breasts, the taut and then
sagging skin, the elongating nipples and the
tearing of flesh, and then of heart—

'Parenthood is the only love born of fear,' say friends
as they cup soft and still forming skulls, as they reach
palms out in warning as knees are skinned on
playground mulch. The swell of tears.

I fear the choice.

An old colleague and mentor in her fifties once
cried in the storeroom at work while reminiscing.
She wished that she'd had a child; instead, she chose to
buy a beautiful boat and travel the world.

Then there is my mother, who loves her five children,
still loves the child that she miscarried thirty years ago.
What is her advice for a woman my age, in this era?
'Have none,' she says. 'Or if you must, have two.'

There could be rapture or resentment or fulfilment or
regret. No matter the choice, life will change. Or maybe
I needn't choose once the cities and creatures born long
before us are destroyed by those of us already born.

I don't fear breaking laws. I don't fear buildings marked
only by numbers, and placards held by men and women
brandishing them with the gusto of people advertising
pizza deals. I fear the crossroads.

I fear the choice.

Monica Dux
My silent scream

For young people, horror films have a special power. Yes, they're scary and intimidating, but they're also incredibly exciting, precisely because they're illicit.

In my early teens, there was one horror film that terrified me more than the others, not only because it touched on all sorts of forbidden subjects, but because we were told that it was all true.

It was called *The Silent Scream* and if you went to a Catholic school in the 1980s or 1990s, it's highly likely that you'd have seen it. I never did, although among my classmates it was rumoured that the school had a VHS copy, hidden away in the library. So the threat of a screening was always there.

What made this film so sensational was that it was billed as a documentary in which you'd see an actual abortion occurring. Or, as we Catholic kids understood it: a real live baby murder.

This was a snuff film, then, but one that had the approval of our teachers.

But what really haunted me about it was the eponymous scream itself, evoking the tagline from another horror classic, *Alien*: in space, no one can hear you scream.

Well, apparently the same was true of in utero shrieks. Those poor little babies, screaming silently as they were killed by godless abortionists. What greater horror could there be than that?

Made in 1984, just over a decade after *Roe v. Wade*, *The Silent Scream* was a graphic retort to the liberalising of abortion laws in the USA. It soon became the anti-choice film de rigueur, a triumph of anti-abortion propaganda intended to change the hearts and minds not just of the young, the impressionable and the pregnant, but also of legislators.

And it did become a blockbuster of sorts, gaining wide distribution through churches, schools and community groups. In the United States, *The Silent Scream* also screened numerous times on national television, while here in Australia, it was still being shown in Catholic schools decades after it was produced.

Ronald Reagan even screened it at the White House, and reportedly said that if everyone in Congress saw it, abortion would be outlawed immediately. That didn't happen, but its legislative impact was profound, contributing to the decision by some US states to enact legislation that required women to view an ultrasound of their pregnancy before being allowed to have an abortion.

The final measure of the film's success – how many minds it actually changed – is harder to quantify. Certainly, it did have a significant impact on the way the contemporary abortion debate has evolved. And it was highly successful in traumatising generations of Catholic school children. Myself included. Even though I'd never even seen it.

One of the driving forces behind the film, was its narrator, Bernard N. Nathanson, a doctor who had helped set up the National Abortion and Reproductive Rights Action League, before swapping sides in the 1970s and joining the National Right-to-Life committee.

The idea of using ultrasound technology to further his recently adopted cause was exceedingly clever. Ultrasound imaging, still new and dazzling to the general public, meant that for the first time we were able to peer inside a pregnant woman's body, and view her foetus. Best of all, the resultant images proved readily amenable to manipulation and interpretation. All of which was a boon for anti-choice activists.

As has often been observed, what we see in a foetal ultrasound is highly subjective. The 'baby' floating around the screen, that so delights expectant parents when they get their first scan, is really a magician's trick. Because the 'baby' you're seeing is actually only a few centimetres long, and is being presented completely out of context, divorced from its placenta, and the rest of the mother's body. So the image you get is entirely focused on the Unborn. Almost as if the mother isn't there. Which, once again, is just the way anti-abortion activists like it.

Trading on this, *The Silent Scream* claimed to give us a new perspective on abortion, for the first time depicting the procedure from the 'victim's' point of view, making the foetus into the hero of the film – albeit a tragically doomed protagonist.

While the film was not specifically made for us Catholics, its approach resonated perfectly with the official Church stance on abortion, which explains why it was such a hit with Catholic RE teachers. According to Church doctrine, the primary objection to abortion is that the foetus has a soul. Indeed, according to Catholic theologians, a soul is present from the moment of conception. And it's the soul that makes a person special and sacred. So to perform an abortion, no matter how early in the pregnancy, is to kill a person.

The problem for anyone relying on this logic is that, if you don't believe in souls, or in God, or in their sort of God, the argument loses its force. Jesus says abortion is murder, but I don't believe in this Jesus guy. So we've hit an impasse.

The genius of *The Silent Scream* was that it made no appeal to spiritual or religious belief, but instead confronted you with the evidence, replacing faith with science and technology, and using that to arrive at the same conclusion. Look for yourself. Here's a living thing. Small, vulnerable and human. A person, or so it seems. And then the wicked abortionists murder it!

A horrifying spectacle, whether you believe in souls or not.

Since high school, I've cleansed myself of most of the toxins left by my Catholic past. And as far as abortion goes, I've been passionately, vocally pro-choice since my late teens. The two children I subsequently birthed have only deepened my understanding of the importance of women's reproductive autonomy.

Still, a Catholic education has a way of getting under your skin. Intellectually, you might know something is true, and insist upon it with real conviction. Yet in your gut there's still a vague discomfort. Because, as all good propagandists know, the best time to plant the seeds of belief is in childhood. And once those seeds have worked their way into you, good and deep, it's hard to dig them out again.

As a result, I've always been obsessive in my use of contraception (also a sinful practice, according to the Church). Because for me, the idea of that screaming foetus has always lingered. A little kernel of dread at the very idea of it. Even though the logical part of me knows that the whole idea is ridiculous.

It's often observed that the scariest horror movies are the ones where you don't actually see the monster. Instead, your imagination fills in the blanks, and creates something far more awful than even the cleverest special effects person could possibly conjure. So, in a similar spirit, I decided that it was time for me to watch *The Silent Scream*. To confront that imagined monster.

Thanks to YouTube, it proved a very easy thing to do. And so, one afternoon, with a cup of tea in hand, I finally saw *The Scream*. Or, rather, I didn't. Because, of course, it turns out that it never existed in the first place.

The film opens with chilling organ music, the stuff of B-grade schlock. Which is appropriate, since there's something very hokey about the whole production, from the scary font used for the title card, to the opening zoom in to a door with a nameplate on it: 'Bernard N. Nathanson, M.D.'

And there's our Bernard, standing by his desk, shelves full of serious looking books. The message is clear: our narrator is white and in late middle age, he owns loads of books and he has his very own nameplate on his office door, so he must know what he's talking about.

Addressing the camera like *The Simpsons*' Troy McClure, Nathanson launches straight into it, telling us that, since the 1970s, the science of foetology has 'exploded', because of a 'host of other dazzling technologies'. All this dazzle has taught us that a pregnancy involves not a foetus, but an actual baby. The only reason we ever thought differently was because we couldn't see it. How silly of us! But now, thanks to ultrasound, we know better.

We then cut to a woman getting one of those new-fangled scans. There's gentle music in the background, and the woman looks happy – presumably because she's not getting an abortion. 'The abdomen is now suitably draped,' Nathanson adds, confirming that it's all above board. He couldn't take a peak at her lady parts, even if he wanted to.

From here on in, Nathanson spends a lot of time playing with a plastic model of a twelve-week foetus, insisting again that it's just like a fully formed human being in miniature. He handles it affectionately, as if he's about to give it a cuddle.

A twelve-week foetus's bodily functions, he says again, are just like ours. It is 'another member of the human community, indistinguishable in every way from any of us'. Except for the fact that it's five centimetres long, lacks a cerebral cortex and cannot exist outside of the womb. But hey, other than those small differences, these guys could be driving your Uber, or making a skinny flat white at your local cafe, and you wouldn't bat an eyelid.

Amidst all this we see a woman having an abortion. But the discretion that was shown towards the happy woman getting an ultrasound is forgotten now. No coy draping for the abortion woman. We don't see her face either, or her body, just her legs in stirrups with a doctor pushing into her, blood streaming down her inner thighs. The image is graphic and violent, as if she's being violated. Which is precisely the point. Because this image is cautionary. Look at this horror, it says. If you get a termination, this will be you!!!

When we come back to Nathanson he's wearing a lab coat. Things are obviously getting serious now. Here he explains how an abortion is performed, showing us the various instruments that are employed, including a device that he tells us is used for crushing the foetus's skull. Nathanson seems particularly focused on the skull crushing part.

And now, finally, it's time for the film's climax: the actual abortion, seen via ultrasound. Nathanson settles down next to a television set, with his plastic foetus beside him – suddenly a much larger plastic foetus, one that really does look like a baby – and describes what we're seeing on the screen. Which is just as well, because to me it looks a lot like grey, grainy fuzz.

'The child is moving quietly in its sanctuary,' he explains. He then tells us to look out for a 'shadow at the bottom of the screen', which is the suction instrument, there to bring about this child's 'imminent extinction'. This 'child' he insists 'does sense aggression in its sanctuary'. In support of this, Nathanson points out that its heartbeat has sped up to 200 beats per minute, although I have no idea whether this means anything since I have no idea what a foetal heartbeat rate should be. Nor, I assume, would most viewers, especially Catholic school children. But he has the white coat, and the books, so who's arguing?

According to Nathanson, the baby is now trying to get away from that big scary pointy instrument. 'There is no question that this child senses the most mortal danger imaginable.' Again, I have to trust what he's telling me, because I can't actually see very much.

And now, the big moment arrives. Nathanson pauses to point out the foetus's open mouth. Its screaming mouth. The silent scream itself!

But hang on, was that it? I don't think I saw anything that looked like a scream. I know it's meant to be silent, but is it invisible as well?

Seems I'm not the only one who's had that reaction, because Nathanson says he's going to show it to us again, in freeze frame. Just in case we missed it. But once again, I'm stumped. Not horrified – just a little annoyed.

In fact, I feel cheated.

Because there was nothing to see. I don't mean, I *intellectually* know that the foetus wasn't screaming, even though it looks like it was. I mean, there's literally nothing that even resembles a scream. Nathanson could equally have told me, 'And now the foetus is singing *Yankee Doodle Dandy* while tap dancing. Here, I'll freeze frame it on the good bit!'

Because all I saw was more grainy fuzz. The ultimate moment, the thing the film trades on, the idea that haunted my young Catholic psyche, proves to be a blurry washout.

I shouldn't have been surprised by any of this, because I already knew that *The Silent Scream* is a breathtaking concoction of misinterpretation, misinformation, and wilful lies – as accurate a depiction of abortion as *My Little Pony* is a nature documentary about equine behaviour.

But I had expected them to try a bit harder with the manipulated visuals.

Immediately after *The Silent Scream* was first screened on US television it was slammed by many in the medical community for its profoundly inaccurate depiction of a termination, and its false claims about the physiology of a twelve-week foetus.

Planned Parenthood convened a panel of experts to counter the claims made in the film, including the idea that it is possible for a twelve-week foetus to experience pain (it's not), or that a foetus of that gestational age could carry out purposeful movements (again, it can't happen).

Nathanson's overwrought description of the procedure was also challenged on factual grounds, as were his references to the 'crushing instruments' that are supposedly required to remove the foetus's head. The panel pointed out that if performed properly, a termination at this stage of gestation requires nothing more than a suction cannula. Maybe Nathanson was just a particularly ham-fisted doctor?

But even beyond the factual errors, there is something particularly tricksy in the way the visual 'evidence' is presented. For example, the ultrasound footage has been slowed down, and then sped up to make it look like the foetus's movements become intentional and frantic. So the supposedly recoiling foetus is nothing more than a special effect – and a pretty rudimentary one at that.

And what about the scream? Well, first of all, you can't scream without air in your lungs. Which pretty much rules it out right there. And in any event, according to the American College of Obstetricians and Gynaecologists, the neural pathways of a foetus are not sufficiently developed until well into the late stages of a pregnancy. So air or no air, it's simply not possible for a twelve-week foetus to scream. If you can see mouth movement, or you think it looks like the foetus's mouth is open, it's almost certainly a reflex, unrelated to the termination that's taking place.

As some doctors pointed out, it's possibly not even a mouth that Nathanson is pointing to during the abortion sequence – it could just as likely be the space between the chin and neck that he's indicating. But then, *The Silent Chin Flap* just doesn't have quite the same ring to it, does it?

If the scream is such a grainy washout, then why *were* so many children upset by this film? It can't just be Nathanson's creepy relationship with the plastic foetus, can it?

As a kid, most of my knowledge about the film came from my brother, who'd seen it twice. Being a year older than me, he'd started bringing all sorts of astonishing information home from school.

When my brother first told me about *The Silent Scream*, his account was confused, but also layered with hinted at meanings that he didn't quite grasp himself. The film was so charged with tantalising but forbidden adult stuff, stuff that neither of us properly understood. My brother didn't even fully understand how conception worked, so how was it that anyone deemed it appropriate to show him a film that featured the supposedly bloody and horrific end consequences of an unwanted conception?

Once you've actually seen the film, the decision to show it to children becomes even more inexplicable. There's that woman in the stirrups, the overwrought narration, the insistence that we are watching a murder, the misleading, ghoulish claim that a skull is being crushed. Any one of these details might be deemed sufficient to award the film an MA rating. But there's something worse than all that.

Near the end of the film, flashing on the screen, are images of what are most likely stillborn babies, or perhaps very late-term terminations, all in various stages of decay, some dismembered, others in plastic vessels. There is absolutely no context for these images, no explanation. Just more schlocky, B-grade horror organ music.

And these images really are awful. But of course they have nothing whatsoever to do with the twelve-week abortion that the film purports to observe. They might as well have shown close ups of open-heart surgeries, or corpses in a morgue. So it's a simple piece of manipulation. Not subtle, not clever, but probably very effective. Particularly when you show it to a class full of naïve young teenage Catholic boys like my brother. Twice.

To paraphrase Stephen Fry, any God who would deny women their bodily autonomy is no God that I would care to worship. But in the end, that's a matter of faith. We can argue with the religious, insist that we live in a secular society, and point out that their views, based on personal faith alone, should have no role in determining what the rest of us can and can't do. But in the end, the religious person will believe what they believe because those beliefs are based on something that's beyond the rational.

By contrast, *The Silent Scream* claimed to be grounded in science and technology. It purported to be rational, and used our collective respect for science and technology to fool us. Of all the many reasons I find it despicable, this is the greatest, the one that really makes me furious.

You might think people who justify their beliefs with reference to an invisible person in the sky are silly or deluded. But they're not necessarily dishonest. By contrast, *The Silent Scream* is just a cheap con job. Nasty, manipulative and disingenuous. Like a tacky horror movie, it trades on our worst fears, while also exploiting our best selves – our desire to protect the vulnerable.

Sadly, the film shows no similar compassion for the women who are featured. There's the Happy Pregnant Woman Getting an Ultrasound, the Violated Woman Getting a Messy Abortion, and of course the sad women who appear later in the film, the Women Who Regret Having a Termination, looking off into the distance, pained, like they're concentrating on doing a particularly difficult poo. But none of these women are given a voice, an opinion, or even the personhood that Nathanson works so hard to award the foetus.

Which, once again, is just the way the anti-choice brigade have always liked it.

Catherine Deveny
How abortion set me free

I discovered I was going to have an abortion during my youngest son Charlie's first swimming lesson at the Brunswick Baths. He was five years old. I was about to turn forty.

As he bobbed about with the other little monkeys in the calm blue water, I was in the toilet marvelling at the stick I had just pissed on, delighted, amazed and surprised I was pregnant and rapt I was going to have an abortion, smug I was still fertile. I felt a flush of excitement. Like most, FOMO (Fear Of Missing Out) had always been my motivation for doing all things conception, gestational, birth and lactation related. Charlie was my last child. I thought I'd missed out on my chance to have an abortion. How do you make God laugh? Tell him your plans. I could finally tick having an abortion off my bucket list.

Charlie was born in the bath nine days before Christmas in 2002 – I delivered him myself, unexpectedly. My then partner

Marz said, just after I lifted Charlie out of the water, 'Bloody hell, that looked like a magic trick.'

He was our third boy. I'd be lying if I didn't mention that I was a teeny bit disappointed, only for a second, that he wasn't a girl. Odds being odds, I assumed I'd have a sheila and I'd been a bit keen for a girl (FOMO again). Years earlier, I'd been a bit disappointed I hadn't been pregnant with twins when I had my first ultrasound with Dom, and then again with Hugo. Then, when I went for the first ultrasound for Charlie, knowing I wanted no more than three kids, I was hoping desperately there was only one child. 'Tell me there's only one,' I pleaded to the radiographer as she scanned away on my wet, sticky tummy. 'Only one,' she said. 'Thank God,' I exhaled. That's one part of fertility we still can't control.

When Charlie landed earth-side, the final part of my children story was complete. I remember during the very happy weeks after Charlie's birth feeling relieved, content and light. 'Here lies Catherine Deveny born 1968 – mother of Dominic, Hugo and Charlie.' Uncomplicated vaginal births, no sick babies, unexpected disabilities or stillbirths. I was a maker of men, a boy factory, a white bloke dispenser. I think if I had kept having children they all would have been boys.

If Charlie was a girl he would have been named Antonia and called Nina or Noni for short. The disappointment of having another boy was over in less than ten seconds, and knowing what I know now with three sons fifteen, seventeen and twenty years old I would have only wished for boys. And wished for those boys, these boys, my boys.

I remember thinking, 'This kid born in the bath is going to be a full-on, dead-set, water baby.' He wasn't. He hated the water. After his water-birth he didn't put his head underwater again until he was about four years old.

Getting pregnant with Charlie was an accident. A happy accident. Marz and I had always thought we'd have two, maybe three, kids. I was keen for three. Dom was born in 1998 when I was 29. I got pregnant again when Dom was ten months old but it was a molar pregnancy which developed into gestational trophoblastic choriocarcinoma resulting in chemotherapy and not being allowed to get pregnant for eighteen months. I finally got pregnant and gave birth to Hugo, and so for six months there were two little ones strapped into the car seats on the back seat – what a joyful time that was. I'd always see that spare seat and think 'there's still one missing'.

So when I got pregnant with Charlie, our umming and ahhing about having two or three was suddenly over. Marz had a vasectomy two months after Charlie was born. Done. Strapped in. Let's fly this thing.

Marz and I had fourteen very good years and then the wheels fell off. We eventually split up after three very messy years of trying everything to see if we could patch things up and make it work. I had a relationship or an affair – I am not sure what it was really – during those three years. We were splitting up and it was all very messy.

As I am writing this now, fifteen-year-old Charlie popped his head in and I told him I was writing about him and explained this book. He didn't know I had had an abortion – I hadn't kept it from him, he just hadn't registered it. 'So, were you and Marz still together?' he asked. 'Kinda, sorta, not really sure,' I said.

I am not embarrassed about my abortion. I'm very, very proud of it. I am very proud my intellect overrode how I had been raised to think and feel and how, despite so much brainwashing, I could see past the bullshit to what *I* wanted, what *I* needed, and what *I* thought.

I wasn't sucked in by the romantic 'it's meant to be' or 'blessed' reason for creating another human, or tempted by the lure of having the identity of being the mother with all the children, nor was I interested in the convenient excuse to opt out of career and independence.

I have seen hundreds of women in terrible situations convince themselves to have a child they did not plan and were unable to properly care for with irrational illogical reasons that had been programmed into them from birth purely to oppress them. These emotional landmines resulted in these women truncating their lives, not living to their full potential, and impacting on their other children. For many, these unwanted pregnancies kept them in dysfunctional relationships, perhaps with a misguided belief the baby would solve everything. These women live their lives and many have gone to their deaths suffering a clusterfuck of cognitive dissonance. Having an abortion meant I had escaped.

During the three messy years after the fourteen good ones, I had this affair-relationship with a D-grade celebrity. We'd known each other for twenty-odd years. There had always been a huge sexual attraction. He was a rake, a sleazebag, a player with Narcissistic Personality Disorder. Not my usual type. Our intoxicating, exhilarating and exhausting rollercoaster went for about 18 months. Look up the word limerence if you want to understand it better.

Psychologically, I understand it – my father had a personality disorder and I assume I was drawn to this bloke we'll call Clancy (I have NO problems telling you who he is; the only reason I don't is because he'll get a massive thrill) because he had a similar psychological make up to my father, in an attempt to resolve my dysfunctional relationship with my creepy mess of a father.

It was all so heated, glittering and breathless; we shagged a couple of times and lo and behold I got pregnant. No, we weren't using any protection and no, I am not entirely sure how it happened. I was almost forty and he was convinced of his coitus interruptus technique. Clearly I wasn't that fussed about getting pregnant. I did not want to get pregnant but my revealed preferences illustrate that I wasn't fussed. If I didn't want to get pregnant I would have used protection.

I remember coming home after the first time I slept with Clancy. It was mid-January and I sat on the front deck watching the boys play in the twilit midsummer garden and I felt triumphant. Marz and I had been struggling for a while and sleeping with someone else had somehow broken the seal. I felt free and mature and adult. I felt released.

I am a very progressive person. I have never married, my children have a hyphenated surname (my name first), and I have been financially, socially, economically, intellectually and creatively independent my whole life. But I was raised Catholic and like that glass you drop on the floor you're sure you've cleaned up all the shards of until one pierces the bottom of your foot, sometimes you . . . yeah, well, that. Perhaps it was less Catholicism than 'family values'. My family of origin had been broken, disadvantaged and dysfunctional. I was determined to do a better job of it. Despite the business with Clancy, I am a very loyal and monogamous person. The affair was out of character. I can only describe it as looting in a war zone.

My mate Lou recently asked about it: 'What do you make of the whole Clancy thing now all these years have passed?'

'It was unavoidable, it was a baptism of fire, I had to go through it.'

The affair with Clancy was more about having a break from a long line of expectations as to what a mother and a good girl was than it was about my feelings for him. It wasn't him I was attracted to but what he represented, and becoming pregnant and having an abortion was an extension of this liberation. I come from a long line of Catholic women who were seen only as slaves, incubators and service providers. Women's worth was exclusively about their bodies, their fuckability, and their ability to serve the church and the patriarchy by pumping out more Catholics, more tax payers.

The preoccupations with kids, and particularly girls', bodies and sex lives was considered so normal that no one questioned it. No one.

When I was a child, if I was in the bath and it was getting cold and I needed to force myself to get out I'd say, 'If you get out of the bath by the count of ten you won't be a lesbian, be pregnant before you get married, not be a virgin on your wedding day, be a prostitute or have an abortion,' and out I'd spring. I'm not proud of it, but it's the truth. That's how I felt back then. All these things were considered shameful and unforgiveable.

Despite religion being nothing more than a Trojan horse for racism, sexism, toxic masculinity, violence, homophobia, oppression and discrimination, and the Catholic Church being simply a wealthy, powerful 2000-year-old child sex ring that doesn't pay tax, the 1970s was one of the better times to be a Catholic. It was all rock masses, ponchos, guitars and hip priests with sideburns to sell the illusion of the progressive Catholic Church, but the truth was it was the same shit in a different bucket.

In the early 1970s, our whole parish (along with hundreds of other parishes) was routinely bussed into the Right To Life anti-abortion rallies in the centre of Melbourne. Margaret Tighe, the president of Right To Life, was a household name. The buses were provided and paid for by the church. There were thousands of Catholic families at these rallies singing 'We Shall Not Be Moved'. Parents pushed babies in prams as the bigger kids ran alongside. It was exciting and fun. Great family day out. Killing babies? What kind of an animal would do that?

As we passed Melbourne Town Hall chanting, banner waving and feeling holy, there was a group of women on the corner of Swanston and Collins Streets, maybe eight or so, with short hair, wearing overalls and holding signs that said 'HER BODY HER CHOICE' and 'WOMEN'S RIGHTS ARE HUMAN RIGHTS'. The crowd was booing them as we passed. 'Who are those ladies?' I asked loudly. A priest turned to me and said 'They're no ladies, they're lesbians'. Other adults laughed. This may provide you with an insight into the deprogramming I have had to do.

The 'you must be a virgin before you marry' trope was very, very strong. I am not sure what my fear was. Going to hell? God not loving me anymore? My parents being (even more) disappointed? People thinking I was common? Cheap? A slut? I have no idea. It was a rule that seemed lodged in me.

Any fears about somehow ruining myself has always, eventually, been overtaken by FOMO on experiencing rites of passage. In the years and months leading up to having my cherry popped I talked to lots of people, hoping they'd help me make a decision. I even talked to two priests in search of some form of permission.

Then I realised, like the Good Witch Glinda said in *The Wizard of Oz*: 'You've always had the power my dear, you just had to learn it for yourself.'

Having sex for the first time felt similar to when I had the abortion. I was unmarried and just had sex – I ripped it off fast like a Band-Aid. My virginity was something I didn't have to worry about anymore. It was gone. You can't unscramble an omelette. I had sex out of marriage and I didn't die. In fact, I looked exactly the same, and the whole physical experience was as underwhelming as the emotional experience was liberating. The same thing could be said for my abortion.

I remember organising the abortion. I woke up and got the kids off to school. It felt exciting. I took a cab up to Bernard Wiener's famous Fertility Control Clinic alone – Clancy was to pick me up. I sat in the waiting room full of couples. I was seeing a whole other side of the world. I was called into the doctor and saw the ultrasound. They prepped me and then wheeled me into surgery and I said, 'Please don't tell anyone'. I was a very high-profile columnist at the time.

The staff in the theatre seemed very chummy and up. One of them said, 'What happens here, stays here. We could blow the lid off Melbourne with what we know'. I came out of the twilight sedation, had a biscuit and a cup of tea, and Clancy picked me up. We went to a terrible three-star hotel for a few hours and then he drove me home. I was back at home by the time the kids got back from school.

I was happy to have the abortion. At the time I was, in some very unevolved way, happy to be connected to Clancy. He had to pick me up from the abortion clinic because somehow we were connected to each other. I know, I know – I am not proud of it – I am just doing my best to be as accurate and truthful as possible. We were joined in some way. My relationship with Clancy helped set me free.

The next day I stood on stage at a rally and addressed 15,000 teachers at Rod Laver Arena with my kids standing by my side.

A year after the abortion I had my tubes tied. It was a deeply meaningful ritual for me. I didn't want any more children and I was drawing a clear line in the sand.

What surprised me was how liberated I felt having sex after my sterilisation. For my whole life sex had been linked with pregnancy and pregnancy had been linked with potential shame if it was unwanted. Suddenly here I was having sex – fabulous, beautiful, life-affirming sex with no way I could get pregnant. Sex purely for pleasure with no chance of pregnancy.

I told a gay mate of mine all this and he said, 'as a gay man I find it bizarre the idea that sex could cause pregnancy'. That moment was a revelation. I had never separated the two.

To have sex when I choose, have children when and with whom I choose, to have an abortion, and finally to have a tubal ligation, is a right I am aware of and grateful for every single day, and I do not take it for granted.

The sexually transmitted inconvenience of children has been used and continues to be used to reduce women to being slaves, incubators and service providers. Don't underestimate how many old men want women they don't know to have unwanted babies simply to support their own power structure.

When we think of the huge advances over the last century, I cannot think of one greater or more important than fertility control. Those who have tirelessly fought for this right have changed the lives of people still not even born. I can never thank those people enough.

Every parent willing, every baby wanted.

Jess Scully
Still dancing

Dirty Dancing was the wallpaper in my house growing up. My grandma Rosa was obsessed with it, so my sister and I watched it more times than any other film, with only Indiana Jones giving it any kind of competition.

If you're a woman over thirty, odds are you've seen it – and maybe it was as formative for you as it was for me. Who didn't feel like Baby, awkward and eager, well-intentioned but oblivious, wanting desperately to fit in? As Britney Spears might say: not a girl, not yet a woman. That 1980s take on 1950s style shaped my love of big hair and three-quarter-length pants, the soundtrack can still trigger tears and singalongs, and I've never seen a log on the ground without trying to dance along it.

Much, much later I realised something else: almost everything I knew or felt about abortion was gleaned from watching *Dirty Dancing*. I suspect I'm not the only one. At first, I didn't understand why Baby needed to borrow money from her dad to give to Penny. I didn't quite know how Penny went from being the sexy blonde bombshell that steamed up the dancefloor alongside Patrick Swayze's Johnny, to a tragic figure: a limp, ashen form bleeding out in the background of that dramatic scene in the staff quarters. I couldn't work out how Baby had disappointed her father so deeply, just by being friends with Penny, and being involved somehow in whatever had happened to her.

As I got older, pieces of the puzzle started to come together, and I started to work it out: my family's favourite movie was a heartwarming romance with a botched backyard abortion as the core plot device.

Abortion was never something that was discussed in our house or at school. For twenty years, in my mind abortion happened like this: a desperate, secretive drama, that, if it didn't kill you, would leave you forever scarred and tainted. It wasn't something people talked about out in the open.

When it happened to me, the reality was somewhere between this melodramatic hush, and going for a job interview.

I was starting a new job and ending an old relationship: the timing couldn't have been worse. The thought of bringing a child into the mess of my life at that time, into that crumbling share house and dissolving relationship, was so unfair to everyone involved, that I didn't hesitate to turn to a termination.

In one sense, it was as mundane an experience as any other specialist visit in a nondescript office building, across the street from the New South Wales Parliament. Inside, an office suite lamp-lit in the middle of a bright spring Saturday, half-closed venetian blinds and a wood veneer desk. As the doctor started to ask me a very formal set of questions, I could tell this was a very specific dance we had to do.

'The state of New South Wales requires that I document why you are having a termination,' she said. 'There needs to be a reason for a termination that meets specific legal requirements. What impact would continuing this pregnancy have on you, physically, financially and psychologically? Would it cause you significant distress?'

'Are you sure of your decision today? Can you tell me why you're sure?'

With her questions and my answers, we were dancing around a law that stood between me and a freedom, the freedom to choose what happened to my own body, the right to chart the course of my own life. I was anxious to make sure I got the answers right: what if I couldn't prove, somehow, that my distress was real, that this would be a terrible outcome for me and for this kid? But of course, we limped over the bar, a relic and a reminder that women's bodies are contested territory.

The procedure itself was unremarkable – I just remember waking up groggy and spending the afternoon on the couch with a hot water bottle – but that lamp-lit room is the part that sticks with me. The questions that were an incantation to unlock bodily autonomy, and those specific words, had to be traded so as to climb over the barrier that the New South Wales Parliament has stubbornly kept in place, keeping us in the past. By keeping abortion officially illegal, our governments are keeping us in those back rooms, in this half-light, shrouded in shame and secrecy.

The world has moved on and has benefitted from generations of women claiming our right to be treated equally, to have our contributions recognised, and to make decisions about our own lives. And yet our laws don't reflect that. The disconnect has real impacts on people's lives and their capacity to make free choices and realise their potential.

In that sense, we're not that far from that story I grew up with: we're living 21st-century lives with 1950s laws.

Louise Swinn

In conversation: Jenny Kee and Grace Heifetz

Jenny Kee remembers what she was wearing. The first abortion – Philip, London – she was nineteen. It was the swinging sixties, 1966, and she had a swinging boyfriend. There was no question of having the baby. 'It wasn't a steady relationship. It had to end.' Philip provided the money and supported the decision. 'I remember that it was a decent doctor.' Artist Martin Sharp, a dear friend, visited her in hospital. She wore a Victorian nightie. 'Look, I'd been lucky up to that point. From sixteen to nineteen I was like a wild child. I wasn't taking precautions.' Jenny is always candid: 'I have no filter,' she laughs.

The second abortion – Michael, London – Jenny was 22. She had been seeing Michael – also an artist, broke – for three months. 'I asked Martin Sharp for the money for the abortion but he wouldn't lend it to me. (*Oz* founder) Richard Neville gave it to me, though!' It cost about £45, and she wore a Jordanian dress. It was 5 July 1969, and from the hospital she went straight to the Rolling Stones concert in Hyde Park.

The third time Jenny was pregnant – Michael, Sydney – she was 27. It was 1974 and she had just started the iconic Strand Arcade store, Flamingo Park Frock Salon, with Linda Jackson. She went to the gynaecologist because she hadn't had her period and she had a bit of a tummy. She found out that she was pregnant. 'Michael was over the moon. I was too, but at the same time I had just opened the shop. We looked at each other, and I remember thinking: I can run the business and have a baby. But we'd just started the shop . . . I remember saying *fucking hell*!'

Jenny was six months pregnant when she put on her first fashion parade. She concealed her stomach with a beautiful green Chinese embroidered coat. 'It had plenty of room in it.' She gave up smoking, and worried about the drugs they'd been taking.

'I had two beautiful women (business partner Linda Jackson, and photographer Fran Moore) by my side, as well as my mother. Michael was in ecstasy that I was pregnant. He was at home being an artist. He wore pink shirts, and I just knew she was going to be a girl, and I wore pink – everything was pink. I blossomed. It was a beautiful pregnancy.' Jenny looks at her daughter, Grace, born in 1975, 'You were meant to be, darling.' Jenny laughs, 'but then I ate too much chili crab and got toxaemia (pre-eclampsia) from too much salt.'

For a special video for Grace's 21st birthday, Jenny interviewed her own mother and discovered that her own mum also had an abortion in Sydney in the 1950s. 'It would have been the hardest thing in the world for a woman who loved children, but my father was a gambler. I don't remember

Mum ever in that bedroom – she slept on the sofa – it was an unhappy marriage. The abortion would have been a big secret.' Jenny was the second of three children. Her mother wasn't able to have that fourth baby but she doted on Grace, her new grand-daughter. 'She was beyond in love with Grace. Grace was the fourth child, you see.' Grace and Jenny pass around a photo of Jenny's mum, strong and defiant and beautiful.

'When Michael rolled in after joints and whiskey and she had been babysitting, she would just pray that he would get Grace safely home.'

Grace grins with the recollection of the strong, non-judgemental bond she had with her grandmother. 'As a teenager after I had been out all night, she would bring me freshly squeezed orange juice!'

Grace had her daughter, Estella, in 2004. 'Jenny and Stella straightaway had the same kind of bond as me and my grandmother.'

The third abortion – Michael, Sydney – changes the air in the room. Where the first two were had-to-haves, this one is a painful recollection. It was 1978. The year before, Jenny and 22-month-old Grace had been involved in the Granville rail disaster, a train derailment that resulted in 84 deaths. 'We were in the first carriage that split in two. And to hear those words now is very different to having lived through it. Grace fell out of my hands once . . .' Here, Jenny pauses. 'But I was so driven and so creative, and Granville brought out more creativity in me.'

'Michael wasn't practical and lived in a fantasy world – he played golf four times a week! I had a beautiful, incredible baby, and I got pregnant again. And I was thinking: how can I take two children down to Sydney on the train now, after Granville? And with Michael – he was a fabulous father but he was difficult, smoking dope and painting beautiful art. But part of me wanted to have the child . . . Well, I had another abortion because I couldn't cope. How could I cope with a three-year-old and a baby? Two children – he wanted the romance of that – but fuck that. I knew I couldn't do it.'

'My dear friend Gabby took me in to have the abortion and I can remember sobbing, and the crying was because I knew I wasn't being supported by my partner. That was a huge thing. And Grace was divine, and she fitted in like a glove with everything Fran and Linda and I did. Every time Linda made an outfit for us, she made a little version for Grace. It was a beautiful world but I could see that another child wasn't going to be easy. My adrenalin was running on empty. And I was very ambitious – we were heading right to the top of the game. We were creating Australian fashion.'

'These two women, and mum, were by my side with Grace – we were in love with Grace. But I knew that I could not have another child with Mike.'

'So the first two had to happen, but this third abortion was hard. It was with a beautiful man who was a great father to Grace, but he was an addict. He hadn't been supportive after Granville. That third abortion was traumatic.'

The fourth abortion – Michael, Sydney – it was 1983 with a riot of colourful prints. Jenny visited a clairvoyant who told her she was pregnant. 'I said, WHAT?' She was still married to Michael, and would remain so until 1990. 'But the writing was on the wall. I couldn't do it again.'

'I feel blessed that I can talk openly with Grace,' Jenny says. They are clearly close. Of her father Michael, Grace says: 'He was a great father, but on his own terms.' Grace went on The Pill when she was seventeen. 'I was terrified of getting pregnant.'

At some point Jenny went on The Pill, then the copper coil. 'And then I had my tubes tied. All good.'

She is philosophical. 'The regret was the third abortion. Not regret exactly – there was no other way. I reflect on this now through my spiritual practice (Jenny is a devoted Buddhist of 33 years) and ponder these decisions, but I have no judgement, this is the way it was and how it had to be.'

Grace adds: 'Having such strong women around me allowed me to be honest and real, and nothing has ever been too taboo to discuss. I only hope I can pass this openness on to my own daughter. I think we are on the right track.'

Samantha Maiden
RU486 in Australia

The first woman to take RU486 to terminate a pregnancy in Australia was 43 years old, a divorced single mother from Cairns. She had just discovered she was six weeks pregnant. It was an unplanned pregnancy.

Cairns obstetrician Professor Caroline de Costa calls her 'Joanne' in her book, *RU486: The Abortion Pill* (2007). Joanne was about to make history, opening the door for thousands of other Australian women to gain access to a medical abortion, an option already available to many other women around the world for decades. It was 2006.

The doctors were nervous. In fact, Joanne did not know that she was the first woman in Australia to be prescribed the drug for an abortion.

'We said, "we know this is a very safe drug and we are prescribing it for you," but we were very anxious,' explains Caroline de Costa.

'Mike [Dr Mike Carrette] unwrapped the package of mifepristone and as we both watched, Joanne took a sip of water and swallowed it down.

'We gave her our mobile phone numbers and sat staring at the mobile phones waiting for them to ring – and here if it doesn't work it's catastrophic. But in about three hours she rang and said, "It's fine. It's all over and I am so happy."

'We knew it was safe. But we had Tony Abbott breathing down our necks. And we just knew if someone ended up with a severe haemorrhage in hospital . . . well, we didn't want anything like that to happen. And it didn't happen because it was a safe drug.'

Not everyone agreed. Critics, including feminist Renate Klein, who describes herself as pro-choice but anti-RU486, described it as 'a chemical cocktail'.

RU486 was originally developed in the French laboratories of the company Roussel Uclaf in the 1980s. It is a synthetic steroid. It works by blocking the effects of progesterone, the hormone which is required to maintain the lining of the uterus during pregnancy. By removing that progesterone, the lining of the womb breaks down, ending the pregnancy.

It would take another six years for the drug to be listed on the Pharmaceutical Benefits Scheme and for headlines to predict: $12 abortion pill. That price point never arrived.

But Joanne's choice that day in Cairns set in train a policy experiment that would also see demand for surgical abortions dramatically decline in Australia. It's a development that continues to pose challenges for policymakers in states where abortion is largely privatised and the only private providers have shut up shop.

In Tasmania, the only low-cost provider closed at the end of 2017, forcing women to travel to the mainland for an abortion, or pay an exorbitant fee.

Of course, Joanne didn't know that at the time. She knew she had had a previous episode of thrombo-embolism – a blood clot had formed in her leg which doctors had warned if it occurred again posed a serious threat to her life. She knew she did not want more children and felt ill-equipped, given she was a single mother, to care for another child. She knew she wanted an abortion.

Joanne was not the first woman to use RU486 in Australia but she was the first to use it for an abortion. Trials conducted by Professor David Healy of Monash University had previously set off a political firestorm. It prompted the Harradine Amendment, which decreed that the use or import of the drug was prohibited without the personal permission of the federal minister for Health.

As feminist Anne Summers wrote in *The Drum* on 12 June 2013, conservative Tasmanian Senator Brian Harradine, a former Labor MP inspired by the teachings of B.A. Santamaria and the Democratic Labor Party, had demanded prohibitions on RU486 as his political price for supporting the Telstra privatisation.

'Harradine, an old DLPer schooled in the tough tactics of leveraging maximum advantage, demanded two things: an amendment to the *Therapeutic Goods Act* to require specific ministerial approval for the importation of RU486 and other similar abortion drugs, and the introduction of the AusAID Family Planning Guidelines which prohibited any family planning agencies in developing countries that received Australian aid money from providing any form of advice or counselling on abortion,' Summers said.

'No other drug was subjected to this ministerial veto, and the Catholic Harradine was seemingly unmoved by the statistics that showed that a woman dies every eight minutes in the developing world as a result of unsafe abortion.'

Professor de Costa's activism for RU486 and greater choice for women to obtain surgical abortion was sparked by those restrictions.

'Not only restrictions, it was just impossible. Doctors didn't even know about it. Some obstetricians did, a few of us did. It just wasn't on the radar and women didn't know such things existed,' Professor de Costa says.

'But when I came to Queensland, I was working full time in 1999, doing outreach on Cape York – I had a particular case with a woman who suffered very much from the fact that she had not been able to terminate a pregnancy she wanted to terminate early on. She ran into a lot of problems with pre-eclampsia at 36 weeks and I did a caesarean for her and the infant died. It was her third experience like that. She knew about it and she said, "I wanted an abortion and they said I couldn't have it and I've heard there is this drug. And wouldn't it be a good idea if we had it?" And I said, "you're absolutely right."

'And I began to look at it more and learn about it more and I went to a conference in San Francisco in 2005 and just became convinced that we needed to get it.'

She met up with Democrats Senator Lyn Allison and Liberal MP Sharman Stone.

'I don't want to overstate my role, but I think the fact there was a woman professor of obstetrics who was saying this is safe and has been used and I can show you the evidence kind of gelled the whole thing towards the end of 2005. And then they got the private member's bill together,' she says.

'But that was never going to solve the problem of actually using it because no drug company was prepared to market such a controversial drug. And that was when I realised there was this loophole in the TGA legislation. My colleague Dr Mike Carrette and I used that to import the drug and use it here in Cairns.

'We had a lot of support from the TGA, although they were very quiet about it. I used to get these kind of deep-throat kind of phone calls from them saying, "never mention this or ask a question about this but this is moving on".'

Even the United States, with a powerful pro-life lobby, had access to RU486 since 2000. RU486 had been available in France and Switzerland since 1988, the United Kingdom since 1991, most other European countries since the early–mid 1990s. But not Australia.

As a doctor working in Sydney in the 1990s, Professor de Costa didn't see a great deal of problems around access to abortion.

'Although we weren't able to do it in public hospitals, I didn't see it as a big problem. I was annoyed by the Harradine Amendment but I didn't see it impacting enormously on my practice then,' she says.

Dr Michael Wooldridge was the Health minister at the time. But his replacement in the portfolio, Tony Abbott, would spark further debate when he described abortion as a 'national tragedy' in 2004. In a speech titled, 'The ethical responsibilities of a Christian politician,' he described abortion as 'the easy way out.'

'The problem with the contemporary Australian practice of abortion is that an objectively grave matter has been reduced to a question of the mother's convenience ... To a pregnant 14-year-old struggling to grasp what's happening, a senior student with a whole life mapped out or a mother already failing to cope under difficult circumstances, abortion is the easy way out,' he said. 'Aborting a foetus is not morally identical to deliberately killing a living human being, but it's not just removing a wart or a cyst either.'

'Even those who think that abortion is a woman's right should surely be troubled by the fact that 100,000 Australian women choose to destroy their unborn babies every year.

'Why isn't it regarded as a national tragedy approaching the scale of Aboriginal life expectancy being twenty years less than the average of the general community?

'No one wants to bring back the backyard abortion clinic or to stigmatise the millions of Australians who have had abortions or encouraged others to do so.

'But is it really so hard to create a culture where people understand that actions have consequences and take responsibility seriously?'

Professor de Costa believes that it was that speech that helped galvanise activists to campaign for RU486.

'I think the speech made people angry enough to say "how are we going to do it?",' she says.

In late 2005, Tony Abbott declared he would not approve the use of the abortion pill RU486 in Australia. Mr Abbott cited advice from the Chief Medical Officer that RU486 has a higher rate of 'later adverse events' that could require urgent intervention, than surgical termination.

Soon, senior Liberal women were openly challenging the Health minister about his stance. Senator Helen Coonan, who held the Communications portfolio, warned that there needed to be further debate about the pill in late 2005.

'We've got some advice from the department on a very specific question, that is how it relates to women in rural and regional areas,' she said.

'Ultimately, safety is what it is all about and I think we need to have a discussion about it.'

The AMA described Mr Abbott's comments as 'plain wrong'.

Four female senators proposed the bill, to make RU486 more accessible in Australia. It would strip the right of the Health minister – at the time, Tony Abbott – to veto the drug. It was a rare conscience vote with former Prime Minister John Howard and Tony Abbott opposing the reform. Mr Howard argued that politicians should continue to hold the power, rather than health bureaucrats.

'There is just a whiff in this whole debate of this being a little too difficult and controversial, so let's give it to somebody else,' Mr Howard said. 'Plainly, this is not a normal drug.'

But Treasurer Peter Costello and Opposition Leader Kim Beazley supported the change. The debate was intensely personal.

'It is galling listening to the men, and it is mostly men, who have such contempt for women who terminate unwanted pregnancies," Democrats senator Lyn Allison told Parliament.

Liberal Senate leader Nick Minchin, a conservative, disclosed his own personal experience with abortion. 'A former girlfriend of mine had an abortion when we were in a monogamous relationship, and I cannot divorce that experience in my life from this consideration,' he said.

Nationals Senator Barnaby Joyce was characteristically blunt. 'RU486 is going to kill mothers. The first one that dies is the responsibility of the people in the chamber who voted for it,' he said.

Liberal Senator Judith Troeth, who co-sponsored the bill, disagreed with Tony Abbott's warnings. 'I think he's stereotyping women as political warriors, with that frame of mind when they think about getting an abortion,' Senator Troeth said. 'They are simply looking for a solution.'

Senator Allison argued that Mr Abbott could not be trusted to control access to abortion drug RU486. 'It is also a great pity for Tony Abbott to keep talking about 100,000 abortions a year,' Senator Allison said. 'Firstly, that figure is not correct, it's nowhere near that. I think he's done himself a lot of harm and it's a great pity because I think he's a very intelligent man,' she said. 'But people are saying to me, how can we leave this decision to a minister who so readily plays with the truth?'

Liberal MP Ian Macfarlane supported the bill, arguing it was about freedom of choice. 'There are those who have attempted to take the high moral ground in this debate by saying support of this bill equates to support of abortion,' Mr Macfarlane told parliament.

'Simplifying the debate into one about abortion ... overlooks the rights of Australian women and it betrays the freedom of informed, individual choice.

'It also neglects the opportunity for experts to seek a less traumatic process for those women who have made one of the toughest decisions a human being can ever make.'

Mr Costello delivered an emotional speech revealing that he had been faced with the option of abortion eighteen years ago when his wife Tanya, who was pregnant, was unconscious in hospital. 'I think it is common knowledge that when my wife Tanya was pregnant and unconscious in hospital, some eighteen years ago, I was faced with this terrible situation,' he told parliament.

He determined to continue with the pregnancy. 'I have no doubt that the law should not have prevented such a choice – that the law should allow a choice, whether physical or mental health of the woman is at risk,' he said.

In February 2006, the House of Representatives overturned the Harradine Amendment. But removing Harradine legislation did not immediately result in access to RU486.

'Within the extensive legislation governing the role of the TGA there is provision for private doctors to apply to import and use particular drugs for their own patients, in certain serious medical conditions,' Professor de Costa says.

'In late 2005, Dr Mike Carrette and I lodged an application under this legislation to be permitted to use mifepristone – RU486 – for the purpose of medical abortion in early pregnancy, in our own practices in Cairns. This was a complex process involving much paperwork but six months later (and two months after the overturning of the Harradine Amendment) this permission was granted to us. We were able to obtain a small supply of RU486 from New Zealand colleagues and we have been using the drug in Cairns under the Authorised Prescriber guidelines.'

By 2012, Professor de Costa estimates that there were 85 doctors prescribing RU486.

Professor de Costa then wrote to every obstetrician in Australia asking them to join her in offering the drug. In the beginning, only three doctors replied. All were women – one doctor was in Westmead, a doctor in Melbourne, and Joan Dickinson, a professor in Perth.

Even today, it's still a special status drug, which means that doctors need to go online and do a two- or three-hour course to gain registration.

'So you have to find a registered pharmacist who will prescribe the drug,' Professor de Costa says. 'There's no other drug in Australia that gets this kind of treatment and we are now working on getting it normalised so that abortion gets into mainstream medicine.'

The big question for women remains: why is it so expensive in Australia? Despite promises of $12 abortion pills during the early debate, most women in Australia pay hundreds of dollars, in some cases up to $700 or the full cost of a surgical abortion.

'It's so expensive because it cost Marie Stopes a lot. I think they invested more than a million dollars,' Professor de Costa says. 'And then they spent a whole lot on the online training and the 24-hour access hotline. They say they want to make it the same as surgical abortion so that women don't feel they have to take the cheaper option.'

While Marie Stopes is not-for-profit, the recoup of that investment remains controversial.

Now that RU486 is widely used in Australia, a more accurate debate can also be had over side effects and complications.

'It's well under 5 per cent. In 1 per cent of cases it doesn't work. So nothing happens. In that case she can have another go or have a surgical abortion,' Professor de Costa says. 'There's always bleeding, it's like a heavy period. Some women will not expel all the placental material and they will bleed more.'

Melinda Tankard Reist, a critic of the drug, argues that 'RU486 is not the "safe" DIY method for women it is claimed to be.' She cites four examples of women who have taken RU486 to procure a medical abortion who experienced cramping, nausea and loss of blood, among other side effects.

'Here, the TGA has been informed of 132 cases of ongoing pregnancy requiring surgical abortion, 23 cases of haemorrhage requiring blood transfusion and 599 cases of incomplete abortion requiring surgery. This means about 1 in 30 women will need a second termination procedure. Other negative outcomes include cervical tearing and uterine perforation,' she wrote in the *Sydney Morning Herald* on 11 August 2013.

'A South Australian study found women undergoing "medical" abortion had more symptoms, reported higher pain scores and had higher rates of emergency admissions. After discharge they had more nausea and diarrhoea. According to an earlier British study, women who saw the foetus were most susceptible to psychological distress, including nightmares, flashbacks, and unwanted thoughts related to the procedure.'

In response, Marie Stopes said that as part of their observational study involving 13,345 women and published in the *Medical Journal of Australia* (September 2012), over 6000 women from the study reported on their pain, bleeding and overall experience of medical abortion. Most women said that the bleeding (83.8 per cent) and pain/cramps (76.2 per cent) and the overall experience (90.3 per cent) was either as expected or better than expected. Most tellingly, 78.0 per cent of respondents said that they would use the method again. In line with the training, certified medical practitioners are required to provide the patient with information outlining the possible side effects of bleeding and cramps, nausea and vomiting, diarrhoea, and fever and chills.

'These side effects are well documented in all product materials for medical practitioners and patients. Patients are provided with information to take home with them describing the common symptoms of the abortion process, how to manage these, when to seek further medical advice and care, and the additional risks that may arise from using this treatment,' Marie Stopes International medical director Philip Goldstone said.

'Ms Tankard Reist has repeated an accusation made previously by Renate Klein that a woman had died in a Marie Stopes Clinic in 2010 as a result of sepsis from a medical abortion. We consider this accusation factually inaccurate. A woman did not die in a Marie Stopes Clinic in 2010. We are aware of the tragic death of a woman from sepsis. However, following a review of medical reports and other evidence, the Coroner's office did not proceed with an inquest and closed the case.

'In fact, the article in question, whose principal author is a fully qualified medical practitioner, states that "This woman suffered fever and flulike symptoms about six days after taking mifepristone, but unfortunately did not seek medical advice, despite urging from family members." In no way, here or in any other publication on the matter, has Marie Stopes International ever "attributed" this death to the "woman's own negligence" as Ms Tankard Reist claims. It is important for clinicians to understand, however, that this death occurred in the setting of untreated infection.'

There was little debate at the time about the impact RU486 would have on demand for surgical terminations. But it wasn't unexpected, according to Professor de Costa. 'No. Because that was what was happening overseas and happening in the United Kingdom,' she says. 'So it was always going to reduce the number of surgical abortions. It's not the fault of RU486, it's the fault of people not providing surgical abortions when needed that must be addressed.'

In Tasmania, it was the departure of the state's only low-cost surgical abortion provider, Dr Paul Hyland, that underlined the challenges where abortion is not available in the public system.

He blamed the popularity of RU486, arguing that the market simply wasn't there to run his business. 'Back in 2000, there were 25 to thirty surgical terminations a week and that's slowly dropped due to the combined effects of contraception and managing it earlier,' he said. 'No private provider is going to do it so the government is going to have to do something about it, bearing in mind their budget, values and politics.'

Labor's Catherine King also believes that the drop in demand should have been anticipated. 'It's not surprising this has happened but I guess without proper planning this was always the way it was going to go,' she says. 'I think at the time, remembering the debate, the sense that everyone had was that surgical abortion would continue to be available both privately and publicly and you could have more availability. And clearly that's not quite what happened. I don't think that's the sole reason in Tasmania. I think there appears to be a real unwillingness in that state to address public provision.'

In smaller jurisdictions like Cairns and Hobart, the demand for surgical abortion has dropped off since the introduction of RU486. In places where abortion is largely privatised, services have had to close, ultimately limiting choice and causing women to travel hundreds of kilometres to access legal abortions that could be offered for free in public hospitals.

If Bill Shorten wins the 2019 election, Labor wants to involve the states and the Commonwealth in national sexual and reproductive health policy mapping of where the shortages are.

'It's got to be available where people are. So in some circumstances a standalone clinic is suitable, in others within a public hospital, or private clinics, or medical abortions via GPs. Depending on what suits any woman and her partner if he's involved at the time,' King says. 'The model really has to be accessible. We need a new sexual and reproductive health strategy and that's got to go through COAG [Council of Australian Governments] with the states and territories. We've seen some really big gaps emerge but I don't fully understand where those gaps are. I think this is about sexual and reproductive health. So it shouldn't just be about termination services.'

But the situation in Tasmania was rendered more complex by the Health minister Michael Ferguson, a pro-life conservative, who opposed the criminalisation of abortion. Critics argued that he did not seem in a great hurry to restore the provision of surgical abortion in Tasmania.

In 2018, Labor pledged to provide a $1 million standalone 'reproductive health hub', to fill a service gap left by the recent closure of the state's main low-cost private abortion clinic.

'If it's in the public hospital it should cost nothing. Cost shouldn't be a barrier for women accessing a termination,' Ms King said.

Asked if she believes abortion should be available in all public hospitals in Australia, Ms King is unequivocal. 'Yes I do,' she says. 'Legalisation I think sends that signal very clearly. But the next piece of work that we have to do is about the availability. And I think that's where we've got a lot of work to do. I don't think anyone predicted that the cost of RU486 would be such a barrier for women.'

Rosie Waterland

The slutty whore from whoresville making us all look bad

My face must have looked exactly how the over-achieving sperm inside me was making my stomach feel, because the nurse giving me my results didn't even take a moment to assume that this was a life event I was thrilled about.

'Oh. Um. Oh. I'm so sorry. It's positive. You're pregnant.'

When someone says, 'I'm sorry' instead of 'Congratulations', you know that you are definitely too young to be pregnant.

I wanted to vomit. Not because I was terrified or shocked or anxious to find out that I was knocked up at 21, but because whatever little swimmer had managed to successfully plough its way into me was now having some kind of epic sperm-gastro problem that could only be explained by it having eaten bad fish of some kind. Not only had my egg been infiltrated, it had been infiltrated by an obviously defective sperm with a stomach bug. And now all I wanted to do was vomit, all day, every day.

That's how I knew, actually. I can remember the exact moment I knew I was pregnant. I could just feel something wrong in my body.

I got a hot flush while sitting on the toilet at work, and was really suddenly hit with a wave of nausea like nothing I had ever felt before. It was the kind of nausea that takes away any sense of dignity that a person has – I literally took off my top and bra, lay down on the cold tiles of the bathroom floor with my pants around my ankles, just praying for the feeling to pass, and being absolutely certain that no other person in the history of time had ever suffered like I was suffering in that exact moment.

I spent the next ten minutes throwing up pretty violently (this wasn't 'cough a little while a boy holds your hair back' throwing up, this was heaving, 'the blood vessels in your eyes burst' kind of throwing up). It was graphic. Once I was done, I sat back on the toilet, a little worried to be honest, as I didn't know if vaginal tinea was a thing but if you're ever going to get it, it would definitely be after lying naked on the floor of a public cinema bathroom. I closed my eyes and took a deep breath, trying to compose myself. And as I sat there, entirely naked now except for my shoes, the words just flashed across my brain: YOU'RE PREGNANT.

Fuck.

I peed on a stick as soon as I finished work and the two blue lines immediately came into focus. *Immediately*. Like they were shoving the certainty in my face. They didn't even give me the decency of some ambiguity.

Fuckity fuck shitburgers.

I threw up again, because the initial vomit had clearly only been some kind of vomit welcoming ceremony, designed to introduce me to a new, vomit-focused way of life. And from that moment on, the vomiting did not stop. It was all day, every day. That's why I became convinced my egg had been fertilised by a defective sperm with a stomach bug. I was so nauseous I could barely stand upright. And then, a few days after peeing on that stick, I was still trying to hold in vom while sitting opposite the very concerned-looking nurse who had just taken my blood.

'This isn't something you wanted, is it?' she said, appearing to be even more upset than me. I almost felt obliged to give her some kind of comforting hug.

'Not really, no.'

We both sat there in silence for a second. I tried to decide if a 25-year-old nurse could answer my question about the possibility of a single sperm having gastro, but she seemed to be really emotionally affected by my test results, so I thought it best not to add to her stress.

'Okay, so, um, thanks,' I said, and left the tiny room.

Fucknugget.

I hobbled over to the doctor's room. He reacted the same way as the nurse.

'So, what are your plans?' he asked.

'Oh, abortion. Definitely,' I quickly replied.

He nodded, and reached behind him for a pamphlet that was hidden behind a pile of other pamphlets – the pamphlets on show at the front clearly weren't meant for slutty girls who had screwed up their lives.

He handed it to me, without speaking. It was for a place called the 'Pre-Term Clinic', also known as the 'You Fucked Up So Bad the Doctor Hides This Pamphlet Behind the Other Pamphlets Clinic'.

'So . . . Do I just . . . Can I just walk in or whatever? This afternoon?' I asked. I was clueless. As far as I was concerned, I was getting that thing taken out immediately. I didn't like that my defence system had been compromised. Also I just really wanted to stop the vomit.

'Well, you're only at about four weeks, so you may have to wait a while yet. But make an appointment to discuss it with them.'

Wait a while yet? Say what now?

'Why would I have to wait a while?' I asked, panic rising along with more vom.

'You really should speak to them about it,' he snapped back. He really, really did not want to be talking about this with me.

I took my naughty girl pamphlet and left, dialling the 'Pre-Term Clinic' number before I was even out the door.

The clinic was less than a kilometre away, across the city, in an unassuming, nondescript building. It certainly wasn't immediately obvious that it was an abortion clinic. There weren't even any protesters, which, to be honest, I was mildly disappointed about. I really wanted to see someone holding up a graphic sign while singing Bible hymns through angry tears. But there were just a few office workers. A cafe. That's about it, really. A perfectly normal city street.

The only sign that this was a 'special' kind of clinic was the prison-like locked security door. You couldn't just walk into this place. You had to push a buzzer, after which someone would look at you through a camera and ask you to identify yourself over intercom. If you had an appointment, they'd buzz you in to a locked glass area, where the staff at reception could get a look at you, and decide if you were a legitimate woman in need, or a crazy person with a graphic sign singing

Bible hymns through angry tears. If you passed the visual test, they unlocked the final door and let you through.

In my appointment, it was confirmed that I would indeed have to wait to get this thing out of me. The lovely yet no-nonsense female doctor told me I wasn't 'far enough along' to get the termination done at that early stage. This was bizarre information to me. Not far enough along? I was supposed to let it get bigger? Allow the hostile take-over to continue?

Apparently, yes. I needed to be at least six weeks, but preferably eight, to guarantee that the 'procedure' would be successful.

I burst into tears. 'That's a month away!' I cried. 'I'm so sick and I'm throwing up more than I ever have in my life and I seriously think the sperm that broke through has gastro and I don't know how it beat the others when it's clearly defective and I can't take this for another month seriously I can't!'

'We really don't like to do it any earlier than that, I'm afraid,' she replied, politely ignoring my near-hysterical babbling.

'But what if it's a bad sperm?' I implored. 'I seriously think a bad one got through. It is not normal to be this sick. It's infecting me!'

She took a deep breath and smiled – the kind of polite smile that people give when it's taking everything within the deepest depths of their soul to be patient with the idiot in front of them.

'That's just morning sickness,' she said. 'Nausea is totally normal during a pregnancy, especially at this early stage. It's not really possible for a single sperm to . . . have gastro.'

She started rattling off something to do with ginger and lemonade and taking deep breaths, but I was done listening. As she continued to talk about what the termination would involve, all I could think was how stupid I had been to let this happen. My grandmother, my mother and my older sister had all been pregnant before 21, and I was so cocky in my belief that I would avoid going down that road. And now, not only had I failed to break the family curse of becoming a host body before 21, I was also essentially homeless. And directionless. And I couldn't afford to dye my regrowth. What a fuck up.

After years of being sent back and forth between my alcoholic mother and a variety of different concerned adults willing to step in, I was finally removed from her care permanently at fourteen. My uncle took me in, sent me to a very fancy boarding school, and tried to give me some stability and consistency in what was left of my childhood. At twenty, though, that childhood was over, and he asked me to move out.

I didn't really have anywhere to go, so I just sort of floated around for a while, staying on different couches. I spent half my time on my best friend Tony's fold-out in Kings Cross, and the other half going between my older sister Rhiannon's house and my mum's house, both in Liverpool in Sydney's west. I'd stopped going to drama school because I couldn't afford the fees my uncle had been helping me with, so now I could basically be described as: Rosie, homeless cinema worker, cleaning up popcorn and busting guys getting secret hand jobs off their girlfriends during *The Fast and the Furious* movies.

I was hoping to work enough that I could afford to move into a share house close to the city, at which point I would re-assess and try to actually do something with my life. I wanted to go to university, be a writer, maybe even put that time at drama school to use. But at that stage, I was living across three different couches and pulling clothes as needed out of the boxes I had stashed in my mum's garage.

What a perfect time to get pregnant.

It was a one-night stand. A guy I met on Purple Sneakers night at a bar called the Abercrombie, in Chippendale. (Pause while every guy who went to Purple Sneakers back around 2009 tries to remember if they hooked up with me. If you were a skinny hipster and an arsehole, probably.) We made out a bit. Then he mentioned that he lived close to my sister, so we got the same train home together. Then I accidentally got off at his stop instead of my sister's and accidentally went to his house and accidentally had sex with him. I was on The Pill, and we used a condom, so that defective little sperm must have been really fucking determined. I didn't have this guy's number; I didn't even know his last name. It was just a random hook-up that I didn't think would be memorable in any way.

And now I was the one sitting in an abortion clinic, being told I would have to leave this thing inside me for another month before I could do anything about it. I was also the one who had to worry about paying for it, since it was going to cost around $800.

'I'm sorry, *how much*?' I said, thudding back to reality upon hearing such an unexpected number.

'That's if you get a general anaesthetic,' the doctor replied. 'Which means you'll be put completely to sleep during the procedure. But most women just get the twilight sedation, which means you'll still be asleep, but it's not as invasive as a general. It's more like a light sleep.'

'And how much is the twilight sedation?' I asked, praying for a much lower number.

'About $400, so half as much. I really recommend that option for you. There's no reason you would need a general.'

So I had to pay $400 to be 'put to sleep but only kind of' and then, from what I could gather, have something that acted like a vacuum shoved up into my uterus. Apparently there wouldn't be pain, but 'discomfort', which everybody knows is code for 'there will definitely be pain'.

This was bullshit. If men had to get abortions, they would come in chocolate form, be less than $10 and available at every convenience store.

I booked in for a termination, performed under twilight sedation, for four weeks time. Then I caught the train to my mum's house and spent the night puking.

Then I spent the next day puking. And the next night puking. And the next day after that. It just wouldn't stop. After a few days I realised I wouldn't be able to leave my mum's house. I could barely walk to the bathroom without being sick, let alone catch the train into the city to clean up popcorn at the movies. I lied and told them I had pneumonia and wouldn't be able to come in for a couple of weeks. Then I left the couch and went upstairs to one of Mum's spare bedrooms. It had a single bed that had apparently belonged to some flatmate Mum had been sharing with for a while. Other than a bedside table, the rest of the room was empty. It was very sad and very, very grimy. The kind of room you imagine the police raiding to find evidence after a creepy man with a thin moustache gets busted masturbating on a train. And the only evidence they find is a collection of ceramic clowns. But I was desperate, and if I was going to be staying at my mum's for a while, I needed to be in a room where I could close the door to escape her drinking. I couldn't find any sheets, so I lay a towel down on the mattress to protect me from the germs of what I was now convinced was Masturbating Train Man's bed. I covered myself with a doona riddled with cigarette burn-holes and tried to sleep.

A few days later, the nausea still hadn't relented. I spent my days trying to sleep, waking up, puking, trying to eat, puking, trying to sleep again. My older sister Rhiannon, who'd had a daughter, told me that maybe I should go to the doctor, because she did not remember being that sick during her own pregnancy.

But the doctor at the clinic had told me it was normal, so I just decided to stick it out. I developed complete tunnel vision to get through it: I just had to last four weeks until it would be over. And half of the first week was already done. Rhiannon brought over a crappy little TV from her house. It only picked up Channel Nine and Channel Ten, but I switched it on and bunkered down. TV could get me through anything.

I hoped that at some point the nausea would stop, but it just kept going. I was still having trouble getting up. I would go downstairs to the kitchen to mix chicken stock with water, but I'd have to pull a chair over to the stove because I couldn't stand for the ten minutes it took the water to boil. It was like being permanently carsick, but the car could never pull over and also it was spinning. If there is a god besides Oprah, he was certainly punishing me for having sex with a guy just because he lived close to my sister's house.

Mum was working during the days and was drunk most of the nights, so I was pretty much on my own. Every couple of days when Rhiannon had time, she would bring me Gatorade and soup, but other than that, it was just me and my little TV, picking up Channel Nine and Channel Ten.

The first week passed. Then the second. Then the third. I actually felt like I was being tortured. I was desperate to get out of the house, but every time I tried to stand, nausea took over. I was starving, but every time I tried to eat, nausea took over. I was exhausted, but every time I tried to sleep, nausea took over. Nothing made it better. I'd lost weight. I was pale. I hadn't showered. I knew the Channel Nine and Ten daytime schedules by heart.

The day before my appointment, I'd had enough. I called the clinic, in tears, and begged them to let me bring it forward a day. I'd barely heard the word 'yes' before I was on the phone to

Rhiannon, pleading with her to come and pick me up and drive me into the city.

I had to lie down in the back seat of her car for the 45-minute drive. I was so weak she had to help me walk to the clinic. At that stage, their prison-like security door was not holding me back from getting in that building – I would have smashed my way through if necessary. I was tapped into some Hulk-style determination to have this over with.

When inside, I was first taken to a side room to see the doctor. I told her what I'd been going through the last four weeks – that I basically hadn't left my bed since I'd been there last, and that it was probably a bed that a Masturbating Train Man with a ceramic clown collection had slept in, so clearly I was serious. I told her that I hadn't been able to stand up in the shower, let alone work. All I'd eaten was dry toast and soup and sips of Gatorade, and even that had been impossible to keep down. Even sitting upright in front of her at that moment was taking it out of me. 'Oh,' she said, concerned. 'That's not normal. It sounds like you have Hyperemesis gravidarum. It can be very serious. You really should have called or seen your GP.'

This time, I was the one to give the polite smile that people give when it's taking everything within the deepest depths of their soul to be patient with the idiot in front of them. But I was too faint, and too damn sick to get angry. Not to mention, last time I was there, I had rambled hysterically about an individual sperm having gastro, so I couldn't really blame her for not having taken me more seriously at the time.

Most people have only heard of Hyperemesis gravidarum because it's the thing Kate Middleton had when she was pregnant with the first of her royal spawn. Buckingham Palace mentioned it in a brief, polite statement, which made it sound like Kate was having a bit of a hiccup but was otherwise well.

I know different. If Kate was going through anything like what I went through, there is no doubt in my mind that she is probably the first person in history to have ever yelled obscenities at the Queen from the bathroom floor.

I can just see the Queen, in her sensible pastel two-piece suit, inquiring as to whether Kate would bother getting out of bed today, since ribbons that open flower shows don't just cut themselves. Kate, in a room down the hall, would wipe vomit from her face and yell, 'GO CUT A RIBBON WITH YOUR DICK, LIZ' before burying her face back in the decorative Wedgwood toilet. I think the Queen would like her spunk.

HG is officially described as 'a complication of pregnancy that is characterised by severe nausea and vomiting such that weight loss and dehydration occur. Signs and symptoms may include vomiting several times a day and feeling faint. It is more severe than morning sickness. Simple things such as taking a shower, driving or shopping may feel impossible.' (Thanks Wikipedia! Also, thanks for my Bachelor's Degree.)

Unofficially, I would describe HG as 'so torturous I didn't care that I was sleeping on a mattress that was probably once owned by a Masturbating Train Man with a ceramic clown collection'. That's how badly I needed to be lying down, all day, every day.

I was sent into another room to get an ultrasound, which the technician told me was to make sure everything was in order for the 'procedure'. I thought it was strange that she didn't just say the word. Abortion. We're all here to get abortions. We're in the building; I think we know the word. She also turned the screen away from me so I wouldn't 'have to see' what was on it. I told her I didn't mind, and I honestly didn't. I wasn't in a mindset yet where I understood that this could be a painful decision for some women to make, because to me, it was nothing but a relief. Not because of the sickness I'd endured, but just because I didn't want to be pregnant. It was my body, and I didn't want this to be happening to it. I didn't feel guilty, or conflicted, or tormented. I just felt relief.

I went back out to the waiting room and sat next to Rhiannon. One woman was crying at reception. Rhiannon told me that she and her boyfriend had been in a huge fight out the front on the street, and now she was telling the staff that she didn't think she could go through with it. She wanted to terminate; he didn't. He had stormed off and she was worried he would break up with her if she had 'the procedure'. She was worried a man would break up with her for exercising control over her own body. I was just thinking how relieved I was that I didn't have to deal with something like that when my name was called.

Go time.

I was led into a small changing room, and given a bag with a paper gown, paper slippers and paper shower cap inside. I was told to change into those, put my clothes in the bag and hang the bag on the hook. Someone would come and get me in five minutes.

Once I had changed, I sat on the little bench, waiting. The bench was high, and I felt like a little girl, with my feet swinging above the ground. I was also embarrassed, because I couldn't reach back far enough to tie the gown together properly. There were two doors – the one I came in through, and one on the other side that I assumed lead into the operating theatre. It was so strange, sitting there waiting, nervous and full of adrenalin, feeling small and naked and unable to stop my feet from swinging back and forth. It's funny that it's called an operating theatre, because waiting in that little room did remind me so much of waiting to go onstage; crammed into a dark space, full of nervous energy and suddenly so aware of your body, your breath, quietly waiting in the calm before the storm of the brightly lit stage.

The other door opened, and the bright lights of the theatre room hit me. There were about three or four people in there, all in gowns, all with masks over their faces. A nurse took me by the hand and led me to the bed in the middle of the room. I put my legs up in the stirrups. I was given the drugs and I fell asleep.

The next thing I remember is like remembering a dream. I was suddenly very aware of immense pain in my body. It felt like someone was inserting a blunt knitting needle in and out of my vagina. It was being inserted deep, and fast, and I wanted it to stop. I was confused, and I couldn't open my eyes. I tried to sit up, but someone held me down. A nurse held my hand. I remember her saying over and over, 'It's all right, honey. It's all right. It's nearly done. It's nearly done.'

The pain was excruciating. I hate saying that, because I don't want to scare any woman who makes the choice to abort a pregnancy. But that was my experience. I woke up, I couldn't move, and I felt like something long, thin and hard was repeatedly being shoved deep into my vagina. It was excruciating.

Then I was sitting in a recliner chair in a different room. I don't remember how I got there, but my bag of clothes was on a table next to me. There were other women lying in beds and chairs like mine – maybe about five or six in total, all looking as dazed as I'm sure I did. A nurse brought me over some crackers and a glass of juice, and I sat for a while, trying to piece together what had just happened. I looked at the clock; about 45 minutes had passed. I could remember being in the dark little changing room. I could remember getting onto the bed and putting my feet in the stirrups. I could remember . . . Pain. A lot of pain.

I could remember moaning and wanting it to stop. I could remember a nurse holding my hand. And then, in the middle of my confused haze I suddenly noticed it: it was gone. The nausea was gone. THE NAUSEA WAS GONE!

My body finally felt like my own again. I stood up, and didn't keel over with the need to vomit. I had my life back. I changed into my own clothes and went out into the waiting room to meet Rhiannon. I just wanted to get the hell out of there. And I wanted to eat. I wanted to eat all of the food and I wanted to eat it immediately.

'Well, where do you want to go?' asked Rhiannon, clearly a little taken aback at the sudden change in me. I was one person going into that clinic, and a very different person coming out. This person who could walk. And eat. This person really wanted to eat.

'Take me to Cabramatta,' I said. 'I really want to make peking duck pancakes.'

Now, I don't remember any of what happened next, but the way Rhiannon tells it, I walked around Cabramatta shops like a mad woman, buying all the ingredients to make peking duck. Then she took me back to Mum's house, where I proceeded to prepare the duck, talking nonstop the whole time about feeling like I had been assaulted by a knitting needle while unable to move, before stuffing my face with duck pancakes for ten minutes and promptly falling asleep.

I woke up the next day happier than I had been in a long time. I went back to work cleaning popcorn at the cinema, soon moved into a share house close to the city, and started studying creative writing at university. None of which I could have done if not for my 'procedure'.

Do I wish it hadn't happened at all? Of course. Do I wish RU486 had been available at the time? Definitely. Do I wish I had picked the full general anaesthetic over the bullshit 'you may feel some discomfort' twilight sedation option? Absolutely.

But I do not regret my abortion at all. AT. ALL. I have never felt sadness, or grief, or even conflicted. I was never ambivalent. I only felt relief. My life today is what it is because I was allowed to make choices about what was best for my body.

I got pregnant. I didn't want to be. I was in a position to change that. What a privileged position for a woman to be in.

And I never slept on that Masturbating Train Man's mattress again.

(PS – get the general anaesthetic.)

Now, here's the part of my story people usually get very uncomfortable with (besides forcing them to imagine Kate Middleton screaming the word 'dick' at the queen): less than a year later, I got pregnant again. I knew it as soon as I got that familiar wave of nausea.

Yeah . . . fuck.

Fucking shitburgers fuckity shit fuckbag.

I don't have a lot to say about this one, really. I only bring it up because almost every time I've read a personal story about abortion, it involves being emotionally scarred beyond repair, and it also only involves going through it once. It's almost like you're allowed to talk about it, but only if it was a one-off event that you will never forget and be tormented by for the rest of your days. That is the price of admission for telling your story. Safe, legal and *rare*, remember? One is forgivable, but two? You're pushing it. You're taking advantage of the system feminists fought hard to protect. You're a slutty whore from whoresville making us all look bad.

Well, I am the slutty whore from whoresville making us all look bad.

Yes, I felt like an idiot at the time, but I'm not paying the price of admission to tell this story. I've had two abortions and I wasn't emotionally scarred by either of them. It may not be the story people like to hear, but I'm still allowed to tell it. Because while I completely understand and empathise with the women who did struggle, and continue to struggle, with their choice to terminate, I know there are just as many women like me. Women who have felt nothing but relief. Women who have had more than one. Women who feel guilty that they don't feel guilty enough. Those women have stories too. And I never hear them. So:

I've had two abortions, and I regret neither.

(PS – the second time, I got the general anaesthetic.)

Van Badham

Waiting Room: a villanelle

In that clinic, women sat beside me.
The waiting room was silent with respect
– and yet,
there are those who'd seek to chide me.

Outside, camped saints. Chanting echoed wildly –
The holy crowd cried 'Save!' . . . but not 'Protect'.
In that clinic, women sat beside me.

Pious leaflets lied. What grew inside me?
Truth: sometimes, heart and body don't connect
– and yet,
there are those who'd seek to chide me.

Please, no prayers; my choice was not made idly.
I walked in there alone but won't forget:
In that clinic, women sat beside me.

None promised what they won't provide me.
The cold room knows; what's honest is correct.
– and yet,
there are those who'd seek to chide me.

You 'sidewalk' saints – curse, condemn, deride me –
I'm pro-life – my life! – mine! – without regret.

In that clinic, women sat beside me –
– and yet,
there are those who'd seek to chide me

Bri Lee
An absurd threshold

Your name is Emma and you are four weeks into a two-month road trip around Australia when you realise you may/might/could be pregnant. It's just that you packed a couple of boxes of tampons and haven't had to crack them open yet, and you're peeing at 4 a.m. before check-out for the next leg, in a shitty but quaint motel in Hughenden in the north of Queensland, and you think, 'Fuck,' and slump down, resting your head on the toilet roll.

The road trip is for work (you are a freelance photographer and right now a location scout for Netflix Originals) with times and dates firmly scheduled. They're not making you pull trucker-style all-nighters to get across the bigger states, but you'd have to call HQ to request any booking changes at this late stage, and you really don't want to do that. You want to do this job well so you can be their 'go-to girl Down Under' like the loud American producer said, and besides, you're probably not even pregnant, this is just some anxiety. Periods have never been reliable for you and you've been on The Pill since high school. So you get your phone off the sink beside you and look at the date, September 13, and then you scroll backwards through your social media accounts trying to remember the last time you had your period and wore one of your three corresponding fuck-off outfits, but pause at the photos from your friend's wedding on the first weekend of July and realise that must have been it. You'd had food poisoning (vomiting three mornings in a row) then a mad hangover (vomiting a fourth morning in a row) but still got laid, messily, after the reception. You'd put on some weight since then but you'd also cancelled your gym membership and shrugged off that softening as a not-in-your-early-twenties-anymore thing.

Maybe you'd like to call your mum and talk about it, but you won't, because it's four in the morning, and besides, talk about what? Switch apps to Google Maps: *Hughenden Pharmacy*. There is one but it won't be open before you need to leave town. One pharmacy! Imagine if you lived in town and had to go to the pharmacy for a morning-after pill. Everyone would know. Maybe they wouldn't even sell it. They're not obliged to. That reminds you, you need to get off the fucking toilet and get going. When you stand up and pull your pants up you hear a baby cry through the thin motel walls from the room next to yours. *Fuck that*. Flush and roll out.

From Hughenden it's a four-hour drive back out to Townsville. You get the coastal shots the producers want there then piss and get a coffee at the truck stop, find a pharmacy for a test kit, and kick yourself for peeing too early, so get started on the almost five hours to Cairns with the kit sitting on the passenger seat judging you. You think about the 'father' and resist the urge to check your phone on the long, abandoned strip of highway to see if he's still on Tinder. It's weird to think of how many dudes don't even know they could have been dads already. Around the half-way point you've stopped feeling guilty about him not using a condom. You get regular checks, it's chill.

By the time you get to your motel in Cairns it's dark and you're cranky, and when you pee on the stick it's supposed to tell you how many weeks pregnant you are, if you are, but it just says '3+' which is pretty bloody useless if you're taking a test because you've already missed a period or two. Still, it's confirmation – you're pregnant, but you knew that already. The smiling women in the pamphlet look like every yoghurt and life insurance commercial you've ever seen. The driving has you sunburnt and headached so you crack one beer to drink and you put another one against your head. Next you Google: *Getting an abortion in Queensland*.

The results are confusing. It's technically illegal, but a doctor can decide if you really need one and give you one. The trick, you discover, seems to be in finding the right doctor. Google also gives you a shit-tonne of 'news' results about the bill being put forward to make it legal in Queensland, and you read that the only other place in Australia where it's technically still illegal is your home state, New South Wales. Until that moment you'd been thinking about what you'd do if you had to postpone the second half of the trip to go home for a procedure, but actually it seems like your termination tourism might be covered by tax – you would have had to fly somewhere else for a procedure anyway.

With two days in Cairns before your flight to Darwin you could probably find a doctor to fit you in but the websites for centres in Cairns seem to provide medical termination services not surgical ones. 'For early pregnancy (up to nine weeks) the first tablet is taken at the clinic with your doctor. Twenty-four to 48 hours later you take a second medication at home to bring on the miscarriage.' If it's after nine weeks it's gotta be a surgical operation. Regardless, you're going to need to get an ultrasound, blood tests, all the rest. You get hopeful when you see an option to just do the second part over the phone but there's a snag:

Cairns Doctors also offers a limited number of medical abortions via Skype for rural and regional women unable to travel to an abortion provider, at an out-of-pocket cost of $275–$325. To be eligible, a woman needs to be living in a state where it is legal to have an abortion at home (i.e. not NT, SA or ACT), be within one hour of a hospital and have access to secure email and Skype.

Too bad you're flying from Cairns to Darwin on Monday.

At the non-bulk-billing doctor's office who, by some small miracle, squeezed you in at short notice, they do an ultrasound and take some blood. The ultrasound comes back suggesting ten weeks' gestation, and you give them your mobile number to call with the blood test results. The doctor offers to talk to you about your options, she seems chill, but the conversation halts when you explain you're leaving town in two days.

'Can I get it done today or tomorrow?' you ask.

'I'm afraid that's highly unlikely,' she replies, 'the centres aren't open on weekends.'

'What about Monday?'

'There's normally a bit of a waiting list,' she says with a grimace, and you don't bother asking her what regular working women normally have to do.

On Monday at dawn you're on the chartered boat from the coast near Darwin going out to a secret island with perfect-coloured sand to film against Alexander Skarsgård's tan, and you're vomiting your guts up.

'All you cityslickers get seasick!' the captain yells over the outboard motor and you just give him a grin and wipe your chin, spitting bile into the sea foam. Back on dry land you scope out the situation to deal with your situation now you're in the Northern Territory. It's legal up to fourteen weeks with one doctor's approval, and up to 23 weeks if you get a second doctor's approval, and after that it's completely illegal unless to save a life. There's a private hospital in Darwin that'll do them, and a public hospital in Alice Springs too, but you're getting sent out to Papunya and Ikuntji (Haasts Bluff), over 200 kilometres west of Alice Springs. If you're anywhere in the NT apart from Darwin or Alice, you're basically fucked.

So you hang tight until your flight to Broome. Yeah, yeah, you should deal with it ASAP, but you've done your research now and in Western Australia where you're going next it's legal to twenty weeks. You'll get there at eleven weeks along. Easy peasy. But there are no services in Broome – you find this out once you're over the border – nor at Exmouth or Coral Bay or anywhere on that most western point where tens of thousands of people live. And it's a fourteen-hour drive to Perth, the closest place with a service provider. If you don't have a car of your own it's a few hundred dollars by bus. Not for the first time you thank God you're not totally broke. They aren't paying you for the trip until it's finished (another reason not to fuck around with extending the schedule) and you've got about a thousand bucks' wiggle room in your bank account once you do a student-style budget for food and petrol. When you chat to a mate back home you decide to tell her.

'Oh my God,' she says.

'I know, I know.'

'At the wedding? Emma, that's so clichéd.'

'I know!' You smack your forehead.

'Do you need money? Do you want me to fly somewhere to meet you?'

'No no no,' you shake her off.

'Mine was fine, but it wasn't as late as yours.'

'I'll be fine too. I'll call you after it's done.'

You're walking down the street on your way to the clinic in Perth when you see a large group of people and your gut sinks. They're holding signs – you can't make them out yet but you don't really need to – and when a car going by beeps its horn they all shout out and cheer. Put your head down, put your sunnies on, put your headphones in. It's not enough. You look up, trying to see the entrance to the building, and a man just a couple of metres away is holding his phone out in front of him.

'Do you think about the human inside you!?' he yells, and you realise he's filming you with his phone's camera, and a shockwave goes through you. You haven't told anyone else back home; what if this footage ends up online? What if he's spreading it around on his anti-abortion online communities? What if someone from your old primary school church is there and sees your face and starts telling your mutual Facebook friends? You're in complete meltdown.

'What?' You say, feigning confusion, pulling your headphones out of your ears, 'I'm looking for the train station,' knowing full well it's right where you came from.

'Oh, shit, sorry,' the man says, dropping his arm again and becoming, shockingly, helpful and patient, giving you directions, 'where are you from?' he asks.

'Queensland,' you say, lying out of some kind of panic that he still has the footage.

'That's why we're here,' he says sternly, and hands you a leaflet with the words PROTECT OUR UNBORN CHILDREN on the front alongside pictures of late-term foetuses. 'Your government wants to condone thousands of murders a year!'

You don't really say anything, just smile again, and walk back the way you came, back to the train, back to your hostel. It's hours before the shock subsides and rage takes its place. The pamphlet says: *At just eight weeks your baby has organs, muscles, and eyes!* You're more than twelve weeks along and apparently it's as big as a plum now. Something about the trimester counting makes you more anxious than you would otherwise be. It says that getting an abortion might ruin your chances of becoming pregnant again in the future when you want a baby, and you know that's not even true. In Victoria, Tasmania, and the Northern Territory you can't protest within 150 metres of an abortion service provider. Queensland had included the provision in its proposals too, specifically saying people couldn't make recordings.

Seven hours by bus to Esperance – no service providers; another nine hours to Eucla and you're getting nervous. At Eucla, the border of Nullarbor National Park hits the ocean, and you take your pictures. It's beautiful but harsh, the cliffs breathtaking but brutal. On one side, looking towards the park, if it's under twenty weeks and you just had enough time and money you'd be fine because the legislation explains situations in which abortion is not unlawful. On the other side once you're in South Australia, looking back, you need to find two doctors to tell you your mental or physical health would be at risk if you continued with the pregnancy, but at least that way you have until 28 weeks. There will be protestors in South Australia too but you're ready for them this time. You've made the appointment in Adelaide and bought a wide-brimmed hat and huge sunnies from the servo.

There aren't as many people this time, and none seem to be recording you, but their sandwich boards are worse; in their eyes you are a murderer. It's not until you hand your driver's licence over as identification that you meet a hitch in the plan.

'I'm sorry,' the woman behind the counter says, 'you have to have been a resident of South Australia for at least two months to have a legal termination in South Australia,' she says, and your knees go out from underneath you. It doesn't make sense. They were the first state to liberalise access to abortion through legislation. Why put a restriction like that in there? Who the fuck tries to get an abortion that doesn't *need* it? Someone gets you a cup of water and you gather your thoughts for a few minutes before leaving.

Outside, the protestors recognise you and think you've had a change of heart, and one woman grabs you, crying, thanking you, and thanking God, for the precious saved soul.

In Victoria it's legal up to 24 weeks. Cool cool, you think, nodding, still plenty of time, cool cool. Shame you're only stopping in Bendigo. You Google 'Abortion Providers Bendigo' and get a newspaper article about a woman whose GP refused to refer her to abortion services, citing religious beliefs, despite the woman having informed the clinic of the purpose of her visit. The article describes the woman's fifteen attempts to make an appointment for a procedure at the clinic. You don't have five days. You will be in Hobart in five days where, ironically, people can't protest outside a service provider but there also just *aren't* any service providers – none that you can find, anyway. None on the island where the law says it's legal up to sixteen weeks. Your work is paying for your flights, but for a woman needing a termination it could be a huge financial barrier. If she got a doctor like the one in Bendigo she might not even know what her options are until it's so late that it's a risk. When you get to Hobart you call your boss and make up a story about Tasmania not being worth several more days of scouting, and you get your flight to the ACT brought forward.

Among the public servants and monuments, you reflect on the fact that the ACT is the only place in Australia where what you do with your body is a question for you and your doctor. The single law about it says that the procedure has to be performed by a qualified doctor. Nobody draws an arbitrary line at a certain number of weeks' gestation. It's the smallest state or territory with a median weekly income of about a thousand bucks compared to the national average of $660. Their rate of tertiary degrees is about 10 per cent higher than the national average. In the one state or territory of Australia where you'd need the least information, time or money to access reproductive health services, you have the most of everything.

From your hotel you walk to the centre. Nobody pickets. The staff are friendly and patient. It's $600 out of pocket and you get a taxi back to the hotel to sleep it all off. Out the window you look across the lush green lawns and think back to just two weeks ago when you were looking out across red earth in Alice Springs. In the Northern Territory after fourteen weeks you would have needed two doctors' approval. What if you couldn't even find one near you who told you the truth and gave you the information you needed? You take a few days off, eat some good meals, go see the Cartier exhibit, so light and relieved and peaceful to not be a mother. When you call your friend back home you cry a little, and she says with such warmth, 'Welcome to the club.'

Driving along the Great Ocean Road up through New South Wales you relax back into how much you love your job. You've found a beach only a couple of hours out of Sydney with the colour of Skarsgård sand your producer is after, so he'll be stoked not to have to drag his team out to Darwin.

The Queensland vote happens when you've just landed back at your apartment on October 17. It's on the television when you're putting your washing in the machine straight out of your bag.

'Here in New South Wales, though,' the announcer says, 'is the only state in which abortion technically remains a crime for both women and doctors, unless a doctor decides a woman's mental or physical health is at risk.'

You're relieved that you don't need to worry about trying to get an abortion in your own state, but the relief is tinged with guilt. How could it not be? For those few weeks of panic when your entire life's trajectory was taken out of your control, you felt for every other woman who'd tried to make the same decision and been stopped.

You have so many questions. Why won't South Australia let visitors get an abortion? Why is one state fourteen weeks, another state sixteen weeks, another state twenty weeks, and another state 24 weeks? Why do you sometimes need one doctor and sometimes two, and why are some doctors allowed to refuse to refer you because of their interpretation of a God you don't even share?

When you package and email your full photo reel to the production team you admire the vastness of the Australian landscape you've just had the privilege of documenting – the sparkling blues, the white sands, and the deep but dusty reds. In one place your abortion is a medical procedure, in another place it could make you a criminal. The only difference was how much time and money you had.

Jane Caro
An old story

When I was asked to contribute to this anthology I immediately said yes because I have been a supporter of reproductive rights for as long as I can remember. Then, of course – as writers always are – I was faced with wondering what on earth I would write about. I have written about my own abortion many times before, not least in my memoir, *Plain Speaking Jane* (2015). And I have spoken about it even more frequently, including on a radio panel where one of my fellow guests was Anglican Archbishop Peter Jensen . . . that was interesting. This time, my concern was how I could approach the topic in a new way.

And then I remembered that all those years ago in 1982, 25-year-old aspiring-writer me had taken the experience of my unwanted pregnancy and termination and used it as the germ of a short story, a story I wrote out in long-hand in my office in the ad agency I was working for, while I should have been concentrating on writing ads. This was long before people had computers on their desk. I wrote quite a few short stories at that point in my life (anything was better than facing a brief sometimes). I vaguely recalled filing those stories away in a drawer and wondered if I could find them now. Eventually I found the tattered and faded manuscripts in a dusty manila folder labelled, helpfully, 'Stories'. I pulled them out and found – intact – the story I was looking for. Bingo! But then I felt a sense of dread. No doubt it was juvenile rubbish. I didn't submit any of those old stories for publication way back then because I thought they were shit. Nevertheless, I sat down to read it. Written so soon after the event, surely it would at least give me some idea of how to begin.

To my surprise, the story was pretty good. Perhaps I was rather hard on myself back then. Perhaps my standards were higher than they are now. I don't know. Anyway, you can decide for yourself because the story I wrote within a few weeks of the abortion I had at 25 is published for the first time below, complete with its original title. Just one medical fact you need to know to make sense of it; in 1982 there was no such thing as the morning-after pill. If you thought you might be pregnant, you had to wait weeks to find out for sure and if you were, there were only two ways out – abortion or motherhood.

The egg

She regarded the brownish specks on the crutch of her knickers as she might a tardy child. 'Where have you been?' she said, out loud. Her periods were normally so reliable she didn't even think about them. Over the last few days, however, she'd thought about little else.

Anna had stopped taking The Pill almost three months ago. It had seemed ridiculous to keep getting her prescription filled – it had been such a long time since she'd even had a date. She felt pathetic and self-deluded every time she'd swallowed one. When the last pack ran out she decided to face facts: she had no sex life and little prospect of one. Anna was only 25 and pretty enough, but she'd never had a real boyfriend and had been on only a handful of dates in her entire life. Obviously, she just wasn't very attractive to the opposite sex. She didn't know why.

'Why fuck my body around?' she'd asked herself as she'd tossed the last packet into the bin, 'When I'm not fucking anything else?'

It was only a month or so later that she'd gone to Blueberries with Jude, and met Mark. It was a bit like washing the car, going off The Pill. Just like the minute you wash your car, it rains, going off The Pill seemed to guarantee you'd get a screw. Not just one screw, either. She'd been out with Mark a few times since. She'd liked the way he hadn't just expected to sleep with her again on the next two dates. She'd begun to let herself hope that the relationship might just go somewhere, especially now that she had finally got her period.

Anna reached for the drawer of the vanity. It was at a slightly awkward angle, particularly when you were sitting on the toilet with your knickers around your ankles. She had to find a tampon by feel, rummaging about. Eventually she found one and unwrapped it. The curse – wasn't that the old-fashioned name for it? It didn't feel like a curse now. It felt like a blessing. You are not pregnant, said the brownish specks on her knickers. You got away with it.

It wasn't as if they hadn't used any contraception. Mark wasn't like that. They'd used a condom and it had torn. Anna had sensed Mark tense up as he turned away from her to remove the prophylactic.

'What's the matter?' she'd asked him, raising herself up slightly in the tangle of sheets, putting her hands on his waist.

'It's torn.'

She sat right up then, wanting to see the object with her own eyes, to confirm the truth, but he stood up and she didn't like to be too pushy about it. He went into the bathroom and she heard him flush the offending item down the toilet.

They hadn't spoken about it again, not directly, though on each of their two subsequent outings Mark had asked her the same question, immediately after kissing her hello. 'Are you alright?'

And each time she had answered the same way: 'I don't know yet.'

She'd wondered about AIDS as well as pregnancy, and supposed he might have too, but that seemed a far more remote possibility. She couldn't really imagine someone with her pathetic sex life getting AIDS. It would be too unfair. Yet, no doubt the same went for getting pregnant.

It was hard to insert the tampon. Her vagina felt dry and resistant. A little of her anxiety returned. Her periods normally started with a wet and bloody rush, the tampon usually slid in with ease. She checked her knickers a second time, to reassure herself. There it was – blood – plain for anyone to see. She would have liked to display it as evidence. Here it is, your honour – Exhibit A, blood on the knickers, proof positive that I am not pregnant.

She got off the toilet, changed her knickers and rang Mark. 'I'm alright. I got my period.'

'Thank goodness,' he replied, and then neither of them could think of anything else to say.

'I'll call you,' he said, after a pause. 'We'll go out – Friday night – to celebrate.'

'Great!' She said, too eagerly. She wanted to see him but did not want him to feel obliged. 'See you then.'

'Yeah, see you then.'

Another pause.

'Thanks for letting me know.'

'I didn't want you to worry.'

'Thanks.'

'No, thank you.'

'What for?'

'For worrying.'

Then they'd hung up, awkwardly, with embarrassment. Anna felt stupid – daggy – as if she'd given too much away.

It was Sunday, so she went to the laundrette as usual. She read a book. She borrowed a video. She rang her mother, making her usual excuses for not having gone home on the weekend. Anna's parents lived in the country and it seemed to her they expected her to catch the train home practically every week. Anna went at Easter and Christmas and even then she went reluctantly. She forgot about her period until she went to the loo again in the afternoon and the dangling string reminded her. She removed the tampon and her heart sank. It was almost clean.

By Tuesday, Anna could no longer make herself believe she had her period. She stopped wearing even panty shields. Her breasts still felt like they did pre-period. They were swollen and tender. They bulged out of her bra. That usually subsided once she got her period. Not this time. This time, if anything, they were worse. On her way home from work she bought a pregnancy test from the chemist. When she got home, she peed on the little stick as instructed and – after the prescribed time – the window in the stick turned blue. She swore at the little contraption, dropped it on the floor and ground it under her heel before throwing it, forcefully, into the bin. It remained resolutely blue. She did not call Mark. She did not call anyone.

On Wednesday she went to the doctor. 'These days pregnancy kits are very, very reliable,' he said.

'But I had a sort-of period?'

'What sort of 'sort-of' period?'

'Very light . . . just a few spots.'

'I am afraid that is also a common symptom of pregnancy.'

'Oh,' said Anna.

After he examined her and confirmed his diagnosis, he said, rather redundantly, 'I take it you are not happy about being pregnant?'

'No.'

'Do you want a termination?'

'Yes.'

'I'll write you a referral.' He scribbled something on a piece of paper and handed it to her. 'Ring this number and make an appointment.'

Anna took the paper, paid the receptionist and scurried away. She felt like a character in a film or book. She went back to the office. She looked at the paper the doctor had given her and called the number. It was for a place called Population Control, which might have made her laugh, if she'd been in the mood for laughing. The woman who answered the phone was brisk and cheerful and asked no more than the necessary questions. Anna was relieved. She didn't want to talk about this; she didn't want to acknowledge it was happening at all. She booked herself in for the following Tuesday, then hung up and tried to get on with her work.

She could not concentrate. She kept thinking of the movie *Alien* – the scene where the creature bursts bloodily out of John Hurt's stomach. It had horrified her when she'd seen the film at the cinema. Like everyone else, she'd gasped aloud, and now she could not get the image out of her mind. She didn't get much work done that day or the next.

Marian – her boss – who sat at the desk opposite, noticed. 'Are you alright?'

It was Thursday afternoon. Marian and Anna were the only two people in Sales Admin and Marian knew practically everything that happened in the department. She could see perfectly well that jobs weren't getting done so it wasn't surprising that she asked about it. But Marian asked her question so kindly that it caught Anna off-guard. The words 'I'm pregnant' swelled up inside her mouth, filling the space between palate and tongue, and for a horrible moment she thought they might escape, but she managed to choke them down.

'I'm fine – a bit off colour, that's all.'

'Do you want to go home early?'

'No, no, I'll be alright.' Anna put her head down, determined to get something useful done before the day was over.

Mark called, as he had promised, and they went out to dinner on Friday night. Anna told him nothing. He ordered a bottle of champagne to toast, he said, their good luck. They slept together again that night and – this time – the condom didn't break. Anna enjoyed the champagne and the sex. She almost forgot about being pregnant until Mark fell asleep beneath her broderie anglaise sheets (Anna liked pretty things). Anna closed her eyes too, but she did not go to sleep. As she rolled over, she was struck by the thought that there were three of them in the bed – mother, father, child.

She huddled into the foetal position beneath the pretty sheets, her knees drawn up to her chin. She lay awake like that most of the night wondering whether or not she should tell Mark the truth. She liked Mark. She liked his springy dark hair and his broad, square hands. He seemed to like her. Probably he had a right to know about this child – his child. Probably he had a right to an opinion about what they should do. But what if he wanted her to have it? What if he wanted to get married? Then how could she get herself out of it? How could she justify herself to herself? Maybe one day she would want to marry Mark and have his children, but not now, not like this. This was not fair. It had never been meant to happen. This was her body's work, not hers. She would not tell Mark. She could not trust him to support her decision.

She went to work on Monday and told Marian that she had to have the next day off.

'I've got to go to hospital for some tests.'

'Oh Anna!' said Marian, immediately concerned. 'Are you alright?' (Funny how everyone used the same words.)

'Yes, yes, it's nothing serious.' Now Anna felt silly for making such an excuse. She felt she'd been melodramatic and self-important. She had not expected Marian to be so concerned.

'Which hospital? I'll come and see you . . . send flowers . . .'

'No! No!' Anna was horrified. 'I'm only going in for the day. I'll be back at work on Wednesday.'

'Don't be silly. Take as much time as you need. Why don't you go and stay with your parents for a few days?'

To her astonishment, Anna's eyes were filling with tears. What was this? Raging hormones? Anna never cried. She did now, though. Tears gushed out, and her nose started to run. Marian jumped out from behind her desk and ran to Anna. She flung her plump arms around the sobbing girl. 'It'll be alright, you'll see. You are young and healthy, and it'll turn out to be nothing, I am sure.'

Anna was frantic to push Marian away. She couldn't stand to be held like this. She ducked under Marian's suffocating arms, leapt out of her own seat and practically ran to the other side of the office they shared. 'I am alright.' She was panting. 'Really, I am. I don't know why I am being so silly. Don't make a fuss, Marian, please, I can't bear it.'

Marian, still crouched on her haunches beside Anna's now empty chair, looked up at her in some confusion. She rose awkwardly, and Anna remembered she often complained about her knees. 'Of course. I am sorry. I didn't mean to upset you.'

'No . . . no, I know.'

'Why don't you take the rest of the day off? I can take care of anything that needs doing here.'

'I'm fine. It's probably just PMT or something.'

'Well,' said Marian, sitting down at her desk again. 'If you are sure.'

Anna was back at her own desk too now, hunched down over her calculator.

Marian watched her for a moment. 'Let me know the results of the tests.'

'I will.' Anna replied, without looking up.

On Tuesday morning Anna stared at her open wardrobe. What does one wear to have an abortion, she wondered. She tried something loose and comfortable – track pants and a T-shirt – but pulled them off almost as soon as she'd put them on. She hated how she looked – sort of desperate and downtrodden.

'I am not a victim,' she said to the clothes as she cast them onto the bed. In the end she wore what she would have worn to work that day. She put on full make-up and took trouble with her hair.

'I am not a victim,' she said again, to her reflection in the mirror.

When she got to the clinic, she was astonished – the place was crawling with kids. Did they do this on purpose, she wondered. The receptionist sat behind one of those high consoles, walled off from the mayhem in the waiting room. Although it was still early, the woman already looked tired and harassed. She said to wait, so Anna sat down in one of the few remaining empty chairs. More and more women came in, most of them festooned with small children. Soon there were no empty seats left so people began leaning against walls and standing about. The place was packed.

Anna listened to the talk around her; she could do little else. She gathered, as she listened, that this was not just an abortion clinic but some sort of women's health centre. There were people here for mammograms, pap smears, contraceptive advice. Anna relaxed a little. She could be here for any of those reasons; no one need know she was here for an abortion.

Anna waited for a long time, clutching the bag containing the sanitary pads and clean knickers she had been instructed to bring. The chairs next to her became vacant and two women with small children collapsed into them. The mothers sighed with relief as they sat down and took up their conversation without missing a beat.

'Brendan was playing in the car last week,' said one of them, inclining her head towards a small blond boy who was pulling all the toys out of the toybox. 'I know I shouldn't have let him, but it was in the garage . . . and, you know, anything for a bit of peace. He didn't have his pants on . . . he's got to the stage where he pulls everything off the minute he has a chance . . . and he went a bit quiet . . . and I knew I should have checked him but . . . Sian was screaming and . . . anyway, when I did muster the energy to check . . . he'd done this big poo! Right in the middle of the driver's seat! I had a fit when I saw it . . . well, you can imagine. It took ages to clean it all up . . . and the smell! Anyway, I reckon kids are like cats – they like to keep doing it in the same place, and he did again a few days later! I have to keep the car locked all the time now.'

The two women laughed uproariously. Anna felt sick. To distract herself, she looked at the couple seated opposite. The man was the only male over four years old in the whole place. I bet she's having an abortion too, thought Anna. Then she felt teary again. That could have been Mark, if she'd given him the chance. She pinched her wrist hard to stop herself crying.

'Anna Cameron?' Someone was calling her name. She got up and went towards the voice.

'Come through,' the voice said. She went through.

She was hurtling along a tunnel very quickly, but she was not falling down, she was falling up. She was being extracted. She popped out of the end of the tunnel like a champagne cork and opened her eyes. She was lying in a cot, staring at a bright, white ceiling.

'Are you alright?' Those words again.

'Yes,' said Anna.

'Are you alright?' Anna was nonplussed. Hadn't she just answered that question?

'Are you alright?' She realised that the question was now being directed to a woman lying in another cot nearby. Then she heard someone being sick and someone else crying. They've done us in a job lot, thought Anna – we're a batch.

But Anna was alright. She wasn't pregnant anymore and at last she was bleeding. She could feel the stickyness on the pad someone had put between her legs while she was still under the anaesthetic.

'Are you alright?' said the voice, getting further away down the recovery room. 'Are you alright?'

They wouldn't let Anna go home for ages. They said they had to make sure the anaesthetic had worn off properly, particularly as she didn't have anyone picking her up. They didn't seem to approve of that at all. They did not like that she had gone through it all alone.

After an hour or so they let her get up and shower and dress, but a nurse had to watch her the whole time in case she fell. Anna knew she wouldn't fall. She felt better than she had for weeks.

Eventually, they let her go back into the outer reception area. The two toilet-training women and the young couple had gone. Anna wrote a cheque and paid for the abortion on the spot.

'You can claim most of it back on Medicare,' said the receptionist, handing her the receipt. Anna left, still smiling, hailed a cab, and sailed home. Maybe the anaesthetic really hadn't worn off.

When she got back to her pretty, neat little flat, she realised she was ravenous. She had not eaten anything all day. She went to the fridge and searched for something to eat that wasn't past its use-by date. Most unusually, she had not done her weekly shop for a while.

She sat down in front of the TV, her back resting comfortably on a cushion, her grandmother's invalid tray on her knees – so-called because when Anna was little her grandmother had used it to serve her comforting food and nourishing drinks whenever she was sick. After Granny had died, Anna had chosen the invalid tray as a memento.

She buttered the toast generously and licked the melty bits off her fingers. She bashed the top of the soft-boiled egg with the back of her spoon.

'This is the only way for an egg to be,' she said to no one but herself, as she brandished a toast finger (or 'soldier' as Granny used to call them). 'Unfertilised.'

Then she plunged the toast right into the middle of the yolk, and it spurted all over the egg cup.

Tony Birch
The manger

The first Sunday in December was marked in heavy red pen on a calendar hanging on the back of the kitchen door. Kathy wasn't tall enough to reach the calendar. She dragged a chair across the floor, stood on it and circled the number 5. She then stood in the centre of the room studying the number. Kathy was transfixed, willing the important date to rush towards her. In the following weeks, as the looming date approached, she sat at the table drawing her own creation of the nativity scene; the Virgin Mary, Joseph, the Three Wise Men, various farm animals, and of course, the Baby Jesus, dressed in a jumpsuit and bib.

Rosie, Kathy's older sister, teased her about the drawing.

'You know, he wouldn't be wearing all that stuff, the baby, not back then, in the olden days.'

'I don't care,' Kathy said. 'We're not in the olden days.'

Rosie pointed to a drawing of an indistinguishable animal. 'What's that one there, by Joseph's foot?'

'It's a rabbit.'

Rosie dug an elbow into Kathy's ribs. 'Can't be a rabbit. They never had rabbits over there when Jesus was born. It's too hot over there.'

'They did have rabbits,' Kathy answered. 'Rabbits are everywhere.'

'Not in the Bible, they're not.'

'How would you know?'

'Because I got a hundred out of a hundred for Catechism. Three years in a row. There's no rabbits in the Bible. I'd know.' She leaned forward and whispered in her younger sister's ear. 'And I don't believe there was any Virgin Mary either.'

The girl's mother shuffled into the kitchen, wrapped in a chenille dressing gown, hair in rollers and fluffy pink slippers. She noticed the look of shock and flushed cheeks on her youngest daughter's face.

'Don't you be whispering lies into that girl's ear, Rose Maree. What did your sister say to you, Kathleen?'

'That there are no rabbits in the Bible.' Kathy snivelled. 'It that true?'

'That can't be all your sister said, turning your face to a beetroot. What else did she say to you?'

Kathy didn't want to contemplate what Rosie had said to her, let alone repeat the words to her mother. She was certain that the thought alone, that Mary had not been a virgin, could only be a sin, even though she wasn't quite sure what a virgin was.

'What did she say?' their mother insisted.

'I said to her,' Rosie answered, 'that if she's lucky, Father Keegan will pick her out to help with the nativity scene.'

'And that's all you said? By the look on her face, I would think she'd been shocked by the Devil.'

'There was no Devil.' Rosie nudged her sister. 'You're just excited, aren't you, Kathy?'

When Kathy wanted to ask her older sister a serious question, she waited until they were in bed at night, when the light had been turned out. Kathy slept in the bottom bunk, Rosie on the top. Kathy drew the bedspread and blankets away, lifted a leg and rattled on the wooden slats of the mattress above her head.

'Are you asleep, Rosie?'

'Yep.'

'Can I ask you a question?'

'I'll ask you one. Could I stop you asking a question if I really wanted to?'

Kathy sat up in bed. 'Tomorrow, Father Keegan will pick the students to help with the nativity.'

'That's not a question, Kath. We call that a fact,' Rosie said.

'Who do you think he will pick?'

'I don't have a clue. And I don't care much who he picks. It will be the goody-goodies, I know that much. That's what Father Keegan always does. He goes for the quiet ones. And the best behaved.'

'Did the Father pick you in your year?'

'You know he didn't. Like I just said, he picked the best behaved, and the smartest. He was never going to pick me. And I'm glad he never did.'

'Why's that? All the girls I know want to be picked for the nativity. They get to sit in the front row at Mass next Sunday and stand up in front of the whole church. You didn't want that?'

Rosie laughed out loud. 'Being forced to Mass each Sunday is bad enough for me, without being paraded around by the Father. You want it, don't you, to be picked?'

Being chosen for the nativity scene was all that Kathy had ever wanted, but not because she wanted the attention of the Sunday congregation. She'd always loved the Baby Jesus, from the Sunday morning she first saw him lying in the wooden crib on a bed of straw, looking up at Mary.

'I don't really care if the Father picks me or not.'

'That's a lie, Kathy. You should be sent to confession for what you just said. Father Keegan will give you three Hail Marys for that one sin.'

'Hey, Rosie?'

'Hey what?'

'Is the Mother Mary a virgin?'

'Why don't you ask Father Keegan while you're at confession. He'll send you off with a full rosary to say and the twelve stations of the cross.'

The next morning, students assembled in the narrow wooden hall next to the bluestone church. Each child sat quietly, the girls on one side of the hall, boys on the other. The nuns sat together on the platform at the front of the hall, silent statues dressed in the white habits and gowns of summer. Father Keegan, tall and broad-shouldered, a mass of silver hair reaching for the ceiling, waited until the room quietened. As he began to speak he tapped the back of one hand with two fingers of the other.

'Today is a special day on the yearly calendar of both the school and church,' he began, as he did each year. 'Today we choose the six students who have shown both in the classroom and their hearts a love for God.'

'Amen,' the hall chorused.

Kathy watched the Father closely as he paced the platform. She nervously pulled at one of her plaits.

'Today I choose the students who will assist me in arranging our annual nativity scene in the church garden for the Christmas season. But firstly ...' The Father paused and inspected the eager faces of students. 'Firstly,' he repeated, 'we remember today that the nativity scene represents a significant day on the Catholic calendar, the birth of Christ.'

The Father stepped down from the platform and stood on the girls' side of the hall. Kathy, seated in the second row, watched him closely.

'Through the nativity scene,' the Father said, 'we celebrate the life of the Immaculate Virgin Mary.' The Father appeared to look directly at Kathy. She dropped her head, certain that he could read her mind. She was reminded of Rosie's comment the night before, and her own questioning of Mary's purity.

The Father raised both arms above his head. 'We celebrate the Immaculate Conception. And we celebrate the birth of the Virgin's son.' He walked along the aisle that separated the girls from the boys. 'Is there anything in our lives more sacred than the Baby Jesus?' he asked.

'No!' came the refrain.

'Do we worship the Baby Jesus?'

'Yes!'

'Do we worship all babies?'

'Yes!'

He marched back to the front of the room, turned and raised his arms again.

'Are not all newborns our sacred gift?'

'Yes, Father!'

Father Keegan walked back onto the platform. Sister Josephine, the head nun from the school, stood and handed the Father a piece of paper. He held it in the air.

'The six children on this list will come to the sacristy after the school bell.'

The first name read out on the list was Margaret Hunter. Kathy was not surprised. Margaret was the top student in her year, her mother volunteered at the church, cleaning the altar, and Margaret was already a favourite of the Father. On Ash Wednesday, earlier in the year, she'd been chosen to veil the church statues with the purple cloth that hid the faces of saints from view until being released on Easter Sunday. The following morning at school she lifted her fringe of golden hair and displayed the ash cross that Father Keegan had marked her skin with.

'It will never leave me,' she solemnly announced.

'Only if you don't wash your face,' Rosie had said. 'And you'll stink.'

Margaret Hunter left her chair in the front row, walked onto the platform and stood behind the Father. As each child's name was called Kathy prayed that her own would be next. But her name wasn't called. Along with the hall full of students she stood and applauded the six chosen students. She examined the faces of the students and thought about the Baby Jesus, convinced that none of the students standing on the platform could love and care for Jesus as much as she did.

That night at home she sulked and refused to eat her tea. Her grandmother, who visited the house once a week, sat across from Kathy at the table. Her habit was to talk about her grandchildren to their mother, without speaking directly to the children themselves.

'What's wrong with Kathleen?' she asked her daughter.

'There's nothing wrong with her, Mum.'

'There is something wrong with her,' Rosie said.

'And what would that be?' her grandmother asked.

'This morning at assembly, Father Keegan read out the names of those to help with the nativity scene. She wanted to be on the list, but her name wasn't called. She loves the Baby Jesus. She thinks he's her own baby, don't you, Kathy?'

Kathy lashed out and kicked Rosie under the table, on the shin.

'Hey, watch it!' Rosie screamed.

'Stop it!' their mother demanded. 'There's over two hundred children in that school. They can't pick you all,' she said to her daughter. 'Perhaps next year?'

'Don't worry about this year or the next,' her grandmother said. 'You're fortunate not to be picked.'

'Why is that?' Rosie asked, genuinely curious.

'Don't be asking such a question,' her mother interrupted. 'Your grandmother is being mischievous as usual.'

Rosie insisted on asking the question again. 'Why is she lucky, Nanna?'

Kathy jumped up from her chair and ran out of the room. 'You're not staying for dessert?' Rosie called out to her sister, before asking the question a third time.

'You'll need to ask your mother,' her grandmother explained. 'And I need to mind my tongue,' she added, not that she meant it.

The following Sunday a crowd gathered around the nativity scene before eleven o'clock Mass. The life-sized statues of the Three Wise Men stood to one side, under a peppercorn tree, with their offerings. Kathy thought they looked tired. The statue of the donkey, which Rosie believed wore the saddest face she'd ever seen on an animal, stared blankly at the gathered crowd. The Virgin Mary and Joseph stood either side of the crib, the Virgin in a powder-blue veil and gown, clasping her hands together in prayer. Joseph wore a fawn tunic and held a hammer in one hand. Between them, resting in the bed of straw, lay the Baby Jesus. He was made of solid plaster and weighed in at a world record for an infant his size. Jesus wore a white crocheted gown, designed and knitted by one of the nuns many years earlier. A wooden collection box sat on a tree stump next to the crib. The parent of any child who wanted to have their photograph taken with Jesus was expected to offer a donation.

Kathy stood behind Rosie, watching as children came forward, one by one, and sat in the bed of straw next to Baby Jesus. Although the Father had ordered that no child was permitted to touch the Baby, some children could not help but caress Jesus.

'Can't see any rabbits,' Rosie quipped. 'Do you want your picture taken?'

'We don't have a camera,' Kathy said.

'It doesn't matter. We can get someone else to take it for you. I can see Mrs Mead from the tuckshop holding a camera. We can ask her.'

'I don't want my picture taken,' Kathy protested. 'Leave me be.'

Kathy had waited so long to be chosen to help with the nativity scene, and now felt cheated. She watched Margaret Hunter closely, expecting to see a satisfying smile on her face. But Margaret didn't seem satisfied at all. She looked miserable.

During the Mass, Father Keegan spoke again about the purity of the birth of Jesus and the need for His followers to protect the newborn *with every drop of Catholic blood.*

'What's he talking about?' Kathy asked her mother. 'Is there going to be a war or something?'

'Be quiet,' her mother ordered, as the Father added, as if on cue, 'we are at war on this matter and we cannot lose.'

When the students were introduced to the parishioners at the conclusion of Mass, they smiled, except for Margaret. She looked ill. Rosie cupped a hand over Kathy's ear and whispered, 'What's wrong with her? I reckon she's in shock or something.'

'I don't know,' Kathy whispered back. 'I think she's being ungrateful.'

After Mass, the crowd around the nativity scene had grown. The kids waiting for their photograph with Baby Jesus pushed and shoved each other. One of the Rizzo twins tried bunking his brother onto the back of the donkey. He fell over the other side, taking the animal with him. The sad-faced donkey fell on top of the boy, who began to cry. Seeing what his sons had done, their father slapped one twin across the back of the head, dragged the other boy from under the donkey and slapped him too.

Kathy watched the chaos in horror, worried that Baby Jesus could be crushed in a stampede. 'This is awful.'

'Sure is. That donkey's tail has broken off. Father Keegan won't be happy about this.'

Kathy looked through the legs of the rowdy children, to where Baby Jesus lay. She was sure she could see the fear on his face.

'Can we go home, Rosie? I don't like being here.'

Rosie noticed her mother talking to Maye Brown, an old friend of hers from the shirt factory they'd worked in when they were both newlyweds.

'Okay. Let's go. Mum will be here all day, talking.'

Kathy took a final look at the Baby Jesus and made the sign of the cross, praying for his safety.

'Did you see the look on Margaret Hunter's face, standing up there in front of the whole church,' Rosie said, as the pair walked home. 'She had a face like a smacked arse.'

'Don't swear like that.'

'Arse? It's hardly swearing. I can say worse than that.'

'Well, don't. I don't want to hear it.'

'Arse! Arse! Arse!' Rosie screamed.

That night Kathy again refused to eat, annoying her mother and providing Rosie with an excuse to tease her sister more about the Baby Jesus.

'She's jealous that some other girl is taking care of her baby.'

'I don't have a baby,' Kathy screamed. 'I'm only ten years old.'

Their mother put a stop to the argument and ordered Kathy to the corner shop.

'I need you to pick up a bag of coke for the boiler. Or we'll have no hot water for a bath in the morning.'

'But I can't carry those heavy bags,' Kathy complained. 'Send her,' she said, poking her tongue out at her older sister.

'I'm not sending Rosie. I'm sending you. Take the old baby carriage from the sideway. Barty Collins will lift the bag of coke into the carriage for you and I'll get it out at this end.'

Kathy went off to the shop, Rosie helped her mother tidy the kitchen and do the dishes.

'I want you to stop teasing your sister,' Rosie's mother ordered, handing her daughter a plate to dry.

'Do I have to?' Rosie said.

'Yes, you have to. She really wanted this and I don't want her upsetting herself anymore. If she doesn't eat soon, she'll fade away to a shadow.'

'Did you see Margaret Hunter today?' Rosie asked.

'Of course I did. The Father called her name and she stood up there with the rest.'

'Did you see the look on her face then? It was like she was going to die.'

'Don't you be silly, Rose. The girl was being shy was all.'

'It was more than that,' Rosie insisted. 'Did you really see her?'

The next morning, a crowd of children gathered in front of the nativity scene in the church garden. Some stood in stunned silence. Others, younger children in particular, were crying.

'Something's going on,' Rosie said to Kathy, as they crossed the street together. 'Let's go take a look.'

'Not me,' Kathy said.

The sisters parted. In the schoolyard Kathy saw Theresa Dove, a girl who sat next to her in class. Theresa's eyes were red raw.

'What's wrong?' Kathy asked.

'It's the Baby Jesus,' Theresa bawled.

'The Baby Jesus? What about him?'

'He's gone.'

'Gone? He can't be gone.'

'The Baby Jesus has been taken. Someone has stolen him.'

Kathy turned and looked towards the church, where Rosie had pushed her way to the front of the crowd. The crib was empty, the Baby Jesus was missing, and the donkey looked more forlorn than he had the night before. Father Keegan was standing with the Three Wise Kings, a confused look on his face. Joseph's shoulders were stooped. Only the Virgin Mary looked as pure and certain as ever.

Rosie met Kathy in the yard. 'The Baby Jesus, he's gone,' she said. 'He's been taken.'

'I know,' Kathy said.

'You know?' Rosie thought about the previous night, when her sister had taken so long to return from the shop with the *baby carriage.* She took her sister by the arm and guided her to a far corner of the schoolyard.

'Of course, you know. You took him,' she laughed. 'Yes! Your stole the Baby Jesus.' She held Kathy and kissed her madly on both cheeks. 'I love you, little sister. You should see the look on the Father's face. I think he wants to die,'

Kathy wrestled herself free of her sister. 'I didn't steal him. Are you crazy? Why would I take the Baby Jesus?'

'Why? Because you're the crazy one. All you've ever wished for is the Baby Jesus. You wanted him all to yourself.'

The accusation shocked Kathy. 'I might have wanted the Baby, but not like that. No one wants a baby *that* much.'

'Really?' Rosie asked. 'Really?'

'Yes. Really.'

Rosie realised that her sister was telling the truth. She was confused. 'I thought you wanted the Baby Jesus more than anything in the world?'

'Not more than anything,' Kathy said, feeling suddenly wiser than her older sister. 'I might love the Baby Jesus, but I wouldn't steal him. That would be a sin.'

Theresa Dove ran across the yard towards the sisters, screaming hysterically, 'they found him, the Baby Jesus. They found him.'

'Where?' Rosie asked.

'Buried,' Theresa said.

'Buried!' Rosie and Kathy screamed in unison. 'Where?'

'He was buried in Margaret Hunter's back garden. Her mother was out this morning watering the rose garden and noticed the side of his face poking out of the soil.'

'My arse,' Rosie said. 'You're making this up.'

'No, I'm not,' Theresa insisted. 'Nola Tracy, who lives next door to Margaret, was in her yard feeding her dog when she heard Mrs Hunter scream out. When she saw the face, she thought it was a real baby. You know, like those ones they find sometimes?'

Every child knew the stories of abandoned babies.

'Where is the Baby now?' Kathy asked.

'Well . . .' Theresa hesitated. 'They say that parts of him are missing, and that Margaret smashed him into pieces with a hammer. Joseph's hammer. It was stolen too.'

'A hammer,' Kathy repeated, shaking her head. 'Why would she do that?'

'I bet she flushed him down the toilet,' Rosie said. 'That's what they do when they don't want them.'

'What does that mean?' Kathy asked, horrified at the idea of a baby being flushed through water pipes.

'He's not down the toilet,' Theresa said. 'The Father has left with some boys from the top year. They had shovels and rakes and were heading for the Hunters' garden. To find the bits and pieces. They say she buried him.'

Rosie began to laugh and couldn't stop.

'It's not funny,' Theresa said.

'I know,' Rosie answered and laughed even louder.

'Your sister is mental,' Theresa said to Kathy. 'She's going to hell,' she added before running back across the yard.

'Why would she do that?' Kathy asked her sister. 'Smash the Baby Jesus with a hammer and bury him?'

Rosie thought about the look she'd seen on Margaret Hunter's face at Mass the day before. She also remembered the words of her grandmother, that Kathy had been *lucky* that she wasn't chosen to help with the nativity scene. She was momentarily consumed by a thought so dark she believed it had to be a sin to even consider it.

Gina Rushton

From the frontline

You'll find women struggling to navigate Australia's patchwork of legal, financial, social and geographical barriers to terminate a pregnancy in the more than 150 articles about abortion access and law reform I've published over the past few years.

A woman who waited days in hospital to terminate a wanted pregnancy; a woman who cancelled her surgical abortion because she couldn't enter the clinic as her relative was protesting outside; a woman who paid more than $4000 to fly interstate for an abortion and was then fired over her online reproductive rights activism; a female politician who had to terminate a pregnancy at 21 weeks for a foetal anomaly and cried in parliament as she called out her colleagues for labelling her a murderer; a woman who explained how traumatic it can be to have a second-trimester abortion; a woman who was harassed outside a clinic as she tried to reach the door to terminate a pregnancy, which was the result of a rape.

In some cases, healthcare professionals have acted as a further barrier to access. One woman told me that her GP refused her a medical abortion because she was 'meant to be a mother', another said her doctor insisted abortion wasn't possible because it was a crime and one said her doctor told her abortion wasn't allowed after nine weeks.

But for the most part, women have emphasised the compassionate clinical care they received from doctors and nurses during what was often a complicated and upsetting time.

These are some of the stories from practitioners I've spoken to who described the personal risks of providing abortions and what it is like to operate within the shadow of the law in states where the procedure is still written into 100-year-old criminal legislation.

Queensland surgeon Dr David Grundmann went to work on the morning of 20 May 1985 at the Townsville clinic at which he was the medical director. He had no idea that by midday he would be holed up in a police station.

'It came completely out of the blue when the police came into the premises and requested that everything be stopped, produced a search warrant and charged me with performing illegal abortions,' Grundmann, 70, told me in 2017.

At 10 a.m. that morning, more than 100 police officers entered two Queensland clinics – one in Townsville and the other in Brisbane – where they seized equipment and confiscated around 47,000 patient files in what Grundmann described as a 'military-like raid'.

Grundmann and surgeon Dr Peter Bayliss of Brisbane's Greenslopes clinic were charged with conspiracy to perform illegal abortions.

The raids, and ensuing legal battle, would shift the parameters within which abortion could be lawful in Queensland by setting a legal precedent.

Grundmann said his main concern on the day was the fate of dozens of women who were travelling from regional and rural Queensland to terminate their pregnancies at 'considerable cost and inconvenience'.

'I was worried my operation would be stopped for a considerable period of time and there would be a lot of women who came to see me who would be seriously disadvantaged,' he said.

'Right up until 2005 we had patients who were refused contraception by their local pharmacists, who were deliberately misdiagnosed as being too late to have an abortion by a GP.'

Until Grundmann opened a second clinic in Rockhampton, patients were travelling from as far away as Bundaberg (1007 kilometres), Weipa (1140 kilometres) and Mt Isa (904 kilometres).

Grundmann escaped prosecution but the battle wasn't over for Bayliss or anaesthetist Dawn Cullen who eventually went to trial once the then Director of Public Prosecutions Des Sturgess found a single woman 'dissatisfied' with her abortion.

Lawyers, doctors, anti-abortion protesters and members of women's organisations overflowed from the public gallery of Brisbane's District Court for the trial, during which Sturgess attempted to convince a jury that Bayliss and Cullen – who had pleaded not guilty – had performed an unlawful abortion.

The jury was not convinced.

Until October this year, abortion was a crime in Queensland and only lawful to 'prevent serious danger to the woman's physical or mental health'.

By 2017, when Grundmann was long retired, there was

only one doctor performing surgical abortions in the 2000 kilometres north of Rockhampton.

'It is not nice what I do, and no one talks about it over the dinner table. In fact, half the people I know don't know what I do because I don't talk about it,' the doctor, who used the pseudonym Grace when I interviewed her, told me.

'I am in a privileged position of having a skill set that allows me to actually step up and do something about something I really care about.'

Grace works at Townsville's Marie Stopes International clinic, which can only afford to open three days a month.

'This practice has been running at a loss for a few years, but we've stayed open because what we do is so important,' she said.

'The population of Townsville is around 230,000, and 117,000 of those people are women. The median age is 34. Do the maths.'

Half of Grace's patients travelled a minimum of two hours to see her and almost a fifth had travelled for more than eight hours.

'It can be an eight-hour drive to get to a regional centre, and the cost is prohibitive for a lot of women. Depending on their gestation it is about $800 [on average] just for the procedure.'

Dr Colinette Margerison works as a GP, medical educator and contraceptive and sexual health consultant across rural and regional Queensland, where she provides medical abortions.

'Some of these rural towns, you can put a service in and all it takes is for that one doctor providing terminations to leave and you've got no service anymore,' she told me. 'If I was to leave, there would be a hole.'

Margerison has to consider the safety of her patients when taking abortion drugs, as they may be hours from medical care if they begin to haemorrhage.

'A lot of [women's healthcare providers] would say that if patients are living in that area and have that potential to have a natural miscarriage, then they should be just as safe, but the difference is that you're making it happen, and you know you're putting them at risk.'

Many patients travelled eight hours to the clinic. If they needed a surgical rather than medical abortion, they then had to drive two-and-a-half hours further to the closest surgical service.

Margerison is the only one of twenty GPs at her regular practice who provides medical terminations.

'The barriers women might face in a clinical setting is if you have people who don't feel comfortable with the provision [of abortion services] . . . I do know there are some clinicians I work with who don't provide contraception.'

For eighteen years, until safe access zones were enacted in New South Wales this year, dealing with religious protestors was a regular part of Paul Nattrass's job as the practice manager of The Private Clinic in Surry Hills, Sydney.

'These protesters tend to talk to people about why they are at the clinic, which is a gross invasion of their medical history,' Nattrass told me. 'Many women are more concerned about protesters than the procedure itself.'

'Even when patients are being discharged after the procedure, they nearly all ask if the protesters are still there and ask to be ushered through an alternate exit.'

When we published a story in *BuzzFeed*, corroborated by footage, of a protestor offering a Chinese-Australian woman entering the clinic help with 'immigration problems, legal problems, medical problems,' Nattrass wasn't surprised.

He said that the protesters targeted most patients, but that it was easier for women with strong English language skills to quickly understand who was approaching them.

'One incident that does stand out is when we had this lady protesting outside and she intercepted a patient who didn't have English as a first language, and we saw [the protester] on the cameras taking this woman across the road to an [anti-choice crisis pregnancy counselling centre],' he said.

'I went across and knocked on the door but no one answered, and when we spoke to the patient later, on the phone, she was still unaware that she hadn't been to The Private Clinic ... she said she was confused as to why we would have told her about horrible dangers of abortion and shown her images of dead babies.'

A registered nurse who used the pseudonym Rosie when she talked to me worked at two clinics in Surry Hills until 2016 – The Private Clinic and Preterm, which has now closed.

'As a staff member, I felt intimidated and threatened by the protestors out the front who eventually learned my name,' she told me.

'They would watch me walk up from the train, it was really predatory, there was nothing you could do.'

The protesters were there for a few hours every day and would approach patients to say, 'You don't have to do this,' or hand out rosary beads, Rosie said.

'This woman came in one day with her young son, who was about four years old, and her partner, and one of [the protestors] said: "Mummy is about to kill your baby brother".'

'That was a new low.'

One day Rosie discovered the protestors had slipped some of their brochures – 'basically just the first couple of Google image results for aborted foetuses and some inaccurate medical information' – into the stack of magazines in the clinic.

'Can you imagine sitting there and waiting for your termination and being confronted with these flyers?'

Dr David Corbett has been an anaesthetist at Albury's

Fertility Clinic for five years and spoke at a rally for safe access zones earlier this year.

'These protesters say they stand there in silent prayer, and no one could argue with that, but the reality is they approach [women] walking in and out and they have been known to go up to patients and tell them that she's "murdering a baby",' Corbett told me.

'As doctors we don't like patients being harassed and we don't like patients being lied to.'

One of the regular picketers also sprays 'holy water' along the footpath outside the clinic.

Corbett said that once, when his wife collected him from the clinic, she was handed a plastic foetal doll by a protester.

'We have a security guard now who protects the women being buttonholed by the protesters, but we also need the exclusion zones.'

The anaesthetist said locals were nervous about taking on the protesters as some were considered litigious.

'There is a lot of bluff and bluster about bringing in lawyers and . . . I think that scares people a little.'

It was more than bluff and blunder for retired obstetrician Pieter Mourik.

Married Albury anti-abortion picketers Roland and Anna von Marburg won $180,000 in damages from Mourik after they claimed they were defamed in 2014 by comments on the Facebook page for which he was a spokesperson.

The case dragged on for almost three years until a settlement was reached in 2017 between the von Marburgs and the Wodonga obstetrician who published an apology on the Facebook page of which he was a spokesperson.

Mourik, who practised in reproductive health in Albury for almost four decades, is staunchly pro-choice.

When I revealed in 2016 that a church-funded cafe in

Albury was raising money for the anti-abortion clinic next door, Mourik told me he was concerned about the anti-choice movement in his hometown. The money was going towards a $30,000 ultrasound machine for the Women's Life Centre – an organisation owned by the Catholic Parish of Holy Spirit Lavington – to scan women with unplanned pregnancies.

Mourik said this was an 'appalling tactic' used by anti-abortion groups 'around the world'.

'It is a lovely cafe but it isn't clear that it is backed by the Church and it is just another way of coercing a woman to continue an unwanted pregnancy by increasing her emotional distress,' he said.

'It is absolutely scurrilous because it is used to manipulate women to continue an unwanted pregnancy which could be far more dangerous to their lives.'

In the first legislative attempt to reform Queensland's abortion law in 2016, abortion provider Fiona Mack said in a submission to a parliamentary inquiry into the laws that she had assisted three women in a single year who came from hospitals unwilling to provide terminations.

'These doctors failed in their duty of care to these women,' she wrote.

One of her patients found out she was pregnant at the same time that she was diagnosed with metastatic ovarian cancer. Her oncologist and gynaecologist would not continue with chemotherapy or surgery 'until she was no longer pregnant' but would not provide her with an abortion.

'She was required to discharge herself from hospital and make her way to our clinic independently. Her sister pushed her over in a wheelchair.'

This year, senators Cory Bernardi and Barry O'Sullivan continued to proliferate their views about abortions after the first trimester in the Senate where they argued that women were terminating pregnancies at the very last minute, right before what would otherwise be a normal healthy birth.

It isn't a new argument by anti-abortion advocates but Queensland obstetrician and maternal-foetal medicine specialist Dr Carol Portmann was furious the misinformation was being spread by not only religious lobbyists, but federal politicians.

'I would hope that if you'd entered politics you would have an ability to separate your personal agenda from facts presented to you and it is disrespectful to women not to look at those facts before opening your mouth and giving unfounded opinions,' she told me.

It was a 'ludicrous fallacy' that any doctor would support a termination in the third trimester for psychosocial reasons.

'In my twenty years experience in Queensland, where I have never been asked by any woman to perform a termination in the third trimester for psychosocial reasons, it is always because a baby has [been] found to have such a severe heart or brain injury, or where the mother's life is at risk,' she said. 'Even in a very late pregnancy diagnosis, or if someone turned up thinking they were at fourteen weeks gestation and found themselves at 30 weeks, they would just have to go on to have the baby.'

Portmann said it was usually severe medical complications that weren't visible in the patient's first or second ultrasound.

'It is mostly brain problems which weren't visible earlier on, and parents know their child will survive for a period of time with no quality of life, whether that is a matter of days or up to a year, and pass away, and parents feel they simply can't watch their child in suffering,' she said. 'These are conditions which are ultimately always lethal.'

I was in Queensland's parliament house on 17 October last year when politicians voted for abortion to be decriminalised.

In the public gallery sat Caroline de Costa who had campaigned for this since 1971.

She was the first doctor in Australia to gain permission to prescribe medical abortion drugs RU486. In 2009, when a Cairns couple were charged for procuring a medical abortion, de Costa was forced to withdraw her service due to possible legal repercussions.

When one of the only doctors providing surgical abortions in Cairns retired and women were being flown interstate for terminations at huge cost, de Costa was on the frontline calling on the state government to fix the situation for months on end.

She has spent decades as a specialist obstetrician and gynaecologist but has always dedicated time and energy to campaign for abortion law reform and increased access to services, particularly for vulnerable women.

Like many women's health professionals, de Costa has had to straddle clinical practice and activism in order to advocate the best care for her patients.

A few days later I spotted her across the room in Melbourne at the headquarters for the Royal Australian and New Zealand College of Obstetricians and Gynaecologists. We chatted about the highs and lows of the two-day parliamentary debate over the legislation in Queensland.

'How did it feel when the bill eventually passed?' I asked.

'Oh, we were sitting there and when it happened we just . . .' she took an exaggerated breath in and exhaled loudly, using her whole body.

She then stood shaking her head, wordless with weary happiness for a moment until snapping herself out of it: 'But of course there's still more to be done.'

Tara June Winch

Letter to my teenage daughter

Every mother, in those first minutes and hours and days, has an instinct to become a mother or not. I was homeless, single, uneducated and 21 years old when I decided to become your mother. It wasn't a difficult decision but an instinctive moment: from the couch to the pharmacy and into the bathroom of a friend of a friend's place. There I had lifted my shirt and pushed my torso forward, side-eyed myself in the mirror and simply knew that the answer was *yes*. Yes, I wanted you against the odds.

Anyone else, in that moment, might have instinctively felt that the answer was no. *No* would have been a decision just as much as *yes*. And yet, not every woman is fortunate enough to be given the choice.

I'm grateful that I had the choice. Maybe my instinct was tethered to my hopes in that I lived in Australia, a first-world country, that I had a book contract, that I was working towards something solid, and that I believed that if I put my whole soul into the writing, I felt I could write a small, humble future for us. I was so sure of it – naïvely, crazily, instinctively sure of it – though still, you should know that I was frightened at times. I worried that the world would not reciprocate all that buoyancy. And it should be frightening because, as every mother in those minutes and hours and days will attest, we make the decision, that commitment to our children, based on whether or not we can give them the world. I couldn't give you what I hoped but I pinned everything on the future – when I looked towards the sky, darkened and overcast at times, I knew the sun shone somewhere and that we would find it, and wherever it was I believed it was *bright*.

And your future was bright, wasn't it? Haven't we had thirteen years of bliss and joy and adventure? You are loved and supported and happy and healthy and thriving – and whip-smart – everything a mother would want for her child, her daughter. You are the best crossroads I ever met.

Now that you are so much older and wiser, I want you to know that the very reason you were born is because of the women that have come before you and me – heroic women, whose footfalls have worn paths. Because precisely for my having had the choice, the choice was mine. That I decided on you. That I had permission to be in control of my body and my eventual baby, *you*.

I want you to always remember that you have permission to be in control of your body, before and now and always. It is yours, your own sacred mass that you must protect and nourish and love. Self-care is the duty you have to yourself. Because so many girls and women do not have that permission over their bodies – even though it is fundamental to a dignified life.

Every girl and woman deserves the right to self-care in that you should *love* your body, thank it for letting you move and create and run and experience pleasure and carry your wonderful brains and hearts and lungs around, that you should *nourish* your body, in order to keep it running, with fresh nutritious food, with clean water, with unpolluted air, and with the right amount of fuel that it needs, and finally, that you should *protect* your body, that inseparable from the need of self-care is the absolute right to self-government, of not only your mind, but of your physical vessel, the only boat in the miraculous, wondrous life we each have.

And yet so many of your sisters around the world, by coercion and tyranny and warfare and broken laws and backward beliefs, cannot practise self-care. They cannot practise self-care because the world is not free of virginity testing, of genital mutilation, of illegal and unsafe abortion, is not free of child marriage and gender-based violence and sexual abuse, and racism and modern slavery.

The year you've become a teenager, 25 million women around the world sought an unsafe abortion. About 17 million teenage girls, mostly in low- and middle-income countries, gave birth, and roughly 3 million teenage girls had unsafe abortions around the world.[27] Not all teenage girls can attend school or see a doctor or have ownership over their minds and bodies.

I'm sorry that you have inherited the times as they are and I'm sorry to be so bleak – but you and I cannot talk about being a female without acknowledging the experience of others, and your existence is affected and affecting to the planet and other people beyond your school and village and home. I cannot right the wrongs for you outside our home.

Just as I cannot tell you about being Australian or French anymore without acknowledging the whole world. Because that's the way you've been raised, that's the time of your life – that is your life; you straddle not just two countries, not just two languages, but your ethnicities, your culture, your history and your ancestors, and the world beside.

You stand among a generation of young women who will change so much. I want you to know that I believe in your ability. You have the right to be whatever you want to be, you are not helpless or weak because of your gender, you are the opposite precisely because you are female. Because you are a privileged female.

I hope that you'll never have to use the services you have rights to. I hope you use your privilege to vote and shout and break glass ceilings, kick down walls and own your sexuality, make great progress, navigate your education and your career, and always lift your fellow sisters up along the way. Kick and break and vote and shout and own yourself alongside them.

I can't remember what it was like to turn thirteen, but I can remember being scared around that age. I remember being afraid of the night. I know you're not afraid of that – in the evenings you hear our laughter or the spin cycle in the laundry, the doors and windows being locked, and the kettle whistling for bedtime teas. But, sometime in the future you may be scared of the night. Your friends might be scared of the night too. I hope you keep yourself and your friends safe. I hope you never, ever come to harm or the threat of it. It is horrific, to be scared, but I cannot protect you from every threat, neither from feeling troubled. I can only remind you that you have the right to not feel those things. There is never justification for your being made to feel less, to feel afraid or threatened. I'm glad you enjoy karate classes every week; I hope that you'll never have to use your skills outside the dojo. But maybe you will, some places and people will not know that you have the right to equality and autonomy.

I hope that you will always announce to the world, unspoken, or spoken when you need, that you have complete ownership of your body.

I can only ask that whatever you do in your life, you are grateful for your privilege. That you remember, even in democracies, your sisters have different rights regarding their own bodies. That everywhere from the Dominican Republic or Malta or Ireland or New Zealand or Morocco or parts of Australia, your sisters aren't afforded the same rights as you are. I want you to believe that those laws are not justified, that they are not right at all. I want you to look back and remember where the world as it is for you now comes from, what people have done to shape this point in history, this point in time where you now live – what soldiers, politicians, wars, natural disasters, racism and religion and protestors and activists and rebels, and even teenagers, have done to afford you this great life that you live. That your privilege always came at a price – someone's freedom or someone's oppression. I want you to question whether we should no longer treat those imposters the same – why shouldn't triumph, and not only disaster, be available to all? I just ask that you are aware of the world, not just your circle of friends, and your family unit, or your Indigenous mob or your sisters but to be aware of the grand sphere and the race you are a member of. I ask that you remember that your privileges come with your obligations.

One day, when you are an adult, you'll leave your home and discover your very own version of your very own world. I'll be holding a candle for you, some beacon you may not always see, or maybe the light won't be right for the times, but I'll be there. And you'll be out there making your choices.

I hope that you are happy, that you are resilient enough to overcome adversity, that you are strong enough to argue, that you are bold enough to follow your dreams, that you are courageous enough to take the travelled road as well as off the beaten track, that you find light in the dark, that you care for the less fortunate and hold fast through whims, that you know yourself and that you make your own choices, with your own great and instinctive mind and body.

And I hope you inform wherever you go and lift your sisters up along the way. They deserve the choices as much as any other person.

I'm here for you, I'm listening to you, I'm with you for all the minutes and hours and days.

I love you,

Mummy.

Eleanor Limprecht
Her history, my silence

When I was researching my second novel, *Long Bay*, I read everything I could find about abortion in the early 1900s: the desperation of women seeking to end their pregnancies, the incredible risks they took to avoid unwanted pregnancies, and the violence of the methods of termination. I was writing about the true case of an illegal abortionist in Sydney named Rebecca Sinclair who had gone to prison for manslaughter when a woman in her care died. At one point my PhD supervisor Debra Adelaide asked me: why this topic, why this novel? We spoke about limitations, about the way lack of choice can cripple you. I didn't mention my own abortion.

I thought about it, though, as I researched and wrote. Not for a moment had I imagined dying on the operating table in Virginia, not for a moment had I wondered if the procedure would kill me.

I was twenty years old, six months off graduating from university, when I discovered I was pregnant. The boyfriend – let's call him John – was also a student. He was a musician and poet, but the talent he had was frequently smothered by substances. He wrote me love poems on little scraps of paper, pursued me. I had not figured out what I wanted and thought that if someone wanted me that was enough.

We got drunk, we smoked pot from a blue-swirled glass pipe and he ranted against the world, how screwed up it all was, how empty and shallow. He was sensitive, see. But there was also a disconnect between feeling and doing, his black moods, the escape into pills and alcohol and emptiness, and after a short time I knew that I had to pull away from him. I was terrible at ending things; I had not learned to speak my mind. And then I missed my period, and my breasts felt as tender as a bruise, and I took a home pregnancy test.

The plus sign appeared, hazy first, like the answer on a Magic 8 ball, wavering then definite: outlook not so good. I was drinking too much and taking recreational drugs. I was about to leave John, and now he was the father of this embryo – this possible child inside of me.

When I told him he cried. It was December 1998 and we were lying on my blue and silver velvet bedspread with my crimple-eared mutt sprawled between us. He railed against the unfairness of it happening to us, but he wanted to keep the pregnancy. He said we would make it work. I stroked my dog's silky ears, avoiding his gaze. I struggled to look after my dog and myself, how would I look after an infant? How would I look after him? I told him I wanted to have an abortion.

I had been to the Planned Parenthood in my small, American college town before for birth control pills, but this time I felt as though everyone knew why I was there. I felt like I had a scarlet letter sewn to my chest: the A not of Adultery but of Abortion. The nurse said that I would have to drive forty minutes east to a Planned Parenthood clinic in a small city and have the procedure there. It would cost $400. They did a test to confirm my pregnancy and showed me pamphlets about *What Would Happen* and *Other Options*, and then gave me the number of the clinic to call for the appointment.

I made the appointment. I had final papers and exams to finish and then I would have the procedure. John said he would pay for half, he said he would come. My friend Nicole would drive us.

On 21 June 1909 a small, black-clad woman stood in the dock of the Central Criminal Court at Darlinghurst Courthouse in Sydney. She had light brown hair, brown eyes and spoke very softly, so her solicitor had to repeat her words.

'I am,' she said, '23 years of age. I am innocent of this awful charge.'

This awful charge was wilful murder. Rebecca Sinclair and her husband Donald Sinclair were charged after a 38-year-old woman named Lucy Smith was found dead in their Woollahra home. Medical reports showed her cause of death to be an air embolism after an attempted illegal abortion. Lucy Smith had been three months pregnant.

Rebecca Irwin Sinclair, as she is listed on prison records, was born in Paddington in Sydney in 1885 to Louis and Elizabeth McDowall. She was the fourth of six children – all girls except for one boy. In 1888, when Rebecca was three, her father died. Two years later, her older sister Helen died at the age of six.

In 1905 Rebecca was nineteen and at the roller-skating rink at Prince Alfred Park when she met a dark-haired, well-dressed,

23-year-old man named Donald Roderick Sinclair. After just three weeks Donald Sinclair proposed, and eventually Rebecca accepted. She agreed to meet him at his house in Glenmore Road to be married in front of his mother and stepfather. But when she arrived late, Donald told her that his mother and stepfather had gone to the theatre and that the clergyman couldn't wait either. Instead, he said the clergyman had left a document for them to sign. She signed it.

Donald and Rebecca Sinclair began living as man and wife, but before long gossip reached Rebecca that her marriage was a sham. On 12 December 1905, she confronted Donald, and he said she was foolish to believe other people's tales. But a few days later, he admitted that he wrote the marriage certificate himself. Two days later they were genuinely married, on 16 December 1905, in the Pitt Street Congregational Church.

In coming months, Rebecca discovered that Donald had been already married when he married her. In August Donald Sinclair was charged with bigamy in the Water Police Court. He was found guilty in October 1906 and sentenced to six months' hard labour at Goulburn Gaol. The sentence was suspended because he was a first-time offender.

Rebecca appears to have forgiven Donald, because in 1907 she gave birth to their daughter, Ellen Lillian Daphne Sinclair, in the Benevolent Society's Thomas Street Asylum for 'destitute and homeless mothers nursing their children'. Notes from the Thomas Street Asylum Inmates Journals from Mitchell Library show that Donald Sinclair was listed as her husband when she was admitted, with the word 'emergency' beside her record. Other records show the word 'destitute' beside a patient's name so it could be inferred that Rebecca was ill-prepared for the birth rather than in completely dire straits. In April of the following year, 1908, Donald Sinclair appeared in court on an unrelated blackmail charge, and was sentenced to twelve months' prison.

He couldn't have served the full sentence because he was at home on 26 April 1909 when a doctor was called after Lucy Smith suddenly collapsed at Rebecca and Donald's home.

When the doctor arrived Lucy Smith was lying on a couch, dead. She lived in North Sydney and had three children, aged seven, six and four. She was three months' pregnant and her husband Andrew Smith, a linotype operator at the *Sydney Morning Herald,* said in court that he did not know why she would visit Rebecca and Donald Sinclair. He learned of her death as it came through the *Herald* newsroom.

From the inquest into Lucy's death she was found to have died as the result of an illegal operation. Rebecca and Donald Sinclair were charged with her wilful murder.

At the clinic in Virginia there were young women with their mothers. My mother lived overseas; she did not even know I was pregnant. I had called my sister in Chicago and told her, and she said that if I wanted to keep the baby she could help me out. I knew that I would need more help than she could possibly provide.

In the waiting room John sat on one side and Nicole on the other. When they called my name I went into the operating room without them. I changed into a gown, the medical kind, which opens in the back. There was a paper cup of red Kool-Aid and they gave me Valium to 'calm the nerves'. There was a vacuum aspirator, a cold whiteness, a groggy ache.

On the drive home I was doubled over in the backseat with cramps. At one point we pulled over and I vomited on the side of Interstate 81, eighteen-wheelers rushing past, the jack hammer vibration as they braked at the sight of us. Nicole held my hair back, stroked my back. John stayed in the car.

He went home. I went home. I stayed in bed for a few days, cramping, bleeding, vacillating between self-pity and self-loathing. John came on the second day and sprawled across my bed. He said he hadn't wanted me to have the abortion because he didn't see how our relationship could continue afterwards. I said that was true, I didn't see how it could. He began to cry again. He said he wanted to kill himself. I tried to comfort him, but I was empty. He was upset that his words did not cause me more concern, but I had none left. I had used up every bit of my sorrow.

Rebecca and Donald Sinclair had only been in business for a few weeks performing illegal abortions with a syringe and nozzle and hot water with Epsom salts.

In the Supreme Court of New South Wales, in a case presided over by Honourable Acting Justice Francis Edward Rogers, Rebecca and Donald Sinclair were found guilty of manslaughter by a jury on 21 June 1909. Donald was sentenced to five years' penal servitude and Rebecca to three years' imprisonment with hard labour. What Rebecca Sinclair did not mention in the courtroom was that she was also three months pregnant.

Six months later, as a prisoner of Long Bay Women's Reformatory, she gave birth to her second child, Freda Hope McDowell, returning to her maiden name (though spelled differently). She kept this daughter with her at Long Bay. On 14 February 1910 in the inspection book for the State Reformatory is a note that a cradle is needed from Darlinghurst Gaol for 'Prisoner Sinclair's infant'. On 11 August 1910 there is a note in the inspection book that Rebecca Sinclair and her daughter were to be transferred to Shaftesbury Institution at Watson's Bay, a halfway house which primarily held inebriates.

After their release, Rebecca married Christopher Willis and took his name. She died at the age of 52 and is buried in Waverley Cemetery. The daughter she left when she went to prison, Ellen, became estranged from her. The daughter who was born in prison, Freda, remained close to her mother for the rest of her life.

John and I broke up. I can't pretend that change came immediately, because it didn't. I turned 21. I graduated from college, with honours, and moved to Arizona to spend a year working there. Afterwards I went overseas and travelled. I fell in love, I moved to Australia.

When I was 28 I had a daughter and at thirty a son. I had a miscarriage before my daughter was born and after the miscarriage spent a year trying to fall pregnant. A friend and I discussed this; each of us had gone through an abortion once, and we talked about our fear that it had somehow ruined us for childbearing.

But these are not Edwardian times. This is not what happens, so why do we still feel the guilt? The need for silence? The abortion was not the defining moment in my life, but it did allow me keep living. It gave me the chance to say no without risking my life. I was not ready.

Life is fragile however you look at it. Embryos are fragile: some make it, some don't. I love my children with a fierceness I have not previously known. Would I have loved this other child the same? Of course. Would I have been a decent mother? Possibly. But I would have felt trapped. John and I would not have remained together, but I would have remained tethered – through our child – to him.

It did not come immediately but here is what came, slowly, once I left John: recognition of my own self-worth, so it was not dependent on praise from others. The ability to look after myself. The ability to deal with pain and regret without drugs and alcohol.

I didn't regret my choice, but for years I was silenced by feelings of shame about my abortion. It was part of why I wrote *Long Bay*, but I didn't say as much. Now I want to go back and reassure my twenty-year-old self, my 37-year-old self. The stories of other women's abortions have galvanised me. I am far from alone in making this choice.

In the early 1900s women like Lucy Edith Smith sought abortions knowing that they risked death in the process. Women like Rebecca Sinclair provided abortions knowing that they risked prison. They were both forced into the margins, into illegality, through desperation. Writing about my own abortion seems small in comparison, but in the words of the black poet and feminist Audre Lorde: 'My silences had not protected me. Your silence will not protect you.'

What protected me is the landmark United States Supreme Court decision *Roe v. Wade*, which the Trump Administration would like to overturn. In Australia, where I live in the state of New South Wales, abortion is still a criminal offence. A doctor can only legally administer an abortion if they believe continuing the pregnancy is a risk to a woman's physical or mental health. There are still so many grey areas, governments controlling our bodies, so much that women stand to lose.

When I was twenty I had an abortion. I did not risk my life or my freedom. The sorrow I felt was dwarfed by the relief.

My silence will not protect me.

Jane Gleeson-White

My womb is not *terra nullius*

Any discussion of abortion must start with those capable of becoming pregnant, and our bodies. These days this is rarely the case. Such conversations, often conducted by cisgender men, usually start with religion or morality, and the vicissitudes of eggs recently fertilised by sperm, when in fact abortion is a matter of our human right to reproductive health and safe, affordable medical procedures.

Writing about abortion in 2018 is for me fraught with emotion – not with regret and loss, but with the charged history of my heart, so closely connected to my womb. It raised two of my great and sometimes conflicting passions: my love for my vocation, writing; and my love for the man who eventually became the father of my children. And yes, there was some fear there as well – palpable, bodily fear.

When I first wrote about abortion publicly – in 2012 for the *Overland* blog – I did not feel fear. Today, 2012 seems another age. It was before Brett Kavanaugh was sworn in as a justice of the US Supreme Court, before Trump, Tony Abbott and Scott Morrison. And it was before the defeat in 2017 of a bill in the New South Wales parliament to decriminalise abortion. The End12 Bill, as it's known, would have overturned three archaic sections of New South Wale's *Crimes Act 1900*. It would have brought the laws governing one of the state's most common medical procedures into the 21st-century and in line with the views of 73 per cent of its voters. The bill was defeated by a margin of fourteen to 25. Twenty-one of the 25 MPs who voted against it were men.

2017 also brought a novel I'd read in the distant 1980s – Margaret Atwood's *The Handmaid's Tale* – kicking and screaming into the 21st-century in ways that seemed terrifyingly plausible and disturbingly timely.

But the times have changed in other ways too. In 2012, I was blogging in response to a story called 'I took secret photos of my abortion to empower and educate women' published anonymously in *The Guardian*. It was before the abortion rom com *Obvious Child*, before Emily Letts filmed her abortion and posted it to YouTube, before #shoutyourabortion, We Testify and Youth Testify. In 2018, many more of us are telling our abortion stories in the hope of normalising a medical procedure that must be safely available for all those capable of bearing a child, especially given that one in three of us in Australia, the UK and USA will have an abortion in our lifetime.

The woman who photographed and wrote about her abortion in 2012 remained anonymous – because they were dangerous times for women and those capable of becoming pregnant. It seems, today, that the times are more dangerous still. Almost daily I read deeply troubling stories about the invasion of female reproductive organs by governments and others.

I use the cold scientific term 'reproductive organs' deliberately because I think such terms allow legislators – and all those outsiders who think they have a say in what happens to our bodies – to abstract our wombs from our breathing flesh, from the fabric of our lives and our stories.

Our wombs are not terra nullius. They are not blank tracts for others to write their laws upon. Every womb on this earth is enfolded in a person with their own unique life and story – and the decisions we make for our wombs must be governed by our lives and our stories alone. Not stymied by the abstractions of 'God', 'State' or any other lawmaking entity that does other than ensure our access to safe, affordable reproductive healthcare.

Anonymous published her experience online to show what a safe abortion looks like, to 'help dispel the fear, the lies and hysteria around abortion, and empower women to make educated decisions for their bodies'. She was partly motivated by the fact that her mother had nearly died from an illegal abortion some thirty years before and then spent the months of her recovery 'in silence in a country where she would have been banished, if not killed, for her actions'.

When Anonymous went to have her own abortion, she wasn't sure which was more harmful: the anti-abortion protesters who threatened her outside the clinic or the procedure itself. But once she'd gone through the bulletproof (!) doors, she found a sanctuary.[28]

> Counselled, educated and physically readied, I let go of my anxieties in this safe place. The procedure itself, albeit uncomfortable, was straightforward and passed with ease.

You won't be surprised to hear that Anonymous lives in the United States. The US continues to experience an abortion crisis. Here's how she concluded:

> Within 48 hours of launching thisismyabortion.com, I received a deluge of emails from men, women and couples all over the world confiding in me their own courageous and unique abortion stories. Some told tales of horrific self-inflicted abortions in countries where abortion remains illegal. Others expressed sincere gratitude for my documentation . . .
>
> I hope thisismyabortion.com will be used as a tool to bring a fair, honest, balanced view of safe abortion. We, together, can take a stand for the truth, women's rights and reproductive justice.

In 2012, I wrote that her hope was my hope – and that I, too, had had an abortion. Like Anonymous, I thought it was time we told the secret histories of our wombs. Write them and the full spectrum of their stories – menses, abortions, miscarriages, births, menopause – into the culture, so that no one ever again mistakenly believes that wombs are uncharted entities ripe for government by external forces.

What I didn't write then was that, in fact, I've had four abortions. Each time I got pregnant by accident, I'd thought I was safe: menstruating, using a condom or breastfeeding a new baby.

When I first became pregnant with the man I loved, we were living streets apart in rented studios in Potts Point and Kings Cross. Some hours after the test confirmed our pregnancy, I sat alone on my bed regarding the single room I'd painted shell pink for Botticelli's Venus. I decided this was no place for a baby, with its father living six blocks away in his own single room making art in prized solitude. He wanted the baby but had no intention of changing anything, including our living arrangements; he longed to be a father as I did not long to become a mother.

My decision to end the pregnancy was straightforward, governed by common sense and my work. My writing life had just kicked up a notch: I'd recently started my first job as a writer of prose pieces longer than captions and I was relishing it.

The procedure – a surgical abortion – was equally straightforward. I was lucky to have a job and the money to afford it, and access to a safe clinic. I had close friends to advise me from their own experiences and to accompany me to the Preterm clinic in Glebe. There were no protesters outside – they would come later and abortion centres would become increasingly difficult to find. My initial nerves at the prospect of the unknown and of possible pain were soon calmed by the gentle atmosphere and attentive healthcare professionals. Of the procedure itself – vacuum aspiration with a local anaesthetic – I felt only the sting of a needle and a strange movement in my abdomen. Afterwards I was taken to the recovery room and more kind people brought me magazines, a cup of tea and biscuits. After a couple of hours, I went home. I had some cramping and light bleeding which continued for about three days. I was cared for with the greatest of consideration throughout.

Thinking about abortion also recalled my first tentative explorations of my body. I don't mean childhood investigations of my genitals and budding breasts, but my first ventures into the organised world of feminists intent on demystifying the great procreative powers of my body.

It was 1993. Newly married and freshly pregnant, I joined a circle of women and girls in a hall behind Sydney's King

George V Memorial Hospital in Camperdown. I wanted to learn more about my embodied self and so I was starting with one of the last remaining taboos, which unsurprisingly happened to concern my body and precisely that one feature unique to most of those with wombs: menstruation. Some fifty women sat cross-legged in a circle to talk about blood, led by a prominent feminist elder.

We learned that evening in our menstrual circle – sitting around a scattering of red towelling pads to be used for our monthly bleeding, many of us wearing red as suggested by the organisers – that ancient Egyptian women had known their bodies in ways we modern women had forgotten. With herbs and even with the power of their minds alone, they could abort a pregnancy if required. Without warning, sitting in that circle, harnessed to the power of that group of women and their blood law, I found myself mentally, calmly, releasing the child in my womb. The next day I bled. The following Monday I miscarried, spontaneously aborting our eight-week-old embryo. The ultrasound examination found that my womb had successfully expelled the entire contents of its pregnancy and no dilation and curettage was required. At the time, my husband and I were not yet in a position to bring a new life into our world.

I still have my diary from the day of that menstrual circle. I noted merely that at 7 p.m. on Friday 30 April 1993 I went to a 'lecture'. I was on a mission to learn more about my body but for reasons I never analysed at the time, this foray was of the utmost secrecy.

I wonder now – two adult children, two miscarriages and two more abortions later – if my adventures into my own body were so secretive and fearful because I was investigating a realm that had until so recently in the scheme of human history been the property of men.

In 2013, for different reasons entirely, I began to investigate western property laws governing the natural world. I quickly discovered that they were analogous to the laws governing female bodies.

As recently as 1968, a widely used first year property law casebook made this parenthetical comment: 'for, after all, land, like woman, was meant to be possessed.'[29]

Ancient denigrations of women are well known. Two of the fathers of western culture – Pythagoras and Aristotle – believed women were inferior to men. As Simone de Beauvoir observed, by the time humans came to write mythology and law, patriarchy was definitively established. And so

> it is males who write the codes. It is natural for them to give woman a subordinate situation; one might imagine, however, that they would consider her with the same benevolence as children and animals. But no. Afraid of woman, legislators organise her oppression.[30]

Consequently, there is a litany of foundational law that crushes women. The Hindu Laws of Manu define woman as a vile being to be held in slavery, and Leviticus equates women with beasts of burden owned by the patriarch. The Athenian laws of Solon grant her no rights and the ancient Roman code puts her in guardianship and proclaims her 'imbecility'. Canon law considers her 'the devil's gateway' and the Koran 'treats her with the most absolute contempt'.[31]

Writing only four decades ago – in 1972 – US law professor Christopher Stone had this to say on the first page of his famous article on the rights of nature, *Should Trees Have Standing?*:

We have been making persons of children although they were not, in law, always so. And we have done the same, albeit imperfectly some would say, with prisoners, aliens, women (especially of the married variety), the insane, African Americans, foetuses, and Native Americans.[32]

This was an astonishing aside. There I learned what I had always imperfectly known: that in western law, along with whole groups of human beings, one entire half of the human population had been excluded from legal personhood until appallingly recently. In fact, in the United States, corporations were granted legal personhood in the 19th century decades before women were.

Stone goes on to tell a story about the first woman in Wisconsin who in 1875 thought she might have a right to practise law. She was told she did not, in the following words:

The law of nature destines and qualifies the female sex for the bearing and nurture of the children of our race and for the custody of the homes of the world ... [A]ll life-long callings of women, inconsistent with these radical and sacred duties of their sex, as is the profession of law, are departures from the order of nature; and when voluntary, treason against it.[33]

What is striking about the Wisconsin case, Stone says, is 'that the court, for all its talk of women, so clearly was never able to see women as they are (and might become). All it could see was the popular "idealised" version of *an object it needed*.'[34] (Stone's emphasis)

As he explains about attempts to extend rights to women, or to trees:

> The fact is, that each time there is a movement to confer new rights onto some new "entity", the proposal is bound to sound odd or frightening or laughable. This is partly because until the rightless thing receives its rights, we cannot see it as anything but a *thing* for the use of "us" – those who are holding rights at the time. (3, Stone's emphasis)
>
> Thus it was that the Founding Fathers could speak of the inalienable rights of all men, and yet maintain a society that was, by modern standards, without the most basic rights for African Americans, Native Americans, children, and women. There was no hypocrisy; emotionally, no one felt that these others were fully *people*.[35] (Stone's emphasis)

Barely a century ago, we women were rightless *things* for the use of 'them', felt by no one to be fully *people*.

When counsel was arguing for the unfortunate Wisconsin woman who had the gall to imagine herself a lawyer, her very presence in the court disputed her claim; the court found it 'impossible' even to suggest that a *woman* could be a *person*. The definition of legal person so incontrovertibly signalled masculinity that the court could not begin to imagine how it might apply to a woman. It was so unthinkable that a woman could be a legal person that to call her one was the same as calling her a man. So much so that in the court's view it would then follow that she would be subject 'to prosecutions for the paternity of a bastard, and . . . prosecutions for rape'.

These legal erasures of women made possible such views and practices as those of the 19th-century physician J. Marion Sims, the so-called 'father of modern gynaecology' and 'architect of the vagina' (really). Sims – notorious for his abhorrence of female organs – advocated ovariotomy and conducted medical experiments on enslaved African-American women. According to him, removing women's ovaries enhanced their moral sense and made them biddable, industrious and clean.

Contesting the mass sterilisation this unleashed, in 1906 Ely van de Warker MD advocated the protection of the ovary. Not because he considered ovariotomy to be an invasion of women's bodies – but because '[a] woman's ovaries belong to the commonwealth; she is simply their custodian'. He then calculated the cost of this – not to the violated women, but to the United States:[36]

> Some of this large number have openly boasted, when the lunacy was at its height, that they have removed from fifteen hundred to two thousand ovaries. Assuming that each of these women would have become the mother of three children, we have a direct loss of five hundred and fifty thousand for the first generation and one million six hundred and fifty thousand in the second generation.

Sixteen years later in the title of *The Waste Land* (1922), T. S. Eliot played with the Arthurian legend of the Fisher King, whose wounded genitals blighted the regenerative powers of his kingdom as they damaged his own. Both lay wasted. The poem's opening line, 'April is the cruellest month', makes spring a time not of green abundance but of menace and death. Thus did Eliot diagnose the barrenness of his age, ruined by the senseless slaughter of First World War.

In 2018, the mythological wounds that plague the western world go deeper than a legendary king's genitals. The great mythic – and literal – wound of our age is not to the testicles but to the womb.

In my shell-pink Potts Point studio, I was reading Karl Marx and his contemporary Johann Jakob Bachofen, a Swiss jurist, historian of Roman law and mythographer. I'd discovered

Bachofen in the pages of Oskar Kokoschka's *My Life*. He introduced me to the possibility of ancient cultures ruled by principles of mother right.

Having studied Roman legal texts, Etruscan tombs, ceramics and other materials, Bachofen postulated the existence of prehistoric matriarchal cultures. His mythic views of history were scorned by scholars interested only in a materialist, political-economic approach to the past. But he was taken up by artists, writers, philosophers and poets, among them Engels, Nietzsche and Rilke; he inspired 'searchers of the psyche, and, in fact, anyone aware of the enigmatic influence of symbols in the structuring and moving of lives',[37] as Joseph Campbell put it. Archeologists and anthropologists later found evidence of the matriarchal civilisations Bachofen had deduced, including the cities of Troy and Crete, and hundreds of terracotta figurines of women with pregnant bellies and pendulous breasts.

And Bachofen's view that myth – 'the exegesis of symbol' – was formative in human history is today gaining a new sort of currency with the idea that we are inherently storytelling creatures, an idea which has brought the now ubiquitous belief in the power of stories and narrative, and the view that to change the times we must change the story.

When writing was first used by lawmakers, priests and poets, around 2000 BCE, stories that had been passed down for millennia were recorded. And all of them recount one unvarying myth: a great goddess is separated from her beloved, who dies or appears to die, and falls into the underworld – or winter, a time when light and fertility are dimmed. The goddess descends into the darkness to find her beloved and return him or her to the daylight realm, so life may continue.

This story was changed around 2000 years ago and it seems

that the myth that emerged in its place has a dangerous underbelly: womb bashing. The new myth suppressed the story's female potency – reducing it to a virgin mother – and subverted it with a male god. It retold the ancient story of the cycle of darkness and light, winter and spring, in the form of the Virgin Mary and her son Jesus. Jesus dies and descends into darkness for three days (the number of days of the dark moon). He's then rescued by his father. And as in earlier versions of the myth, his return to daylight coincides with the earth's regeneration. The resurrection of Jesus Christ is winter turning into spring.

Laws that restrict or criminalise abortion and dare to invade bodies capable of bearing new life are rooted in a history of lawmaking that has co-opted the life-giving powers of wombs and installed them in a sky god and his crucified son. As Gloria Steinem said in 2011: 'we got into this jam when some men took control of women's reproductivity . . . man is not god and god is not man and we do not have power over women and nature.'[38]

In an aside, Steinem glossed the architecture of churches where men take over women's power to give birth. They construct buildings with an outer and an inner entrance, a vagina-like aisle, two curved ovarian structures on each side and an altar which is the womb where a miracle takes place. Men in long skirts say: 'You were born of woman in sin, but if you obey the rules of a patriarchal god you will be reborn into the realm of men.' They sprinkle sacred water (birth fluid) over the rebirthed supplicant and say: 'Yes, you can give life. But only we can give eternal life.'

And in return we are plunged into shame and secrecy. US abortion activist and writer Katha Pollitt argues that contemporary opposition to abortion is a reaction to the growing secularisation of American life, to the sexual revolution and to feminism. It's an attempt to suppress 'women gone wild'.

Our potency is formidable – and under threat. No one who

has experienced the labouring womb could ever again consider the so-called 'feminine principle' as passive. The womb is life-giving and life-taking. Every month of our generative lives our wombs prepare for new life. Every month that potential is either fertilised or destroyed. The waxing and waning of life happens daily in our bodies. Life and death are our domain. That is why religions and states are so keen to control us and our wombs.

Acknowledging the real life-giving potential of the womb seems to me a good way of going about life on this Earth. To start changing the story, perhaps we could adopt a metaphor from 12th-century medical practitioner and writer Trota of Salerno. She called menses 'flowers', because 'just as trees do not produce fruit without flowers so women without menses are deprived of the function of conception'.[39] And if menses are flowers, then when we choose to abort a fertilised egg we are surely just plucking unripened fruit and returning it to the great cycle of life.

Emily Maguire
The abortions I have known

Cindy's abortion
An episode of *Family Ties* I haven't seen before is a big deal, because it's the late 1980s and afternoon TV is basically just a repeated loop of the show. But here's something I've missed (or been guarded from) in previous cycles: Mallory's friend Cindy is pregnant and since she can't talk to her own strict mother she talks to Mallory's progressive, supportive dream mum Elise instead. Cindy tells Elise she doesn't know whether to have an abortion. Says it out loud. Using the actual word and everything. I remember so clearly because I had never heard it from the mouth of someone considering it (rather than preaching against it) before.

I think Cindy is terrible for being pregnant and for considering killing her baby and for saying it out loud like it's *fine*. I think Mallory is pretty terrible, too, for being friends with someone like that. And I can't understand why Elise doesn't explain how wrong it is to murder babies and how every time you sin it's like you're hammering the nails into Jesus' flesh all over again.

The episode ends with Cindy going home to talk things through with her mum and we never find out what happens to her poor innocent little baby. I watch and watch and watch every time the show is on (so, all the time) but nobody ever refers to Cindy again. My best guess is she had the abortion and died in a pool of blood and it's too sad to speak about. Mallory probably prays each night for the souls of Cindy and her unborn baby, but prayer is a private conversation between a person and God so it makes sense the audience never sees that.

Annie's abortion

Natalie is not my favourite character on my favourite show, *Facts of Life* (that would be Jo, swoon) but she's the one I relate to the most. Like me, she's chubby. Like me, she wants to be a writer. When I'm a teenager like her, I want to be editor of my school paper, like she is. (I don't understand that the shitty suburban public high school I attend will not have a newspaper, only a semi-regular newsletter warning parents of nit outbreaks and drug rings.)

So, Natalie is a good girl, but this one time she does something bad: she invents a story about someone at her school having an abortion just so she can write an edgy story that will get lots of attention. Problem is, someone at her school actually did have an abortion and now that girl, Annie, thinks she's been busted. Meanwhile the headmaster, Mr Parker, is threatening Natalie with expulsion if she doesn't reveal her source. Should she reveal she made it all up (humiliating) or give up Annie's secret (mean)? She decides on the first option and loses her job on the paper but this is fair enough, because she lied and there have to be consequences for that. There are no consequences for Annie, though, which seems outrageous to me.

But what really gets me is that the episode finishes with this line from smug Mr Parker: 'I know this school and I know these girls,' he says. 'Something like this could never happen here.'

Natalie's sad, knowing expression and the audience's snickering combine to create a pocket of worry in my chest. I am a Christian and only associate with other Christians. If one of them had an abortion, her shame and grief would show all over her face. She would cry all the time and maybe even go a bit mad and start ranting. She might become a drug addict or worse! (I don't know what is worse, but it's something our youth leaders refer to a lot: becoming a drug addict or worse. I take them at their word.) Point is, I'd know.

Or in thinking I'd know, I'd be Mr Parker. Who is wrong.

Erica's abortion

I'm not really supposed to be watching *Degrassi High* because it is about and for teenagers and although I am (barely) one myself my parents would like me not to be. Or not to be the kind that you find in a famously frank and controversial Canadian drama series. The kind like Erica who loses her virginity to a boy she barely knows and ends up pregnant.

In one scene, Erica's English class is debating abortion (because the teacher wanted to 'get them talking', no matter what they're talking about, which is the opposite of my English teacher who insists on silence, even for those of us bursting with nerdy excitement for the prescribed text). As opinions about women's bodily autonomy and foetal rights fly around the room, Erica sits, silent. Nobody realises that the points they're flinging are smashing painfully into her morning-sickness-weakened, terrified self.

I feel sad for her as she wilts under all those beliefs and opinions. But it's her twin sister Heather I agree with. Abortion is not to be contemplated, no matter what. 'It's horrible to think of all those babies dying every day in the killing centres,' Heather says, face contorting in disgust.

Except by the second half of the double-episode, Heather decides her sister, while wrong, deserves her support. She turns up just as Erica is approaching the clinic and the two of them fight through the shouty crowd of anti-abortion protestors together. I keep hoping they'll stop and listen to the (admittedly very creepy) lady with the tiny unborn baby doll, that they'll turn and go home and ask their parents for help and pray for forgiveness, which is definitely what I would insist on doing if one of my sisters was ever stupid enough to end up in that position. But they don't, and I find it tragic. Not only will the baby be murdered, but both girls are destined for hell because being silent in the face of murder is the same as doing it according to Jesus.

The Cider House Rules abortions
This book is inappropriate for someone my age, a teacher who sees me carrying it tells me, which of course makes me more excited to read it. When it turns out that the inappropriate content is a bunch of graphic, brutal, genuinely horrifying abortion scenes, I keep reading anyway because I'd rather have nightmares for months than admit a teacher was right.

There's one woman whose self-administered abortion has caused her internal organs to putrefy, leaving her with intestines like 'fragile jelly'. She's better off than her daughter, whose botched abortion kills her. Another post-abortion woman is suffering 'sepsis and putrefaction ... strong enough to gag' the doctor leaning over her.

I know things are different now. They're different even in the world of that book, so long as the principled, medically trained abortionist Dr Larch does the job. But for so long afterwards, whenever I hear the word abortion, it's the gag-inducing putrefaction and the jellied insides that I think about.

Judy's abortion

My favourite *21 Jump Street* character, Judy Hoffs, is undercover at a high school to investigate threats made against the in-school reproductive counselling clinic by a radical anti-abortion activist group. (An in-school clinic? The nearest thing my school has is Damo who always has condoms on hand, albeit to fill with water and chuck at passing girls.) When the clinic is bombed, Rebecca, a pregnant teenager contemplating an abortion, is injured and miscarries. Visiting Rebecca in the hospital, Judy admits that she herself had an abortion years ago and doesn't regret it.

I am haunted by this episode for months. I am not yet sexually active. No boy has ever asked me out. I've never so much as given or received a flirty look. Nevertheless, every cell of my rapidly changing body screams that I will be having all kinds of sex very soon. Although I'm still a Christian and so don't believe in sex outside of marriage, I really don't feel I have a choice. Fish gotta swim, bird gotta fly.

But if something went wrong and I ended up pregnant, would I be able to do what Judy did, have an abortion and move on with my life, no regrets? I love Judy *so much*, but the thought of terminating a pregnancy just because it's inconvenient seems repulsive to me. Not as repulsive as bombing people, or even standing outside a clinic screaming at scared teenage girls, but not far behind.

That's the other thing that haunts me: even if I could decide on abortion, if I could thoroughly convince myself that I would suffer neither guilt for the rest of my life, nor hellfire for my entire afterlife, would I be brave enough to go through with it? I already knew that women died in bloody agony during and after abortions, but now I also had anti-abortion terrorists to worry about.

Penny's abortion

In *Dirty Dancing*, the movie which I watch every day over the summer holidays, whose dialogue I can recite and whose dance moves I practice until I am more sweat than girl, dance instructor Penny has to have an abortion because she will lose her job if management find out she is pregnant. But the 'doctor' she goes to is a 'butcher with a folding table and a dirty knife,' who uses no anaesthetic and sends Penny away doubled over in pain and gushing with blood. Only the fast intervention of Dr Houseman, summoned by his daughter Baby, saves Penny's life.

A friend's mum, watching the movie with us one afternoon, pauses it to give us a lecture about how bad things were back when abortion was illegal. My friend and I roll our eyes at each other and giggle because what else are you meant to do when an adult talks earnestly about uterine injuries and wire shoved up vaginas? But in bed that night I think about what she said: what happened to Penny happened because the law was brutal and unfair and allowed charlatans to prey on vulnerable women. It wasn't because she'd had sex or because she hadn't wanted a baby. She had done nothing wrong. And since the law here and now was better, if I ever did that same thing that wasn't wrong,

I wouldn't have to face the dirty knife, the folding table, the butcher. No jellied insides or peritonitis or septic stink.

Still, I think, it's cool that abortion is safer now but why should it even need to be? How dumb do you have to be to let yourself get pregnant in this day and age when you can get condoms for two bucks from public toilet vending machines? I already have a small stockpile in the inside compartment of my school bag. I've already practised how to say *If it's not on, it's not on* so it sounds sexily ironic, but so the boy also knows I totally mean it.

I will never be like Baby, who, only moments after leaving the bedside of haemorrhaging Penny, runs and seduces Johnny Castle without a moment's pause to talk about, let alone procure, contraception. If seeing a woman almost die from the consequences of unprotected sex doesn't slow her roll, well, maybe Baby isn't quite as clever as the movie keeps telling us she is.

Very soon after, I discover I'm not so clever either. Or I am, and Baby is, but when you've got hungry eyes and a feelin' that won't subside, well, you could be right in the middle of a goddamn maternity ward and it'd seem like all those screaming women and bawling babies had nothing at all to do with the magic happening between you and your Johnny.

Andrea's (non) abortion

Andrea in *Beverly Hills 90210* (which I watch religiously but pretend not to, because: *dork*) is unexpectedly pregnant. Her boyfriend Jesse loves her, he says, but if she has the abortion she wants, he won't ever see her again. Recently, I have, myself, been guilty of mistaking control for love, but, come on, this is a clear-cut case. Andrea can't see it, though. Again with the allegedly smart girl acting dumb as a box of hair when it comes to love and sex.

So Andrea cries a lot while Jesse stays away. After making her suffer for a while he rides his high horse around to her place and tells her he forgives her. She tells him she hasn't done it yet. She suddenly doesn't want to! Just like that! They kiss and decide to get married. Happily ever after, I guess, but fuck. Andrea and the kid are looking at a lifetime of 'I'm not telling you what to do but if you don't do what I want I'm gone' bullshit now. You'd think some of her friends would be pointing out the whole emotional manipulation thing, but no, they whoop with joy and pretend that breadsticks are cigars. Bunch of arseholes, for real.

Nora's abortion

I buy *Tirra Lirra by the River* at a second-hand book shop for $1 and am excited to find it is about being a woman wanting to make art, which is what I am, I think. Maybe. Early on, the narrator Nora is told a story about Sydney's 'abortion car' which 'collected that day's batch' of pregnant women 'every Monday and Wednesday and sometimes Thursday from Doctor So-and-so's rooms in Macquarie Street, opposite the Botanical Gardens' before driving them to the eastern suburbs for the procedure. The whole thing was 'as easy as puff'.

When Nora needs such a service, however, she's living in London where 'abortion was a matter of whispers, danger and solemn secrecy'. With the help of her friend Olive, she manages to get an appointment with a doctor who doesn't use anaesthetic and speaks to her 'with an almost wild contempt . . . "Stop that noise. Don't tell me it hurts. Of course it hurts. You were willing enough to have the fun, weren't you? Oh, yes! But now you're groaning because it hurts. Hurts! You women. You make me sick, the whole rotten lot of you. There's only one sure way to avoid pregnancy, but oh no, you haven't the decency for that."'

I would have agreed with him once. I mean, I would always have detested him for his cruelty and would once have detested him for his work, but this idea that if you want to have sex you need to be prepared for the ultimate consequence – well, I use to think that, sincerely and righteously. I can't identify a moment when that belief changed, but reading this scene now I am overcome with rage.

Days after her abortion, Nora is bleeding so heavily she has a 'flooded bed', a 'spoilt mattress to be paid for'. Still, though, 'very frightened', Nora says she is 'prepared to die rather than submit myself to medical examination. I mean that quite literally: I was prepared to die.' I know it's an old book but I want to find the doctor who made her feel that way and run him through with a sword. I want to burn down the British Houses of Parliament and the Australian ones while I'm at it. Prepared to die, she said. I can't bear it. I can't.

Emily's abortion

It's funny how life sometimes is exactly like TV. The missed period ignored because you're not that regular anyway. The tiredness and soreness, explained by working hard and partying harder. But then you're in the midst of ringing up a sale and you have to abandon the register before you fill the cash drawer with vomit. And there you are, having an out-of-body experience in the Westfield dunnies. Look at her, this smart girl who's done something so stupid. Look at her, not even able to realise her predicament in any kind of interesting way. Dumb, embarrassing cliché, from the bile dripping down her chin to the dramatic clutching of her terrifyingly inhabited middle.

Unlike any of the women I've seen spewing their way into pregnancy awareness on a screen, I do not have one second of doubt about what to do. The only TV character I identify with right now is the trapped wolf in a nature documentary I watched when I was too drunk to sleep one night last month. The wolf that chewed off its own leg to escape the steel claw. I think of the bare, jagged bone stabbing the snow. The way the wolf whimpered but didn't hesitate, kept moving.

As my school friend's mum once told me I should be, I am grateful abortion is (sort of) legal and that organising it is, with the help of the Yellow Pages, a shopping centre phone booth and a pocket full of change, simple enough. But I know – know in my marrow, in a way I've never known anything before – that I'd do it anyway, anyhow. I would, if it came to it, die trying.

Unlike Erica, I do not tell either of my sisters, let alone ask them to support me on the day. Not that they would do a Heather and lecture me about murder and hell. But one is still a little kid and the other has just announced her pregnancy – a wanted baby, a cause for celebration. If I carry to term, we will make cousins so close in age they could be twins.

Like Cindy, I don't want to talk to my mother. Unlike her, I don't capitulate. I don't talk to a friend's mum, either. Or anyone older than me. I know I should have been more adult than to have got into his situation. I cannot let the real adults know of my mistake.

On the day of my appointment my boyfriend and I call in sick to work and he drives me to the place on the other side of Sydney. The clinic is in an old, fancy-looking house in a leafy, rich neighbourhood. To my enormous relief the street is empty. I will not have to fight my way through protestors bearing posters of dismembered foetuses, like Erica and Rebecca and Judy did. At the front door, I identify myself to an intercom and though I am buzzed in without fuss, the very presence of the security camera and deadbolts make me think about the explosion in *21 Jump Street* and I start shaking.

I am forced to speak to a counsellor before anything else can happen. I don't know if this is because I'm shaking a lot or if it's normal procedure. I tell the woman across from me that I already know everything she's going to say and what I'd like is to skip the chat and get right to the surgery. As I'm saying it I remember that Andrea said something exactly like this to her pre-abortion counsellor, but they made her wait, and her douche boyfriend got in her head and now she's bloody marrying him. I tell the counsellor that if I don't get the abortion today I will resort to measures I've read about in old books. She smiles, like I'm making a joke, and tells me that won't be necessary, I'm all ready to go in.

We've had a hard time coming up with the money and so I am getting the cheaper procedure. The nurse checks that I understand that I will be awake throughout, that the anaesthetic will be local, that I may experience discomfort or even a bit of pain. Yes, I say, I know. I know how it'll be.

Why did I think that? Given that the abortions I'd seen and read about were illegal ones performed by misogynist, punishing butchers and the fictional ones that weren't that, the ones that were, like mine, legal(ish) and performed by kind, gentle medical professionals had never been shown at all? Why did I think I knew anything at all about how it would be?

I didn't know you could be in this much pain and still conscious. I use all of my courage and energy to ask if something is wrong. *Everything's fine*. I ask if I can have more anaesthetic and someone tells me it's nearly over. I sob that it hurts a lot. *It'll hurt less if you relax* they say, which is what everyone said about first-time sex. It was impossible to test the theory then, even more so now. I flash back to the wolf, her mouth dripping with blood and bits of her own leg and think *bitch you have no fucking idea.*

At least, I think later in the recovery room, I didn't have a doctor like Nora's. At least when I said it hurts I was only told to relax and not to *stop that noise*. I wasn't told that I deserved the pain, that I made him sick and had no decency. Poor Nora.

I know she isn't real, but she and the other made-up foetus-expellers are all I have. I am the only person I know who has been through this.

In the weeks following I amend the thought: I am the only person I know *that I know* has been through this. I realise that when it comes to abortion I have never stopped being the headmaster from *Facts of Life*. Even when *I* was Annie, my inner Mr Parker insisted that girls who had abortions could be easily identified from the outside. I was sure that what I'd done must be written all over my face. I was sure, when people talked about abortion in the abstract, that they were talking to me, personally.

Who else felt the same way, I wonder? How many of us sure of our uniqueness in having knowledge about which we could not speak?

Sue's abortion

In Hilary Mantel's *Experiments in Love*, set fifty years ago on the other side of the world, there is a conversation about abortion that echoes one happening right around me. Claire, a first-year university student in London, warns that if her friend Sue has an abortion 'it could do her endless damage . . . Endless,' she repeats. 'Psychological. Damage.'

The narrator agrees, deferring 'to the pieties of the age' but secretly she 'couldn't think what damage would be greater than that inflicted by an innocent wailing itself into the world, from between my unprepared thighs'.

It's what I want to say every time the discussion of psychological damage caused by abortion comes up. The closest I've ever come is to say that I imagine for others the damage caused by forced pregnancy and childbirth would be worse. Behind gritted teeth are words I can't let out: *I would have chewed off my own arm. I was prepared to die. It was hard and it hurt and I would make the same choice again in a heartbeat.*

Xiomara and Paula and Ruth and Olivia and Mimi-Rose and Cristina's abortions

Recently there's been a real change in fictional portrayals of abortion. I'm happy that today the fictional friends helping a girl in my situation understand her predicament would be Xiomara (*Jane the Virgin*), Paula (*Crazy Ex-girlfriend*), Ruth (*Glow*), Olivia (*Scandal*), Mimi-Rose (*Girls*) and Cristina (*Grey's Anatomy*). All of whom have abortions and are fine. Not that their choices are uncomplicated, necessarily, or without conflict or sadness or pain, but there is no haemorrhaging or septicaemia or gushing blood, no bombs or gruesome posters or abusive doctors. There is, in the end, calm and clarity that the woman has made a choice that is best for her and her life at that time.

And unlike earlier abortions on screen, none of these is presented as the defining feature of a character or the most important event in her story arc. The abortion is a single slender plot thread in a long, rich, complicated story. From where I stand, over twenty years after my abortion, it's this that feels radically, wonderfully true to life.

Zoya Patel

Provision: an interview with Dr Kamala Emanuel

Dr Kamala Emanuel, an experienced women's health practitioner who has been providing abortions since the late 1990s, began her interaction with abortion clinics on the other side of the fence, as a protestor.

'My first ever political activity was standing outside the abortion clinic in Tweed Heads with a bunch of other people with signs,' Dr Emanuel admits. 'I was there with my mum, and we wanted to *save babies*.'

Dr Emanuel's voice rises here, her pitch indicating how silly she now feels about this idea of anti-abortion protestors trying to save the innocent souls of unborn children – this is clearly no longer her position today.

'We actually didn't like the way other people were harassing the women going in, and we both decided never to do that again.'

This conservative start is quite an anomaly in Dr Emanuel's career since. Today, she is a well-known voice in socialist politics, having run for the Socialist Alliance for the seat of McConnell in the 2017 Queensland election. Her platform was based on legalising abortion and making it freely available in the public health system, as well as addressing climate change.

So what makes someone go from physically protesting abortions to training to provide them herself?

'In the middle of my medical degree, I had conversations with people about things like women's liberation and poverty, and the environment and so forth. And I shifted quite a lot, and came to embrace the idea that we actually need, women actually need, to achieve our rights. We've still got a long way to go,' Dr Emanuel says.

When she speaks, her passion for this issue is very evident, and I can almost imagine her political awakening, not dissimilar to my own (although I was a teenager when feminism first revolutionised my way of thinking). I know it must have been a difficult transition to unpick her long-held beliefs, and consider the world through this different lens – a lens that takes the onus off the individual and instead looks at our societal structures and systems that rely on inequality to serve the mainstream and oppress the marginalised.

'A lot of things changed for me in a relatively short period. My whole identity had been constructed around my Christian beliefs. I saw myself as a Christian before anything else – gender, class, race, nationality, age or whatever,' Dr Emanuel says. 'When, from a scientific point of view, I could no longer believe in the tenets of the evangelical Christianity to which I had adhered (primarily the literal resurrection of Jesus and the existence of God), I had to be honest with myself and give it up. But I didn't want to. I remember a period in which I felt as if I'd been torn into a million pieces and was waiting for the dust of myself to settle, to find out what remained of who I am.'

This change, of course, affected Dr Emanuel's views on a wide range of issues, abortion rights being one of the last that she contended with. Although it was one of the more challenging issues to grapple with, reproductive rights were ultimately what she decided to dedicate her life to.

'I'd reached a point where I believed I could respect whatever reproductive choice a woman was making, and wanted to be part of providing technically excellent, compassionate and dignified care.'

Perhaps one of the most frustrating things for women's health practitioners to reckon with is the political pressure put upon a service that they feel should not be political – a woman's right to control her body.

Part of what motivates Dr Emanuel is the anger she feels at the way the medical institution controls women's bodies, and how that power imbalance is reified by the structures of the industry.

'I actually really think there is a need for us, from whatever position we occupy, to try to dismantle the unequal power between doctors and patients and between women and men,' Dr Emanuel says. 'And that's what made me decide, yep, I'm going to provide abortions, that's what I'm going to do. And I haven't always been in situations where I've been able to provide abortions, but that has always been work that I have sought.'

This is a bold step for a woman who is already pushing boundaries just by practising medicine, which is still a male-dominated field. In some ways, the prestige associated with being a doctor is negated by choosing to work exclusively on women's health.

Why does this dissonance exist, between the noble field of medicine, and the provision of abortions, or contraceptive services for women? Why is there still such societal distaste for women's rights to control their wombs and what occupies them?

Growing up in Australia, I can reflect on the education I was provided on my reproductive capabilities, and notice how the uterus, ovaries and vagina were all discussed and referred to as being somehow separate from the woman.

Periods are something we 'get', or 'have', not something we 'do'. There is a squeamishness towards this essential part of a woman's reproductive cycle that means that as young women, we are taught to fear our period becoming public knowledge, through a leak onto our clothes or from the discovery of pads and tampons in our school bags.

I still remember catching a bus with boys from a local private school, who would raid our bags for sanitary items, and then scribble on them with red textas and throw them out the bus windows at passing cars. Those boys couldn't think of anything more gross than a pad or tampon – they would squeal as they unwrapped the items from their liners, and toss them from person to person, revelling in the pseudo intimacy of touching something that was intended to then touch female genitals.

I learned to fear my body from my first sexual education class. I feared that this onset of reproductive power, the moment my body would betray me by bleeding, would limit me through this act – no swimming for a week, no praying in my Muslim household, no speaking about it in front of my male relatives.

This fear was extended as I grew older. For years, I was told to fear ever becoming pregnant. Pregnancy would steer me off the correct path for an unwed young woman, I was told by every piece of culture I consumed. It was a message repeated at me from the books I read, where young, unmarried women were shunned and turned out of their homes for being pregnant. It was a message reinforced by news stories about teenage mothers, depicted as wayward and unable to care for a child, continue their education or contribute to society.

But just as pregnancy was feared and maligned in young women, outside the bounds of a societally approved marriage, our solution to crisis pregnancies was equally maligned. The only thing worse than a teenage mother was a teenager who had an abortion.

Despite the fact that our inability to terminate unwanted pregnancies has been the historical cause of so much suffering – women forced to give birth and have their children taken for adoption immediately, young mothers' homes in the UK hiding pregnant girls in shame, attempts at self-terminating pregnancies resulting in death – now that we have medically safe methods of abortion, the stigma still continues.

Dr Emanuel can remember her early days practising as a GP and seeking education on how to provide abortions. It was a hard road, and one mostly travelled alone, despite the historical gains that had so recently been made.

'By the time I was starting out, the trail had already been blazed as far as regards working as a GP with a focus on women's health. In Newcastle, there was the Hunter Working Women's Centre, and in inner western Sydney, the Leichhardt Women's Health Centre. Leichhardt had, I believe, been set up in the early days of the women's health movement that grew out of the feminist radicalisation of the 1970s. It may have been the first of its kind in Australia – certainly one of the first,' Dr Emanuel says. 'So, one element of starting out was an awareness of taking part in a movement to empower women as patients, to approach healthcare as a partner. I felt a strong connection with the ethos of dismantling some of the unequal power that exists in our whole society, from a little space in the institution of medicine, with its patriarchal history. That was extremely satisfying.'

But even with this strong foundation, there were very few paths available when it came to gaining the technical skills required to provide abortions and after-care.

'As a medical student, intern and resident, there was no opportunity to learn in the university or public hospital system of Newcastle where I trained and first worked and lived,' Dr Emanuel says. 'So, early on, when it came to pursuing work focused on abortion provision, I felt somewhat isolated. I'm not sure whether that was a typical experience. I had strong women peers who it was great to have connections with. But although there were pathways to working in women's health that involved GP training, sexual health medicine and/or obstetrics/gynaecology training, without a clear path directly into abortion care, it felt like I was on my own in the path to get the skills for the work I wanted to do.'

This was further exacerbated by the fact that many GP practices created additional barriers for the provision of abortions, even when it was legal in the state.

'Some GPs are told by the owners of the practice where they work – whether as trainees, or as independent practitioners – that they are not allowed to provide medical abortions. It may be an attempt by anti-abortion practice owners to enforce their views. It may be a concern that if the practice gets known as being a place where abortion is offered, there will be some kind of retribution organised by people who oppose abortion.'

There is a religious undertone to the anti-abortion movement, of course. There is a focus on the innocence of a child, and the erroneous assumption that a foetus within the early stages of pregnancy is the equivalent of a living, breathing child. There is also the continuation of the devaluing of women's lives, a trope that has been present in both Judeo-Christian religions and in secular western society for centuries.

A woman seeking an abortion is not worthy of the life she is seeking to protect – her own. Instead, from the moment of conception, the life inside her is more important than hers – it is pure despite her sins.

Ironically, a woman's life is only truly valuable when she is still inside the womb – once in the world, her body is again a vessel for society's opinions, not her own choices.

This attitude is deeply ingrained in the medical institution, according to Dr Emanuel, so much so that even if a woman requires an abortion due to a spontaneous miscarriage, she may be refused in some Australian states.

'The textbook treatment of someone who's having a spontaneous miscarriage, if they're still bleeding and it's not complete, is to offer them either wait and see and let your body do it, or surgery, or medication to help the uterus sufficiently empty more quickly. And they're all reasonable things to choose, but the textbook approach is the pregnant person gets to decide,' Dr Emanuel explains.

But until recently, abortion was illegal in Queensland, where she practises, and the attitude towards women's health was mired in anti-abortion rhetoric.

'It's "oh well, we don't do that here. Unless you're bleeding too much, just take the pain relief and go away".'

Present in this thinking is the ongoing stigmatisation of women's bodies, and the reinforcing of pain and fear as the natural outcomes of our reproductive systems. Just as we're made to fear falling pregnant when society deems us unsuitable for raising children, we're made to fear our inability to conceive when we are finally allowed to actively attempt pregnancy.

A miscarriage is a feared outcome, and infertility signifies a failure as a woman. There is no way to keep our wombs separate from public opinion, and no way to take control of our sexuality and reproductive rights without judgement.

This lack of autonomy extends even to the use of contraception. Dr Emanuel remembers some of her early patients, all of whom came from different walks of life and who had found their way to her clinic through different pathways but who were ultimately seeking some control in a situation of crisis.

One patient that particularly sticks in her mind is a woman in her early middle-age, who had made the choice not to use contraception, knowing that abortion was an option should she have an unwanted pregnancy. This woman had made an informed decision – she knew she infrequently had penetrative sex with men, and that the possible side effects of the contraceptive choices that were available outweighed her risk of pregnancy. Yet, despite having considered this deeply and made a choice for her own body, to seek an abortion having deliberately chosen not to take contraceptive measures is largely seen as grossly irresponsible by our society.

For Dr Emanuel, this case is particularly important because it reinforces the need for us to review the way we talk about contraception, especially in relation to abortion.

'Most people would prefer to avoid crisis pregnancy, and termination of pregnancy does have real (though few) risks and costs. But contraception is not without risks and costs – whether these are the risks of pregnancy or the risks of heart attack, blood clot, stroke, depression, suicide, menstrual pain or acne. And it seems to me that we need to be better at recognising that contraception is voluntary – and of course do everything to offer good care, information and access to ensure that people can find and use what's best for them.'

The overwhelming problem at the crux of how we address reproductive rights is the constant moralising of women's decisions. Contraception is good, but abstinence is better, and abortion is always wrong – the result of irresponsibility on the woman's part, with no mention of the man who inevitably contributed to the pregnancy.

It is this moralising that means that abortion providers play multiple roles.

'I feel as though my role in relation to abortion has several facets. There's the obvious one – the direct care of patients that I've spoken of. Then there's my activist role, as a feminist, something I'd do regardless of whether or not I was a doctor or abortion provider, a political campaigner as a woman and feminist, believing excellent care is our right,' Dr Emanuel says. 'And then as a doctor, I have a role teaching other doctors, in the hope of provoking a self-critical approach to judgementalism and bias, and looking for ways to be at least professional and better yet, compassionate, when it comes to working with women and pregnant people facing a crisis pregnancy.

'I would extend this to contraception too, and the recognition that there is no one-size-fits-all when it comes to contraception, and what matters is not what we do in our personal lives, what contraceptive decisions we make or think we might make in someone else's position – it's their values, experiences and framework that we should be supporting with information to facilitate decision-making that's best for them.

'And finally, there's a role as an abortion and contraception provider, in contributing to the public debates about abortion and contraception, from a technically accurate and well-informed perspective.'

These positions are not lightly held, and require a commitment that goes beyond medical training, and instead speaks to the overarching issue of gender equality, women's bodily autonomy, and the role that medicine can play in empowering patients. Dr Emanuel is one woman, making a big impact in abortion provision – in the decades that she has been practising, some legal reform has already taken place. Now, the battle is one of cultural norms and expectations. In this, she is not fighting alone.

Maxine Beneba Clarke
Weight

they'll spin you this
and spin you that

and they'll tell you
all these
truths
   bout backyard butcher botch jobs
coat hanger clumsiness
and *girls just like you*
wearing baggy sweaters to conceal their carry
giving birth in some high school bathroom
and just letting that tiny babe turn blue

because what else is a girl
from a god-fearing hail-jesus family
gonna even do

they'll tell you bout girls
as young as pollyanna
bleeding out
and caught
   in catatonia

   they'll sing of way back
before women had rights

neighbourhood girls
jumping high

off kitchen tables
     to bring about blood
climbing top of the stairs
and giving their desperation a mighty shove

yeah we know sister
we already been told all that stuff

and besides

don't no good brown girl wanna show like
some big-belly-jane down the block
whose own mama
can't even say her name
ain't not a one of us
wanna live with the shame
of *slut*

   you got choices now though
the white sister smiles

writing the appointment up

but what none-a them campaigners wanna tell you is
us brown girls didn't need no placards
for them not to want *us* to have kids

family planning

we were always right up front the line for this

if you a brown girl
  with an empty fridge
  and scuffed shoes
then places like this
were built
especially for girls like you
  for slum queen poor girl ghetto trash
brown girls with no man
or a where-he-gone man
or to be honest
any brown man at all

for girls like you
with the getting-big-belly blues
  see
clinics like this
uninvitedly moved in

just set up in our neighbourhoods
led by some rich white girl doctor
in a crisp white coat
straight outta some
    fancy eugenics-lab medical school

saying
> *you don't have to worry no more*
got a choice now sister
we'll take care of you

   help you snuff the future
      yet
   they weren't so worried
bout getting us the vote

and i believe
      in prerogative
but the history of it

y'know

approach the steps

push past the old lady
with the wild grey hair
and wide-sad eyes
cradling plastic foetus
howling *save your baby sister*

   with an eerie smile

like maybe if she stop enough of us
she gonna wail herself back
and save hers in time

want your body back
too young don't got no money didn't

love him anyway your family don't know and
how you think you gonna feed it anyhow

so here you are sister
here you are
   ain't no backyard butcher botch job
coat hanger clumsiness
wearing baggy sweaters to conceal your carry
giving birth in some high school bathroom
and just letting your tiny brown babe turn blue
   nah
it's just history
and you

Amy Gray
Against choice

For a suburb right on the city's doorstep, East Melbourne is set in a perpetual doze. While office workers may shuttle through its wide terrace-framed streets on weekdays and it may endure the occasional weekend throng of sports fans, the rest of the time East Melbourne is a languid wave of old people lingering over cream cakes in cafes or standing in line to pick up parcels at the post office.

Back when I lived in East Melbourne, the only murmur of activity to spike the gentility came from shuffling protestors outside a townhouse, noticeable only because it hadn't become a block of apartments. Known as the Fertility Control Clinic, it has been the face of the state's abortion debate since opening in 1972 as Australia's first private abortion clinic.

Each weekday morning as people made their way to work, a small group gathered outside the clinic. As patients approached the building, anti-abortion protesters swarmed them. 'Consider your baby' they'd plead.

These were the days when the group were not constrained by buffer zone laws to protect women from harassment or being filmed. This buffer zone was simply a line painted on the pavement, dividing it in two – one side for pedestrians, patients and security staff, and the other side for the protesters.

Back then, the group, Helpers of God's Precious Infants, would always attend from early morning to early afternoon in shifts, mirroring when patients were admitted for a wide range of procedures (not just abortions). While some made the occasional detour to the laneways to pray loudly, most of the protestors clustered in front of the building, ready to cross the line and interrupt any woman walking up Wellington Parade.

The line became an enduring metaphor for abortion: it was a line the protesters would constantly cross, refusing to acknowledge that they were bound to rules as they waved placards and brochures. It was a line ignored and rarely enforced by the police or council, who would turn up late if the clinic called for help. It was a line many patients desperately hoped would protect them, but rarely did.

A protester blocked a woman with her family, a small child in a stroller. 'There's another way,' the protester said, holding out a pamphlet.

'I have cancer,' the mother shouted as her husband shielded her on their walk in.

Pam, the protester, shrugged, simultaneously confused and upset that someone would consider her rude. She tutted and huffed repeatedly, before launching into a stream rationalising her hurt. 'I just offered a bit of assistance . . . and she said it's cancer, well, why would she be going in there, why wouldn't she be going into a proper hospital, she's going to abort and that's what it's all about . . . she got nasty.'

Malcolm,* another protester, agreed. 'We see this as a killing factory . . . nobody should be supporting an organisation like that, an organisation that kills innocent children.' I point out that, as well as abortions, the clinic provides counselling, STI testing, pap smears, contraceptives and vasectomies.

He disagreed with the list of services the clinic provides. 'It's like saying – and I know people don't like us using the comparison – but it's like saying in the gas chambers in Nazi Germany they might be exterminating hundreds of Jews and others every day but they're giving a nice bath to some people so I think we should support them.'

Motioning to the clinic over the walls, Malcolm said, 'this place has killed over a third of a million babies since 1973. I've been involved since the 1970s in this cause – they don't deny it – and Bert Wainer who was the so-called abortion law reformer boasted that back in the early days he performed fifty abortions a day.'

When asked to back up his calculations, Malcolm said, 'I've had big signs saying "over 250,000 abortions performed here" and they haven't denied it.' To Malcolm, who claims to be trained in economics, this makes it true.

As members of the international Helpers of God's Precious Infants (HOGPI), both Pam and Malcolm are part of a campaign to recriminalise abortion in Victoria. They hold 'prayer vigils' around abortion clinics and outside parliament on sitting days to raise awareness for their cause.

Though many would argue that prayer vigils are a form of harassment, Malcolm believes their tactic of approaching patients outside the clinic has drastically reduced the number of abortions.

'We've been counting roughly the number of girls who go in there first thing in the morning. We know the numbers have declined since we started coming here twenty years ago … and probably nearly halved … it's an average of sixteen now.' This seems less an indication of HOGPI's prayer power than it does the easier access to contraception and abortion procedures throughout Melbourne.

Malcolm disputes this, quoting numbers he can never quite source. 'We've helped over 300 girls from this clinic in the last nineteen years who we've helped through their pregnancy.'

When asked how they get the funds, Malcolm says, 'we help them with thousands of dollars … we have hundreds of supporters. Whenever we have a family or single mother who has serious financial problems … we have an appeal.'

According to Malcolm, their assistance can involve making large purchases on the woman's behalf. 'We help them with cars,' he says. 'Even now, we're helping a woman get a car because her current car is a bomb that doesn't have air conditioning or power steering.'

I have been unable to find anyone who can corroborate that they cancelled an abortion because of HOGPI's influence, or received ongoing financial or personal assistance from them.

Torrey Orton, a psychologist who volunteers as a clinic defender, laughs at any notion that the group is effective at helping or converting patients. From his observation, 'they have next to zero actual turnarounds. They will claim otherwise,' he says. 'They don't have any [financial] resources to even handle turnarounds. If they did they'd be out of business in a week.'

The group's presence is near universally reviled, yet expected by patients. Susie Allanson, clinical psychologist at the clinic, has witnessed the harassment in different forms – she's had anti-abortion protesters stand in front of her car, or wail up hymns to her consulting rooms from the lane below. Torrey recalls the work involved in getting the protesters to stop approaching patients who are trying to park their cars, and all the attempts to secretly take footage of patients.

While we may think of this as a relatively benign nuisance, there have been times when it has become extreme. Like on 16 July 2001 when Peter Knight (not formally aligned with HOGPI) went to the clinic and shot security guard Stephen Rogers in the chest. Even more disturbing were Knight's grander plans for death and violence. Police found various fuels and lighters, thirty gags, and a scrawled note saying, 'We regret to advise that as the result of a fatal accident involving some members of staff, we have been forced to cancel all appointments today.'

Susie Allanson says patients still turned up the very next morning after the attack to have abortions, thankful that the clinic was still open.

For Lauren, a relatively recent patient of the Fertility Control Clinic, 'I was bracing myself for being bum-rushed but they were fairly feeble actually.'

'They came right up to me and stayed in quite close personal space as I made my way towards the entrance,' she says. 'There was lots of muttered things, hearing bits about god and the baby's right to life and a lot about my options as well. You know, the options not including abortion.'

'I told them to fuck off. I definitely felt the heart racing, and braced myself for a fight. I told them quite loudly and firmly to fuck off. And they didn't let up in the personal space.'

This is the sort of stress that most patients face when they come to the clinic.

For Torrey, this is one of many reasons she volunteers as a clinic defender, standing by the entrance with the security guard and providing a friendly and safe buffer from the protesters, in an attempt to minimise stress for both patients and nearby residents.

Torrey describes the time as 'long periods of nothing happening with short bursts of infractions'. He says it took him a while to realise that his job as a tall, imposingly genial man is to 'just stand there and say hi'.

He realises there is a lot of community support for the clinic and its defenders. Locals wave and greet him, telling him he's a good guy. It's one of many motivations to return. 'We have a lot of fun, we get a lot of positive stuff from the passing public.'

According to Torrey, HOGPI's enduring rhetoric of saving people while waving placards of photoshopped dead foetuses shows a willful ignorance as to how their actions impact others. Perhaps they think they can convert the suburb with their claims that the clinic is a killing factory.

'They think they are not disturbing the patients who are coming along, because they think they are already stressed and that therefore they can't be more stressed though stress is cumulative,' Torrey says. It also suggests that they assume all women are sad to abort.

As a man committed to helping the protesters understand their behaviour, Torrey tried to share the Holmes and Rahe Stress Scale with them, to help them see how their actions cause distress to others, potentially creating 'cognitive revulsion'.

Ultimately, however, he knows the group doesn't really care.

Torrey's unpaid shift begins at 7.30 a.m. until mid-morning, and he always takes on two of the six weekly shifts. That's when patients come in for surgical abortions. Other times, the anti-abortion protesters are either not there or keeping a quiet distance behind the line, praying to themselves.

The HOGPI shift also varies, with different people taking it in turn depending on home, work and protest commitments.

The day I attend to watch, the adult members of HOGPI are busy protesting outside the Victorian Parliament because it's a sitting day, but outside the clinic at 7.30 a.m, two schoolgirls stand against the clinic walls. One is in her school uniform and lets the rosary dangle at her hips. The other, in casual dress, holds a prayer book. Together they recite prayers.

There is no attempt to engage with patients. They are focused on their books. I can't help but wonder if this is a usual before-school visit.

The guard opens up shop for the day. No one comes.

Torrey appears. He is a tall, older gentleman. Self-possessed, good-humoured and matter of fact. The face of someone who has done this all so many times that he is no longer surprised. He scoffs at my high heels and, with the practised eye of a veteran, explains the scene.

'As you can see these are the first players,' he nods to the schoolgirls. 'You can tell by the fact that they're standing there (where they are not supposed to) and they're young.' He walks off to get coffee. He obviously doesn't rate the schoolgirls' ability to interrupt anyone.

When he comes back with his coffee, he watches as a staff member tells the schoolgirls they aren't allowed to stand there and threatens to call the police. Pam, the adult protester who has just arrived, appears to whisper to them that they are okay to stand along the wall. The staff member comes out a second time to let them know they've called the bylaw officers.

Eventually, the girls head to school as Torrey baits them about not understanding the law. The girl in uniform screams at him with the full, heady indignation of adolescence, that she has done nothing wrong and knows her rights. Torrey has an indulgent chuckle as they stomp off.

After the girls leave, Pam is joined by Malcolm. Local residents and workers walk by, smile at Torrey and scowl at the assembled protesters as they pass. They are not held in high regard by anyone other than their own brethren and yet, in the case of Malcolm, they have been coming to protest at the clinic for twenty years on an almost daily basis.

What prompts people to keep coming to an environment that doesn't want them there? For Malcolm, 'It's the most important human rights issue since slavery and treatment of the black people, and this is every bit as bad.'

I'm told that one of the security guards refers to Pam as 'the bulldog' but the day I meet her, I can only think of other protesters I've witnessed who appeared more confrontational and hostile. One clinic defender spent hours trying to talk with her before giving up upon realising, according to Torrey, that 'there was nothing home in there except some verses that came from a bishop's mouth'.

But Pam and Malcolm look like people you'd meet at a neighbour's house. Older, perhaps a bit uneducated, but ultimately trying hard to be friendly, helpful people. And still, they hold out pamphlets that no one wants, record women from cameras hidden in their sleeves, brandish signs that upset patients, and equate abortion clinics with slavery and the Holocaust.

It may be for show, but Pam does appear to be genuinely nervous, not wanting to say anything damaging. She admits to morning nerves. 'I do pray. I ask God for help and to know what to say as well. I do want to be true witnesses here to help these people.'

Talking with Pam, you get the impression she is surprised anew every day that people don't want her help. She carries a slightly stiff, scared air, like she's constantly being yelled at, yet she still comes to the clinic. It confounds me that she's branded 'the bulldog' and is described as tenacious and defensive when it seems obvious she would rather be anywhere else than here.

'They're remarkably fearful for people who are sure they are right,' Torrey observes.

There's a dissonance at play with the pair. Talk with them about cuts to single parents' benefits and they are incensed with the injustice of it all; they effortlessly list the harmful effects of poverty on women and families. Malcolm expands on this to a discussion about charitable work in poorer countries after International Women's Day.

I ask him and Pam about the role reproductive health and choice plays in these regions and suggest that women's health is a priority for the UN.

Pam immediately dismisses the notion. 'I don't think contraception really needs to come into it because it is against what we believe in but we also believe in the Billings Method . . . but I don't think it's been introduced in a lot of third world countries.'

Malcolm quickly interjects to share their joint belief that contraception leads to abortion. His eyes remain steady with the gaze of a believer.

Talking with them and watching their thought processes spasm is like watching a car stall at an intersection. They will make a series of thematically connected statements that give an idea of their ideology but the minute talk turns to abortion, the car stalls – it will not move, its pistons will not fire.

Pam spoke of her nursing days and finding a friend on the ground, doubled over in pain from a backyard abortion. She speaks of love for the girls, supporting them, giving compassion, her anger over cuts to single parenting payments. Yet she can't comprehend the vital importance of safe reproductive health and choice for women. 'I really love these girls with my heart and I feel for them all the time.' You don't doubt the love she feels.

Pam tells me later, 'We like to offer assistance but that gentleman got verbally abusive to me. We're here to assist the girls.'

But how do visceral pictures meant to show aborted foetuses help women? 'We do have pictures of aborted babies sometimes and just seeing that picture has caused a few girls to change their mind.'

Malcolm pauses to think it over. 'We don't always have that picture showing but we probably should.'

For Pam and Malcolm, it is their single most important issue. Malcolm says that, 'this is the most important issue for me because it's a human rights issue. If you're not alive, all other rights are meaningless.'

*Malcolm's name changed at his request

Melanie Cheng

A test unlike any other

When I order a test on a patient, I usually have a pretty good idea what the patient wants the result to be. They don't want cancer. They don't want a fracture. They don't want high cholesterol or diabetes. Not so with the pregnancy test. Unlike other investigations in medicine, the result does not indicate the presence or absence of disease. Sometimes I have no idea how a woman is going to react. I once informed a patient that her pregnancy test was 'negative' only to have her look at me with a blank face – *what, exactly, is your idea of a negative result?* her expression seemed to say.

People like absolutes. I've heard colleagues joke that 'you can't be a little bit pregnant'. But I would argue that you can. With my first pregnancy, I walked into my ten-week antenatal appointment happily pregnant, only to walk out, an hour later, with one less heartbeat. At five weeks I'd had what the medical profession refers to as a *missed abortion*. For over a month I'd gone about my daily business believing my baby was doubling in size inside me, when in reality, my baby wasn't growing at all. My hormone levels had dropped and the foetal heart had stopped beating, but I'd had no bleeding. My body had not yet done what it should have done. There was still a small sac clinging to my uterus. I was in a state of limbo somewhere between pregnancy and non-pregnancy – a half-pregnancy, if you will. The procedure I later underwent to empty the contents of my uterus – a dilation and curettage – is strikingly similar to a surgical termination of pregnancy.

Pregnancy tests mean different things to different women. I can see one patient on her seventh cycle of IVF for whom a negative pregnancy test is the final, brutal blow in a long battle with infertility, and fifteen minutes later I can come face to face with a university student for whom an unexpected pregnancy signifies an abrupt end to all of her hopes and dreams. Emotions run high and they're not always what I, or even the woman, expect them to be. A patient can miscarry while waiting for a termination and feel profoundly sad about her loss – the outcome may be the same, but the decision has been taken out of her hands. The miscarriage, like the pregnancy before it, is a reminder of her lack of control in matters of life and death.

The decision to proceed with a termination is rarely an easy one. A lot of women keep it a secret. Many worry about complications. Some agonise that when they are finally ready to start a family, they'll be unable to achieve one. They fear punishment through some terrible and ironic twist of fate.

In 2018, pregnancy and motherhood still loom large in our collective conscience. For many, pregnancy maintains its long-held status as something spiritual and mystical. This was never more evident to me than during my own two pregnancies.

I was shocked by the amount of unsolicited attention and advice I received from complete strangers. People came up to me in the supermarket and rubbed their hands all over my belly. Patients predicted the sex of my unborn child based on how much weight I was carrying. Most people meant well but their advice was rarely evidence-based.

There's no doubt that pregnancy can be beautiful, but it can also be risky. The first birth I attended during my medical training came as a shock – I hadn't prepared myself for how much distress the woman would be in, how much bodily fluid there would be, how dusky the baby would look in those first few seconds before he opened his mouth and screamed. I was not emotionally connected to the couples and I didn't share their post-birth euphoria. I left those delivery suites traumatised, determined to delay my own plans for a family.

Over the past few decades in the developed world, the dangers of pregnancy and labour have been dramatically reduced, but pregnant women remain a uniquely vulnerable subset of our population. For one thing, pregnancy is a state of immunosuppression – a necessary physiological change, which prevents a woman's body from attacking the cells of her baby, but which also makes her more susceptible to serious complications from everyday viruses. And it's not just infections – certain conditions like venous thromboembolism, high blood pressure and diabetes are also more common in pregnancy. That's not to mention the risks of the delivery itself, which have been minimised in countries like Australia, but which are not and never will be zero.

And that's just the physical complications. Pregnant women are also highly susceptible to mental health disorders. Perinatal Anxiety and Depression Australia (PANDA) quotes the risk of anxiety and depression as 1 in 10 in the antenatal period and

1 in 7 in the six months immediately after delivery. So long as we view pregnancy as something mysterious and magical, we risk ignoring these cold, hard, confronting facts.

I'll never forget the time I accompanied a psychiatrist to visit a patient with post-partum psychosis. More than anything I remember the woman's eyes – scared, frantic, lost – and the lies she told us. Because no mother – even one who is being taunted by voices inside her head – wants to admit to the world that she isn't coping. I was a young medical student then. I was single. I didn't have children. Now, as the mother of a four-year-old and a seven-year-old, I know the joy of a cuddle and the delight of a spontaneous and heartfelt declaration of love. But I also know the daily grind of parenting. I understand that exhausted, helpless feeling we get after a string of bad nights. I can relate to the seeming relentlessness of meal-time and bath-time and bedtime routines. I know what it's like to look down at the red face of a four-month-old when they're in the midst of a particularly brutal sleep regression, and to feel terrified by your own emotions – that flash of frustrated rage and the hours of guilt that follow it. And I'm a mother with a supportive partner and family, who wanted her pregnancies and suffered only mild and fleeting episodes of post-natal blues. I can't imagine what it might have been like if I hadn't wanted children.

It's worth pointing out that an unwanted pregnancy is not the same as an unplanned pregnancy. Many pregnancies are unexpected; that doesn't mean they're unwanted. My own conception was described as a 'happy surprise' by my parents. Sometimes after the initial shock, the woman rethinks her plans for the future and decides that she does, in fact, have space in her life for a child. By contrast, when a pregnancy is unwanted it's almost always because the arrival of a baby would cause significant financial, emotional and psychological distress to that particular woman at that particular time.

My work has taught me to live with uncertainty and to never make assumptions. Life is messy. The waters are murky. What's right for one woman may be detrimental for another woman. It's not my job to tell patients what to do, but to help them make informed choices. The key word here is *choice*. The other important word is *freedom*.

Contributors

Van Badham is a writer, commentator, activist, occasional broadcaster, theatre-maker, and one of Australia's most controversial public intellectuals. In addition to a weekly column for *Guardian Australia*, her work has appeared in *The Age, Australian Cosmopolitan, Daily Life, Southerly, Women's Agenda,* Britain's *Daily Telegraph* and in anthologies for UQP, Hardie Grant and Monash University Press. Van's first novel, *Burnt Snow,* was published by Pan Macmillan in 2010. She is active on Twitter @vanbadham.

Shirley Barrett is a novelist, screenwriter and director. Her first film, *Love Serenade,* won the Camera D'Or (Best First Feature) at Cannes Film Festival in 1996. She has worked extensively as a television director, with credits including *Love My Way* and *Offspring*. Shirley's first novel, *Rush Oh!,* was released in 2015. Her second novel, *The Bus on Thursday,* was released in 2018.

Clem Bastow is a screenwriter and award-winning cultural critic. Her work appears regularly in *The Saturday Paper* and *The Guardian,* and she has written for journals including *The Lifted Brow* and *Kill Your Darlings*, and books including *Copyfight* (NewSouth Publishing, 2015) and the upcoming *ReFocus: The Films of Elaine May* (Edinburgh University Press). In 2017, Clem wrote and co-presented the ABC First Run podcast *Behind The Belt*, a documentary 'deep dive' into professional wrestling. She holds a Master of Screenwriting from the Victorian College of the Arts, and teaches screenwriting at the University of Melbourne.

Maxine Beneba Clarke is the author of seven books, including the best-selling memoir, *The Hate Race* (2016) and the ABIA award-winning short fiction collection, *Foreign Soil* (2014). She is the editor of *Best Australian Stories 2017*, and the forthcoming *Growing Up African in Australia* (2019). Poetry is her first love.

Tony Birch is the author of *Ghost River*, which won the 2016 Victorian Premier's Literary Award for Indigenous Writing, and *Blood*, which was shortlisted for the Miles Franklin Award. He is also the author of *Shadowboxing*, and three short story collections – *Father's Day*, *The Promise* and *Common People*. Tony is a frequent contributor to ABC local and national radio, and a regular guest at writers' festivals. In 2017 he was awarded the Patrick White literary prize. He lives in Melbourne and is a Senior Research Fellow at Victoria University.

Gabrielle Stanley Blair is a founder of the beloved Alt Summit conference, and the creator of DesignMom.com, named a Parenting Website of the Year by *Time*. Her book, *Design Mom: How to Live with* Kids, is a NY Times Bestseller. Gabrielle writes at the intersection of design and parenting, hosting compelling conversations on difficult topics – from gun control to mental health. She lives with her husband Ben Blair, and their six children – Ralph, Maude, Olive, Oscar, Betty and June – in Oakland, California.

Meredith Burgmann is a former academic, unionist and president of the New South Wales Legislative Council.

Jane Caro is a Walkley award-winning columnist, writer, social commentator and broadcaster. She has written eleven books, including a memoir, *Plain Speaking Jane* (2015), and a trilogy of YA novels about Elizabeth Tudor.

Melanie Cheng is a writer and general practitioner based in Melbourne. Her debut short story collection, *Australia Day* (2017), won the 2016 Victorian Premier's Literary Award for an unpublished manuscript, and the 2018 Victorian Premier's Literary Award for fiction. Her nonfiction has appeared in *The Age, Meanjin* and *Overland*, among others.

Brooke Davis grew up in Bellbrae, Victoria, and now lives in Perth, where she works as a bookseller. She holds an Honours degree from the University of Canberra and a PhD from Curtin University, both in creative writing. Her first novel, *Lost & Found* (2014) was published in thirty countries. She's currently working on her second.

Caroline de Costa is Professor of Obstetrics and Gynaecology at James Cook University College of Medicine in Cairns. She has practised in Far North Queensland and in western Sydney and has been a longtime advocate of improved reproductive health services for women, and improved access to those services. She has been particularly involved in healthcare for Indigenous women and recently arrived immigrant women and refugees.

Much of Caroline's research over the past twenty years has been in the area of abortion service provision and abortion law reform. She has published extensively herself, and with multiple co-authors, both nationally and internationally, on these topics, and has been active and successful in public movements to reform abortion law.

Catherine Deveny has been a comedian, writer and speaker for 25 years. She's the author of nine books; her tenth, a memoir, *Self-Saucing Pudding*, has been acquired by Black Inc. Books. Catherine is the creator of the enormously successful Gunnas Writing Masterclass. She has published over 1000 columns in *The Age* and appeared on Q&A five times. She is dyslexic and almost failed HSC English with 51 per cent. These days, pieces she writes appear on Year 12 English exam papers.

Monica Dux is a columnist with *The Age*, the author of *Things I Didn't Expect (When I Was Expecting)* (2013), co-author of *The Great Feminist Denial* (2008) and editor of the anthology, *Mothermorphosis* (2015). She was a founding board member of the Stella Prize, and currently sits on the board of the Feminist Writers Festival. You can find her at monicadux.com.au or on Twitter @monicadux

Sarah Firth is a comic artist, writer, graphic recorder and animator based in Melbourne. Recently she received a *Frankie* Good Stuff Award, was a finalist in the Incinerator Social Change Art Award, and her graphic essay on complexity was listed in *The Conversation*'s ten best literary comics in Australia. She has a fat stack of self-published comics and work in upcoming anthologies with Abrams Books, Picador and Affirm Press, and she is currently working on her debut graphic novel thanks to the Creators Fund program.

Jane Gleeson-White is an award-winning writer and author of four books, including the internationally acclaimed history of accounting, *Double Entry* (2011), and its sequel, *Six Capitals* (2014). Her essays and reviews have been published by the *Wall Street Journal*, *The Guardian*, *Bloomberg*, *Wired*, *The Age*, *Sydney Morning Herald*, *The Australian*, *Meanjin* and *Overland*.

Amy Gray is a Melbourne-based writer whose work focuses on feminism, culture and human rights. Her work has appeared in *The Age*, *Sydney Morning Herald*, *The Saturday Paper*, SBS, ABC, BBC and *The Lifted Brow*. She is passionate about elevating all women, whether through her written work or through many years of activism.

Gideon Haigh has been a journalist since 1984, contributed to more than 100 newspapers and magazines, and written 37 books, including *The Racket: How Abortion Became Legal in Australia* (2009).

Claudia Karvan grew up in Kings Cross, where her parents owned a nightclub. In stark contrast to this, she attended a girls' private school in Darlinghurst, which she loved. Claudia began acting at the age of ten in films such as *High Tide*, *The Big Steal*, *Dating the Enemy* and *Paperback Hero,* and started producing television series later in her career, such as *Love My Way*, *Spirited* and *Doctor Doctor*. She loves travelling, salsa dancing and her kids.

Jenny Kee is a pioneer of Australian style, and an internationally acclaimed artist and designer. Grace Heifetz, Jenny's daughter, is a literary agent with Curtis Brown.

Laura Jean is a Sydney songwriter revered for the striking beauty of her music and the strength of her piercing, intimate lyrics. She has been shortlisted for the Australian Music Prize and has recorded with national icons Paul Kelly and The Drones. Her latest album, *Devotion* (2018), a deep pop reflection on teenage obsession, coastal childhood and vivid memory, has attracted fans Lorde and Brie Larson. Laura recently completed a tour of the UK and Europe with Courtney Barnett.

Michelle Law is a writer working across film, theatre and print. Her work includes the hit play *Single Asian Female* and the SBS web series *Homecoming Queens*, which she co-created, co-wrote and stars in. She has written for numerous publications including *Frankie* and the *Griffith Review*, and has had her writing anthologised in *Destroying the Joint*, *Best Australian Comedy Writing* and *Women of Letters*.

Bri Lee is an author, freelance writer and lawyer (non-practising). Her first book, *Eggshell Skull*, was shortlisted for the 2018 Nib Award for research in writing, and Bri received a 2018 Queensland Literary Award. Her journalism appears in *The Saturday Paper* and *The Guardian*, and she is a regular guest on ABC's The Drum and ABC Radio National.

Eleanor Limprecht is the author of three novels: *The Passengers* (2018), *Long Bay* (2015) and *What Was Left* (2013), which was shortlisted for the ALS Gold Medal, and she also writes short fiction, reviews and essays. Eleanor has a Doctorate of Creative Arts from the University of Technology Sydney, where she teaches creative writing.

Melissa Lucashenko is a multi-award-winning Aboriginal author from Meanjin, Brisbane. Her writing is about a better Australia for all of us.

Emily Maguire is the author of five novels and two non-fiction books. Her latest novel, *An Isolated Incident* (2016), was shortlisted for the Stella Prize, the ABIA Literary Fiction Book of the Year and the Miles Franklin Literary Award. She works as a teacher and as a mentor to young and emerging writers, and is the 2018 Writer-in-Residence at the Charles Perkins Centre at the University of Sydney.

Samantha Maiden has worked in the Canberra press gallery for twenty years, covering federal politics. She broke the story of Cricket Australia's sacking of Angela Williamson over pro-choice Tweets for Fairfax. In the early 1990s as a university student she went on Adelaide radio to debate abortion with Father John Fleming and was subsequently referred to in Festival of Light publications as 'an abortionist' for her pro-choice views – she would like to stress, however, that she is not trained as a doctor.

Zoya Patel is a writer and editor based in Canberra. She is the Founding Editor of independent feminist journal, *Feminartsy*, through which she publishes the work of writers from across Australia, hosts monthly feminist reading nights, and co-hosts the Read Like a Feminist bookclub. Zoya writes fiction, nonfiction and memoir, and has had her work published in a range of publications including *Junkee*, *Women's Agenda*, *i-D.co*, *Right Now*, the *Canberra Times* and more.

Tanya Plibersek is the deputy leader of the Federal Parliamentary Labor Party, shadow minister for Education and Training, shadow minister for Women, and the federal member for Sydney. Tanya was previously the shadow minister for Foreign Affairs and International Development. In government, Tanya was minister for Health. Her other ministerial appointments have included minister for Medical Research, minister for Social Inclusion, minister for Human Services, minister for the Status of Women and minister for Housing. Tanya grew up in the Sutherland Shire of Sydney and is the daughter of migrants from Slovenia.

Gina Rushton is the gender reporter at *BuzzFeed News*, where she covers issues that affect Australian women, with a focus on reproductive health and abortion law reform. She has worked previously as a journalist for *The Australian* and has been published in *The Saturday Paper*, *Meanjin* and Brow Books.

Ellena Savage has published and performed hundreds of essays, stories, poems, lectures and artistic collaborations, in literary journals, on the internet, in public parks and at major institutions over the past decade. Her collection of nonfiction experiments, *Blueberries,* is coming out soon with Text Publishing.

Jess Scully is a curator who uses creativity to engage communities in the knowledge economy and with urban life in the 21st century. She was the founding curator of Vivid Ideas, and has worked as a policy advisor, festival director, public art curator, radio host and magazine editor. Jess is passionate about cities and city-making, and in 2016 was elected as a councillor for the City of Sydney.

Anne Summers is an author, journalist and feminist activist. She is the author of many books including the classic *Damned Whores and God's Police* (1975). Her most recent book is *Unfettered and Alive* (2018), a memoir.

Rosie Waterland is a Sydney-based author, columnist and all-round media phenomenon. Her first memoir, *The Anti-Cool Girl* (2015), won the ABIA People's Choice Matt Richell Award and was adapted into ACRA award-winning podcast, *Mum Says My Memoir is a Lie*. She continued to tackle topics from mental health and feminism to awkward sex and body image in her second memoir, *Every Lie I've Ever Told* (2017), as well as her national tours, *My Life on the Couch (With Vodka)* and *Crazy Lady*.

Angela Williamson's career has crossed the public service, Liberal and Labor political offices and the not-for profit sector. Through these roles she's secured outcomes for ocean conservation, environment, Indigenous affairs and women in sport. Her recent experiences in reproductive health advocacy in Tasmania have given Angela her loudest voice – in July 2018, she was sacked as Cricket Australia's manager of public policy and government relations after she campaigned for abortion reform on Twitter.

Tara June Winch is an Australian (Wiradjuri) writer. She is the author of the story collection, *After the Carnage* (2006) and the novel, *Swallow the Air* (2003), which has been on the tertiary and HSC curriculum since 2009. A tenth anniversary edition of *Swallow the Air* was issued in 2016. Tara is the recipient of the international Rolex Mentor and Protégé prize, which saw her mentored by Nobel laureate Wole Soyinka. Her forthcoming novel *The Yield* is out later in 2019.

Notes

1. Bateson, D., 'Medical abortion is fundamental to women's health care', *ANZJOG*, 2017, vol. 57, no. 3
2. Shankar et. al., 'Access, equity and costs of induced abortion services in Australia: a cross-sectional study', 2017, https://www.ncbi.nlm.nih.gov/pubmed/28110510
3. ibid.
4. CommBank survey on a representative sample of 3000 Australians
5. Shankar et. al., 2017
6. Dawson et. al., 'Medical termination of pregnancy in general practice in Australia: a descriptive-interpretive qualitative study', *Reproductive Health*, 2017, vol. 14, no. 39
7. WA Labor for Choice poll, July 2017
8. Data from Children by Choice, Unplanned Pregnancy and Abortion in Australia Conference, 2017
9. Shankar et. al., 2017
10. Swannell, 'Unintended and unwanted pregnancy in Australia', *Medical Journal of Australia*, 2018, vol. 209, no. 9
11. *Pregnancy Outcome in South Australia 2015*, SA Health, Government of South Australia, Adelaide, 2017

12 Coombe et. al., 'Contraceptive use at the time of unintended pregnancy', *Australian Family Physician*, 2016
13 Holton et. al., 'Long-acting reversible contraception: Findings from the Understanding Fertility Management in Contemporary Australia survey', *European Journal of Contraception and Reproductive Health Care*, 2015
14 Efficacy of contraception methods, Family Planning Alliance of Australia, 2014
15 Domestic and family violence in pregnancy and early parenthood, Australian Institute of Family Studies, 2015
16 Equality Rights Alliance, Let's Talk: Young Women's Views on Sex Education, 2016
17 Lim et. al., Young Australians' use of pornography and associations with sexual risk behaviours, Burnet Institute, 2017
18 Sexting Among Young People: perceptions and practices, Australian Institute of Criminology, 2015
19 Mintz, Dr Laurie, *Becoming Cliterate: Why orgasm equality matters, and how to get it*, HarperCollins, NY, 2017, p. 36
20 Mintz, p. 36
21 Mintz, p. 36
22 Mintz, p. 38
23 Mintz, p. 39
24 Chalker, Rebecca, *The Clitoral Truth: About pleasure, orgasm and the G-spot*, Seven Stories Press, US, 2018, p. 27
25 Bamak, Sarah, *Closer: Notes from the orgasmic frontier of female sexuality*, Coach House Books, Toronto, 2016, p. 27
26 Chalker, p. 32
27 World Health Organisation, Adolescent Health and Pregnancy. http://www.who.int
28 Anonymous, 'I took secret photos of my abortion to empower and educate women', *The Guardian*, 9 July 2012
29 Stone, Christopher, *Should Trees Have Standing?*, Oxford University Press, Oxford, 2010, p. 181
30 de Beauvoir, Simone, *The Second Sex*, Knopf, NY, 2010, p. 88
31 de Beauvoir, p. 89
32 Stone, p. 1
33 Stone, p. 3
34 Stone, p. 3

35 Stone, p. 181
36 Van de Warker, Ely, 'The fetich of the ovary', *American Journal of Obstetrics*, vol. 54, no. 3, September 1906
37 Bachofen, J.J., *Myth, Religion and Mother Right*, Princeton University Press, New Jersey, 1973, p. xxv
38 Steinhem, Gloria, 'When women are people... and corporations are not', Bioneers National Conference 2011, https://bioneers.org/gloria-steinem-when-women-are-peopleand-corporations-are-not-bioneers/
39 Brooke, Elisabeth, *Women Healers Through History*, The Women's Press, London, 1993